Sunset

Kitchens & Bathrooms
PLANNING & REMODELING

By the Editors of Sunset Books

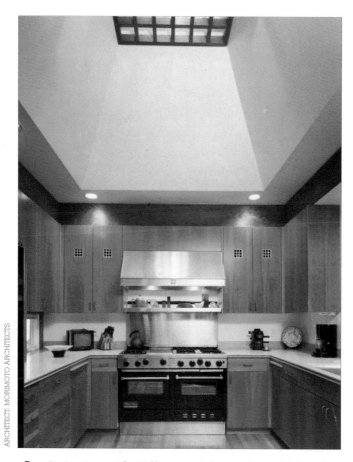

ARCHITECT: MORIMOTO ARCHITECTS

Despite its size, residential/commercial range fits perfectly in this high-ceilinged, very symmetrical kitchen.

Sunset Publishing Corporation ▪ Menlo Park, California

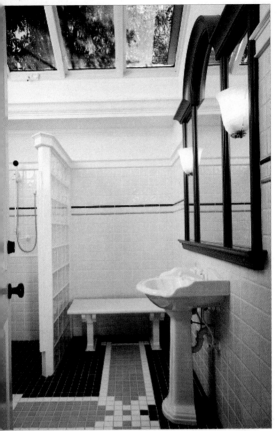

Expansive tiled bathroom captures spirit of yesteryear without sacrificing conveniences of today. Skylight allows natural light to flood room.

A Complete Guide

When people think of remodeling and updating their home, the kitchen and bathroom immediately come to mind. That's why we've combined two popular Sunset titles, *Kitchens* and *Bathrooms*, into one easy-to-use volume.

Whether you just want some new storage ideas for your kitchen or you're planning to rip out your outdated bathroom and start from scratch, everything you need to know about design, materials, fixtures, and appliances is right here.

Cover: Warm wood cabinetry and gleaming surfaces characterize these kitchen and bathroom make-overs. Kitchen design by Morimoto Architects. Bathroom design by Osburn Design. Cover design by Naganuma Design & Direction. Photography by Philip Harvey. Photo styling by JoAnn Masaoka Van Atta.

SUNSET BOOKS
President and Publisher:
   Susan J. Maruyama
Director, Finance & Business Affairs:
   Gary Loebner
Director, Manufacturing & Sales Service: Lorinda Reichert
Western Regional Sales Director:
   Richard A. Smeby
Eastern Regional Sales Director:
   Richard M. Miller
Editorial Director, Sunset Books:
   Kenneth Winchester

SUNSET PUBLISHING CORPORATION
Chairman: Robert L. Miller
President/Chief Executive Officer:
   Robin Wolaner
Chief Financial Officer:
   James E. Mitchell
Circulation Director: Robert I. Gursha
Editor, Sunset Magazine:
   William R. Marken

ISBN 0-376-01340-0.
Library of Congress Catalog Card Number: 94-66501.
Printed in the U.S.A.

Contents

Kitchens

This book walks you through the entire remodeling process, from evaluating your present kitchen to applying the finishing touches. Full-color photos highlight successful kitchen designs. An illustrated showcase of appliances and materials helps you shop more wisely. Finally, for the do-it-yourselfer, detailed instructions on plumbing, electrical work, walls, flooring, and more explain how to do the work.

Bathrooms

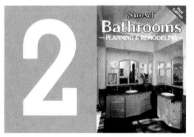

Design a beautiful new bathroom—or update an old one—with the help of complete planning guidelines, full-color photos of winning bathroom designs, and an illustrated shopping guide to cabinets, fixtures, fittings, and surface materials. Then follow the detailed instructions in the back of the book to transform your present bathroom into the bathroom of your dreams.

Sunset

Kitchens
PLANNING & REMODELING

By the Editors of Sunset Books and Sunset Magazine

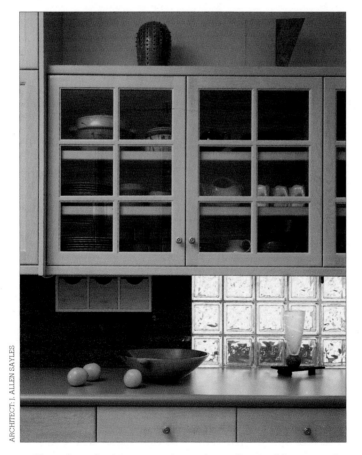

ARCHITECT: J. ALLEN SAYLES

Glass-doored cabinets introduce color and expand the sense of space; glass blocks in the backsplash area maximize light.

Sunset Publishing Corporation ■ Menlo Park, California

DESIGNER: JUDY KENYON

Southwestern-style kitchen features rustic beams and cabinets, hand-painted tiles, and the latest in appliances and accessories.

Book Editor
Scott Atkinson

Coordinating Editor
Suzanne Normand Eyre

Design
Joe di Chiarro

Illustrations
Bill Oetinger

Photo Stylist
JoAnn Masaoka Van Atta

Photography

Michael Bruk: 6 right; **Jared Chandler:** 22 top; **Peter Christiansen:** 27, 28 top, 35 top; **Crandall & Crandall:** 24 bottom; **Stephen Cridland:** 12 top, 26 bottom; **Michael E. Garland:** 2, 35 bottom; **Jay Graham:** 18 top, 22 bottom; **Philip Harvey:** 1, 5, 7, 8 top, 9 bottom, 10, 11, 12 bottom, 14 bottom, 15, 16, 17, 20, 24 top right, 25 bottom, 26 top, 29, 30, 31, 33, 34 top, 34 bottom center, 48, 51 bottom left and bottom right, 64; **David Duncan Livingston:** 23, 24 top left, 32, 37, 49; **Stephen Marley:** 51 top; **Norman A. Plate:** 18 bottom, 28 bottom, 34 bottom right; **Kenneth Rice:** 13 bottom; **Brian Vanden Brink:** 6 left, 8 bottom, 9 top, 13 top, 19 top, 21; **Peter O. Whiteley:** 25 top; **Tom Wyatt:** 14 top, 19 bottom, 34 bottom left.

Cover: Hardworking island capped by a custom-made vent hood occupies center stage in this spacious, open kitchen. Kitchen design by Morimoto Architects. Cover design by Naganuma Design & Direction. Photography by Philip Harvey. Photo styling by JoAnn Masaoka Van Atta.

Editor, Sunset Books: Elizabeth L. Hogan

First printing April 1994

Time to update your kitchen?

Of all the rooms in your home, the kitchen is probably the most complex. Good design and construction are crucial to a successful kitchen; so, too, are your choices in materials, appliances, and accessories. That's why remodeling a kitchen is such a challenging—and creative—project.

This new edition offers a wealth of information to guide you, from design ideas for successful floor plans to actual construction techniques. A special section compares the various products on the market today so you can shop wisely for cabinetry, surfacing materials, and appliances. Whether you're doing the work yourself or hiring professionals for some or all of it, this complete course on kitchen design and construction will provide the help you need.

Special thanks go to Fran Feldman for carefully editing the manuscript. We also wish to thank The Bath & Beyond; Roger Chetrit of Tile Visions; Dillon Tile Supply, Inc.; Menlo Park Hardware Co.; and Plumbing n' Things.

Contents

Special Features

DESIGN IDEAS

Layouts ▪ Materials ▪ Lighting ▪ Storage

Everyone knows a picture is worth a thousand words. That's why this chapter is packed with full-color photos showing kitchen design ideas you can apply to your own situation, whether you're remodeling or starting from scratch.

The first section, "Classic layouts" (pages 6–11), presents basic floor plans and their variations. Even though you may not have a choice of floor plan, study the photos in this section carefully—you're likely to find details that apply to your kitchen. Two related sections, "What's cooking?" (pages 12–15) and "Efficient islands" (pages 16–19), deal with the major building blocks around which modern work centers revolve.

"On the surface" (pages 20–25) shows good ways to use surfacing materials ranging from plastic laminate to stone. "Bright ideas" (pages 26–29) explores natural and artificial lighting, almost always subject to improvement when you're remodeling and an important concern if you're designing a new kitchen. "Storage solutions" (pages 30–35) concludes the chapter.

Warm and welcoming, this kitchen is elevated to living-room status. Earthy red-orange walls, rich verdigris ceiling squares, a copper-hooded cooking island, and prominent display areas draw in family and friends.

Classic layouts

Narrow galley kitchen snugs into setback space at side of house. Accessible through a wide arch on one side, it's a bright corridor of daylight adjoining dining and family rooms. A skylight runs along 16-foot length of room. Glass cabinet doors, wire-glass backsplash, and stainless steel surfaces also reflect light.

ARCHITECTS: CATHERINE ARMSDEN AND LEWIS BUTLER

L-shaped kitchen is accessed through a timbered opening; wide pine planks lead the way. Sink, range, and refrigerator line up galley style; oven occupies adjacent wall. Counter at left stretches working space and doubles as an eating nook.

ARCHITECT: STEVEN FOOTE / PERRY DEAN ROGERS AND PARTNERS

Classic U-shaped layout features residential/commercial range front and center; wings fan out to sink and refrigerator. Tall wall cabinets lift eye toward soffit ledgers and skylight grid beyond.

■ Classic layouts

DESIGNER: LOU ANN BAUER / BAUER INTERIOR DESIGN

Peninsula bounds U-shaped layout on one side, preserving openness and doubling as a breakfast and conversation counter. Small, square island balances layout and provides an auxiliary surface for nearby sink and cooktop.

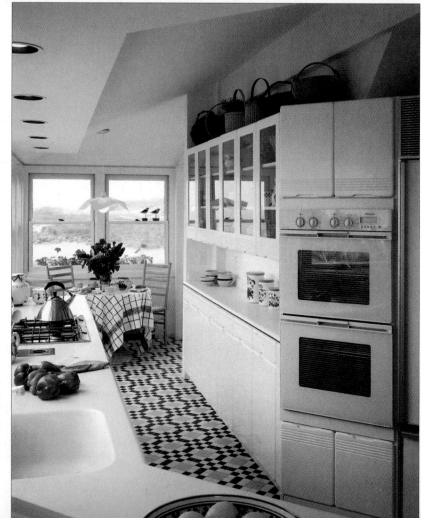

ARCHITECT: REDD & BARBA

Angled corridor setup, defined by molded white European cabinets and matching countertops, leads around corner to bright breakfast nook at far end. Cooktop and integral sink are in center of operations; wall ovens and refrigerator are accessible but out of the fray.

DESIGNER: LOU EKUS

Call it an unfitted kitchen or kitchen suite—here, a luxury of space allows a mix of specialty areas, even a book nook. It's the kind of space that lends itself to relaxing as well as to cooking. Warm cherry cabinets add a furniture feel; hammered tin ceiling blends with contemporary downlights.

Country kitchen sports hallmark open timbers, hanging pots, dried herbs, and open shelving. Granite countertops and freeform backsplashes are augmented by a large, efficient center island. Pine hutch adds a strong accent.

DESIGN: SERVAIS DESIGN & CONSTRUCTION, INC.

■ Classic layouts

Two open kitchens combine great-room feel with a bounded sense of space. Elegant alcove in photo above is screened from living space by an angled peninsula, allowing for conversation but retaining a sense of separation. Laminate-dressed layout shown at right is more modern and open, but angular island still defines kitchen work areas and directs foot traffic.

ARCHITECT: J. ALLEN SAYLES

ARCHITECT: RAYMOND L. LLOYD

Great room has a corridor kitchen at one end, living and dining zones nearby. Room-dividing island houses a cooktop and doubles as an eating counter while screening kitchen clutter from view. Note how materials and trim repeat from zone to zone, visually linking use areas.

Open floor plan brings U-shaped kitchen right into heart of living areas; work surfaces are stepped down out of sight, but cook can converse with company. Like in an airplane cockpit, controls are close at hand; wall ovens and storage pantry are adjacent to kitchen's open end.

What's cooking?

Residential/commercial range commands center stage in room-dividing peninsula; vent hood is wrapped with an overhead cabinet. Thick granite countertops provide range-side work space, and it's only a few steps to built-in bistro table.

Vintage freestanding range, dressed in shameless pink, sets theme for playful "deco-diner" styling, expressed in random-laid backsplash, diagonal floor tiles, and patterned peninsula—a type of laminate once abhorred but now cherished. Even chrome wall fan keeps pace with times.

Simple but serious restaurant range is flanked by hardworking accessories: stainless steel countertops and sink, pot racks, and ceiling-hung open shelves. Small butcherblock table moves with the action; black and white bistro floor adds a touch of fun.

ARCHITECT: PHIL KELLY

Another vintage range—this one older than most of us—is teamed with a burnished copper hood and vent pipe. Six burners, stacked ovens, and a nearby pot rack allow for chef's proficiency; tiled landing zones can stand up to hot pots.

■ What's cooking

ARCHITECT: MACKENZIE C. PATTERSON

Built-in cooking components provide for maximum flexibility and present a trim appearance. Side-by-side 30-inch ovens at left are lodged in double-wide end of a massive kitchen island, directly opposite a six-burner cooktop. Glowing glass-block alcove shown in photo below houses a downventing cooktop and a recessed microwave, flanked by built-in ovens, refrigerator, and freezer.

ARCHITECT: MARK MERYASH, AIA

Porcelain tiles trim backsplash and vent hood above a commercial gas cooktop. An accessory shelf keeps utensils and oils handy. Tile looks great and is easy to wipe clean.

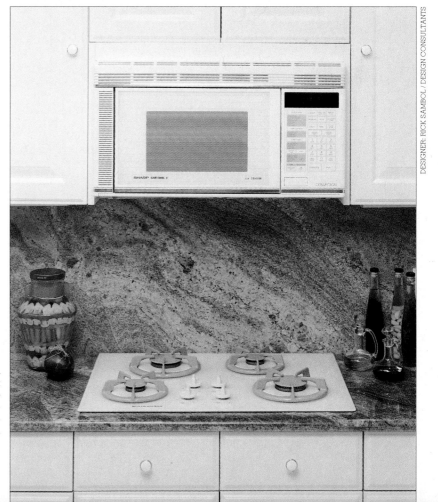

Cabinet-mounted convection oven and a sealed-unit gas cooktop form a compact cooking ensemble; clean white finish is set off by striking granite backsplash. Fan built into oven vents cooktop, too; duct runs through wall cabinet above.

Efficient islands

Islands add work space and augment kitchen style, too. Butcherblock countertop above overhangs a bird's-eye maple base, forming a handy breakfast table; bar sink serves range-side prepping area. Island shown at left is a showstopper but works hard, too, housing a barbecue, a sink, an eating nook, and a chopping block near commercial cooktop.

A cook's dream, this divider not only screens work area from through traffic but also incorporates a massive cooktop and griddle, plus luxurious pot storage on sturdy pull-out shelves. Flanking cabinets add storage space and support granite prepping counters.

■ Efficient islands

DESIGNER: CATHY NASON ASID INTERIOR DESIGN

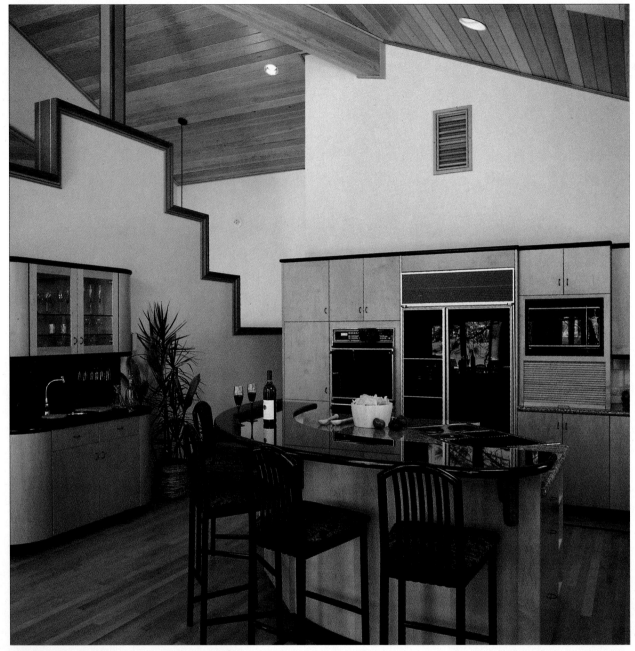

ARCHITECT: FUNG + BLATT ARCHITECTURE

Semicircular, granite-topped island does triple duty: it houses a cooktop on kitchen side, steps up to stool height on outside, and functions as an attractive room divider, marking kitchen space from adjacent living room.

Orbiting mini-island is anchored in center of room, yet pivots to where it's handiest (to cooktop for cooking, to sink for cleanup). Wood-topped unit has a swing-out knife rack on one side, open shelves at rounded end, and closed storage on other side.

ARCHITECT: JOHN MORRIS

Built-in breakfast table and slat benches, anchored to a long kitchen island, show furniture-quality crafts-manship in warm cherry wood. There's plenty of room for eating, doing homework, and loading nearby commercial freezer. Note handy tabletop electrical outlet.

Butcherblock island is heart of a serious cook's kitchen: top provides plenty of surface area and a handy second sink for food preparation; open shelves hold jars of bulk ingredients. Pots are close at hand and provide a striking accent.

ARCHITECT: WILLIAM E. CULLEN

On the surface

DESIGNERS: KALEIDOSCOPE INTERIOR DESIGN / LEDOUX DESIGN ASSOCIATES

Traditional dress for a modern kitchen includes pickled and crackled cabinets set off by floral-patterned wallpaper and a painted brick backsplash. White solid-surface countertops are edged with a complementary green stripe.

Classic cherry cabinets are combined with rustic ceiling timbers, slate-colored porcelain floor tiles, and a brick cooktop surround. Backdrop accents include a stainless steel vent hood, marble and black granite countertops, and a shiny black refrigerator panel.

Oak sets the scene, and green the backdrop. Strip flooring and frame-and-panel cabinets are set off by laminate countertops, printed wallpaper, an aged pine ceiling and timbers, and polished copper accents.

▓ On the surface

DESIGNER: JOSH CHANDLER

Exuberant meeting of materials blends vertical-grain fir cabinets, etched metal countertops, and wood-trimmed carpeting. Main kitchen floor is waferboard, a material meant for house substructures but here sealed and flaunted.

High-tech, high-contrast design mixes brash orange-lacquered cabinets, sparkling black granite countertops, charcoal wall cabinets, and a bright red breakfast table. Floor tiles are marble. See-through glass shelves match other "hard" surfaces, and allow views and light past peninsula.

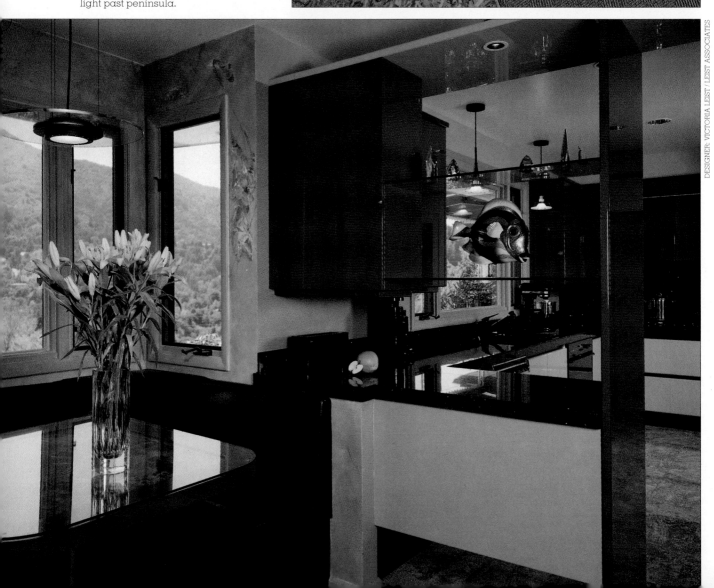

DESIGNER: VICTORIA LEIST / LEIST ASSOCIATES

DESIGNER: STUDIO BECKER

Future meets industrial age: immaculate chrome and steel surfaces are backed by white metal European cabinets, white built-in appliances, and an integral sink and cooktop; floor is concrete. Halogen pendant lights are powered by a chrome ceiling track.

■ On the surface

DESIGNER: LOU ANN BAUER / BAUER INTERIOR DESIGN

Custom touches can make all the difference. Maple cabinets (above, left) are dyed red on top, left natural below; other accents include rippled glass panels and striking backsplash tiles. French paver floor tiles (above, right) are easy on the eye and on cold feet, too: radiant heating pipes run through concrete slab below. Solid-surface countertop (right) is inlaid with strips of green marble tile, repeated in adjacent backsplash.

DESIGN: BAY AREA CONCRETES

While still wet, concrete floor was imprinted to look like gray slate; its texture resists slipping. A grid of rose and black-speckled granite sits flush with surface.

Elegant, uncluttered design features seamless, flush-front maple cabinets, plus black granite countertops, backsplash, and table. Twelve-inch resilient floor tiles are sparked by cut-in color accents that match chair seats.

DESIGNER: GARY HUTTON DESIGN

Bright ideas

DESIGN: TERESA QUIGLEY / SPENDING WIVES DESIGNS
DECORATIVE PAINTING: N. E. LARKIN AND PAINTED ILLUSIONS

A little paint and artistry turn an existing skylight into focal point of kitchen. Faux-painted hydrangeas draw eye up and bounce cool color back into room. Lighting tucked behind frame dramatically illuminates light well at night.

Pivoting roof windows help brighten—and vent—a busy kitchen sink area. Fixed window behind sink is joined by an operable casement unit; also note glass-block accents below and behind wall cabinets.

ARCHITECT: JERRY WARD / WARD ARCHITECTURE PC

Unimpressive views of garage and neighboring apartments dictated changes in old kitchen. Remodel put a band of clerestories over new wall cabinets to bring in ample daylight while editing views.

■ Bright ideas

ARCHITECT: MARK HORTON

Tall glass panels flood kitchen's breakfast area with light and frame vivid views of garden. Instead of a prefabricated metal greenhouse section, architect opted for ganged panes and skylights trimmed with Victorian detailing found elsewhere in house.

DESIGNER: SHARI CANEPA / INTERIOR SPACES, INC.

Sandblasted glass in two-sided peninsula cabinets partially blocks view of dishes and plates, but lets light pass from kitchen to breakfast room. Low-voltage downlights help brighten counter and show off flowers and art in display alcoves on far side.

Pendant lights suspended on bright brass pipes shine on cherry kitchen's countertops and island; during daylight hours, fixtures are augmented by large ridgeline skylights.

Storage solutions

ARCHITECT: I. ALLEN SAYLES

DESIGNER: CHERIE ROSE / THE ROSE COLLECTION

European cabinets come in many guises—from glossy lacquer and laminate to warm wood. Sleek, seamless white lacquer cabinets shown above feature flush fronts, hidden door hardware, and curves at corners. Frame-and-panel pine cabinets in photo at left have traditional faceframe look but utilize European frameless construction.

Cherry cabinets and built-ins show off frame-and-panel styling and traditional faceframe construction. Craftsmanship is augmented by furniture detailing and crown moldings at ceiling, punctuated by an elegant floor of limestone and ceramic tiles.

■ Storage solutions

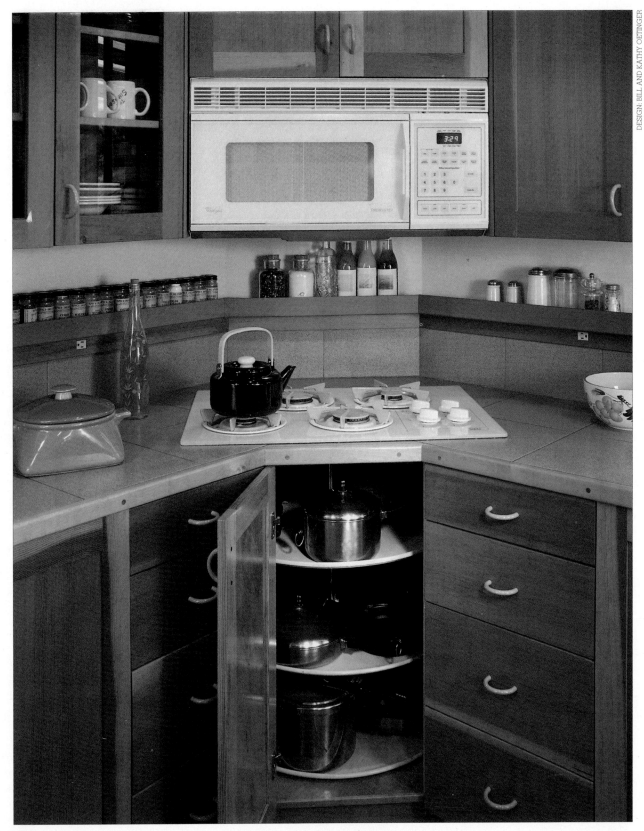

Kitchen corners usually waste space, but not this one: an angled gas cooktop is balanced by a lazy susan below and a microwave above. Wall cabinet layout allows enough space for vent fan and duct behind. Cabinet doors and drawers are built from vertical-grain fir.

Kitchen storage is where you find it. Above, at left, an appliance garage and a microwave oven nestle into a wall cabinet niche; there's space left over for some favorite cook books. Island end in photo above features enough cubbyholes for two cases of wine.

Custom-crafted dish rack was built from solid maple; it tucks between sink and wall unit to left. Open racks and lipped shelves hold accessories securely while placing them on display.

■ Storage solutions

DESIGNER: RICK SAMBOL / DESIGN CONSULTANTS

Racks and drawers bring order to cluttered, hardworking kitchens (shown clockwise, from bottom left): swiveling spice rack housed in a wall cabinet; glass-doored vegetable bins in a bird's-eye maple cabinet; a stainless steel drawer bin for compost scrap; and modular pull-out bins for a pantry unit.

DESIGNER: SUSAN GOLDBLATT

DESIGNER: RICK SAMBOL / DESIGN CONSULTANTS

ARCHITECT: ROBERT LUCHETTI

Baking pans get their own angled slots in convenient storage rack, mounted on sturdy drawer guides behind base cabinet's door.

White-painted open shelves, resting on wooden brackets, convey a rustic cottage look. At bottom, a grouping of narrow shelves, sandwiched between two appliance garages, keeps spices close at hand.

ARCHITECT: ANDY NEUMANN, AIA / SEASIDE UNION ARCHITECTS

DESIGN: BILL AND KATHY OFTINGER

PLANNING GUIDELINES

Decision-making ▪ Design ▪ Floor plans ▪ Products

Warm and earthy . . . sleek and sculptured . . . Whether your ideal kitchen contains a wood stove and open shelves or is the epitome of modern design, it's probably the most important room in the house, as well as the most expensive to equip. More elements—appliances, fixtures, plumbing, wiring, and furniture—fit into a given space in the kitchen than anywhere else in your home, and more time is spent there. Careful planning eliminates costly remodeling mistakes while you turn your dream kitchen into a working reality.

If you're simply replacing an appliance or adding sparkle to your kitchen with a new countertop or floor covering, you'll want to explore the "Kitchen showcase" (pages 54–63); it offers suggestions about equipment and materials. When you're considering major remodeling, such as moving a wall, you may want professional advice before settling on a new design. Perhaps you'll need help with the actual building. In any event, you'll need to have any major structural, plumbing, or electrical changes approved by your local building department. For more information, see pages 52–53.

This chapter discusses the entire remodeling process— from initial planning to final design, from evaluating your present kitchen to drawing floor plans for a new one. You can select and adapt the ideas that best apply to your own project.

Owner designed and built, this kitchen strikes a balance between modern efficiency and country charm. Vertical-grain fir cabinets blend with 12-inch tiles atop floor and countertops; wood is repeated in overhead beams and tongue-and-groove ceiling. Peninsula maintains open feel while screening main work centers from foot traffic.

Getting started

The success of any kitchen remodel depends on how well it suits your family—not only today but also in the future. Who uses your kitchen? Is it a setting for family gatherings or the private domain of a gourmet chef? By answering the questions on these pages and making detailed notes, you'll be able to assess your kitchen needs.

Complete the kitchen inventory below. Then review your notes, assigning priorities to desired additions and improvements. Organize your priorities under "must have" and "would like" lists; you can always rearrange your priorities later, but these lists will become your most important planning tool, even if you decide to hire a professional designer.

Consider not only details, such as appliances, but also the room's overall appearance. Is your idea of the perfect kitchen a cozy room with warm wood surfaces, potted plants, and comfortable chairs that invite family gatherings? Or do you prefer an easy-to-clean stark-white base of operations? Do dishes parading across lengths of open shelving appeal to you, or do they simply mean extra cleaning chores?

A KITCHEN INVENTORY

Space allocation and layout. The three major kitchen elements—sink, stove, and refrigerator—form what kitchen designers call a work triangle (see page 43 for details). More trips are made around this triangle than to any other area of the kitchen. The next time you prepare a meal, observe how much walking you do between the sink, refrigerator, and stove. Is a wall oven conveniently located? If you share the kitchen with another cook, can both of you work comfortably without getting in each other's way?

Consider the layout of the room in relation to traffic. Do you have to walk through the kitchen to reach the family, dining, or laundry area? How many doors open into the kitchen? Do any of them interfere with the opening of an appliance or cabinet? Efficient kitchen space allows cooks to work unhindered by pass-through traffic.

Work surfaces. Lack of counter space is a limitation in many kitchens. When you're preparing dinner, do your mixing bowls, pots, and salad greens vie for counter space with a lineup of small appliances? Are dirty dinner plates often stacked where you would like to set clean dessert plates? Do you have a convenient work surface beside the refrigerator for unloading sacks of groceries?

And while you're analyzing your present work space, look at the condition of your countertop. Is it easy to keep clean? Do you have a heat-resistant surface by the range, a special surface for rolling dough, or a sturdy top for chopping and mixing?

The height of a work surface should be comfortable for the cook. Is your counter so high that you're unconsciously straining to reach it, or so low that you're bending over to work?

Storage. Kitchen storage should provide maximum access for maximum use of equipment. To determine how well your storage space meets this requirement, take an inventory of all items stored in base and wall cabinets. Are items that you use daily, such as spices, bowls, and utensils, conveniently located? Where do you keep lids, large pans, and other odd-size items? Are any cabinet shelves tall enough for large vases, jugs, and jars? Do you have pull-out drawers in deep base cabinets, lazy susans in corner ones? Is it easy to reach the top shelves of your wall cabinets? Do you need a pantry to store quantities of dry or packaged foods?

If you're fairly happy with the way your storage units function but dislike their appearance, you can refinish them. If you're planning to buy new appliances, though, you may need to replace your cabinetry— dimensions of appliances may differ.

Appliances. Outdated or worn appliances are one of the major reasons people choose to remodel. Survey each appliance in turn—does it need replacing, or would a simple facelift do the job?

How convenient is your sink for both preparing and cleaning up? Is it large enough to hold big pans or mixing bowls? Does it have a garbage disposer? Would you prefer a sink with more compartments, or one that's made from a different material? Do you need an additional sink?

Does your range or cooktop have enough burners for your needs? Are the burners far enough apart to hold several large pots at the same time? Do safety lights show that burners are on? Is your oven large and well insulated? Would you like to add a microwave or convection oven? Would you prefer a wall oven rather than one beneath the cooktop? List the features that you would choose in a new range or oven. Note that changing from gas to electricity or vice versa can be expensive unless you already have both utilities in your home.

Is the refrigerator large enough for your needs? Is it noisy? How often must you defrost the freezer section? Is

When you think of decorating style, be flexible. Don't limit your definition of style to such convenient labels as "country French" or "contemporary." Usually, a room is a combination of many styles.

Study the photographs on pages 6–35. Take inspiration from them—you may find ideas you'd like to adapt to your own setting. Varied styles in appliances, fixtures, and cabinetry are also illustrated and described in the section beginning on page 54.

To collect more ideas and learn more about products, visit stores and showrooms displaying kitchen appliances, cabinetry, light fixtures, wall coverings, and flooring materials. Consumer and trade publications also offer helpful information on design, decor, and home improvement projects.

As you accumulate notes, clippings, photographs, and brochures, organize your remodeling ideas in a notebook. Choose a binder with divisions or file your material in separate envelopes. Organize by subjects, such as layouts and plans, color, appliances, cabinets, and so on. Then review your remodeling goals and adapt the categories to suit your project.

---

it energy efficient? Does the door hinge on the far side of the nearest counter? How easily can you open the crispers? Are drawers and shelves adjustable and easily removable for cleaning?

How well does your dishwasher serve your needs? Is it large enough? Does it get your dishes clean? Are the shelves and racks convenient for your use? Is it too noisy or expensive to maintain? If you're thinking about buying a new dishwasher, be sure to investigate such features as energy-saving cycles and safety handles.

Ventilation. Few things are more unpleasant than having yesterday's cooking odors greet you as you walk through the front door. A good exhaust system rids a kitchen not only of cooking odors but of grease and heat as well. How efficient is your system?

Lighting. Working in a poorly lighted kitchen is not only fatiguing and depressing, but also dangerous. Do you have ample natural and artificial lighting, or are your only light sources a small window and a ceiling fixture? Are you always working in your own shadow? Can you see into drawers and pantries? Is there a separate light source for the eating area?

Electrical outlets. Older homes usually don't have a sufficient number of electrical outlets to support the burgeoning collection of small appliances people own today. Does your kitchen have enough conveniently placed outlets? As you answer this question, think about any appliance purchases you might make in the future.

Heating and cooling. If your kitchen turns into a sauna in summer and you cling to the range in winter, your heating and cooling needs aren't being met. Before you make any changes, you'll need to know the location of ducts and outlets. If vents are located near the ceiling, do you have a fan to circulate the air? Is the air conditioning adequate?

Walls and ceiling. A fresh coat of paint or some attractive wallpaper can give new life to any kitchen. If you're considering changing the cabinetry, the walls and ceiling are likely to need new surface treatment, too. New countertops or flooring may also mean a change in the color scheme. Look carefully at the condition of your surfaces. Do you like the color of your present paint or the pattern of your wallpaper? Are there cracks or chips that need fixing? Is the ceiling too high or too low?

Flooring. When considering kitchen changes, pay attention to the floor. What is the condition of your flooring material? How easy is it to clean? After checking the surface appearance, note any sloping or uneven areas. They may indicate that the subflooring needs repair or reinforcement before the floor can be resurfaced.

Eating area. Whether your eating space is a counter with stools, a breakfast nook, or a table and chairs in one area of the kitchen, it's usually the place your family gathers. Is it used for activities other than meals? Do you have sufficient space for all activities? Is the lighting adequate? Is it out of the work triangle and traffic pattern?

Work or entertainment area. Today's multiuse kitchen often includes a desk or alcove for bill-paying, scribbling phone messages, or planning menus and grocery lists. Do you need shelves above the desk for a cook book collection? Will you be housing a personal computer? Do you need ready access to a television, compact disc player, or intercom/security system?

Special needs. If elderly or disabled people use the kitchen, consider their needs. Does the kitchen have a low counter for sitting to chop vegetables or cut out cookies? Is there a stool to pull up by the range for stirring food? Are doorways wide enough for a wheelchair? Is the eating area set up for wheelchair access? What about the height of the sink?

Your present plan

Before you begin thinking about solutions for your kitchen's problems, it's a good idea to make scale drawings of your existing kitchen and any adjacent areas that you may want to incorporate into a new design.

The process of measuring the kitchen elements and perimeters will increase your awareness of the existing space. Scale drawings also serve as a foundation for future design and may satisfy your local building department's permit requirements. And if you decide to consult a professional, you'll save money by providing those measurements and drawings.

These pages show you how to measure your kitchen, record those measurements, and draw a two-dimensional floor plan to scale. You'll also learn how to make elevation drawings of each kitchen wall.

Tools & materials

Listed below are some inexpensive tools and supplies that you'll need for measuring your kitchen and completing your drawings. You can find these items at hardware, stationery, or art supply stores.

- Retractable steel measuring tape or folding wooden rule
- Ruler or T-square
- Triangle
- Compass
- Graph paper (four squares to an inch)
- Cardboard
- Tracing paper
- Masking tape
- Pencils
- Eraser
- Clipboard or pad with 8½ by 11-inch paper

Measuring your kitchen

Since even a fraction of an inch counts in fitting together kitchen elements, accuracy in measuring and recording measurements is vital. Before you begin, draw a rough sketch of the kitchen perimeters (including doors, windows, recesses, and projections) and any relevant adjacent areas. Make your sketch as large as the paper and record the dimensions directly on this sketch—when you sit down to draw your plans, you'll find that a labeled sketch is easier to use than a drawing with an accompanying list of measurements.

Measurements should be exact to ⅛ inch. Don't worry about showing those fractions in the scale drawing. When the work begins, you or your hired workers will be using the written measurements; the scale drawings will simply serve as maps. It's simplest to write your first measurements in feet and inches.

Take care that the tape doesn't sag while you measure. If it proves difficult to keep taut, find a partner to help you or use a folding wooden rule. Double-check all dimensions.

Measuring for floor plans. A floor plan of your kitchen gives you a bird's-eye view of the layout of permanent fixtures, appliances, and furniture in the room. To make this two-dimensional drawing, you'll need to measure all the walls, as well as the appliances, fixtures, and furnishings.

First, measure each wall at counter height. Here's an example, using a hypothetical kitchen: Beginning at one corner, measure the distance from the corner to the outer edge of the window frame, from there to the opposite edge of the window frame, from the window frame to the cabinet, from one end of the cabinet to the other end, and from the cabinet to the corner. Note the locations of all electrical outlets and switches. After you finish measuring a wall, total all the figures; then take an overall measurement. The figures should match. If there's a difference, recheck your measurements.

Next, measure the fixtures and appliances along each wall. Note the depth and width of each appliance, adjacent counter area, and base and wall cabinets. If the appliance is freestanding, such as a refrigerator or range, measure the distance it extends into the room from the wall. Also note how far the doors open on all appliances. When measuring counter depth or width, be sure to include any trim, backsplash, and hardware or other part of the cabinet below that might project beyond the counter's edge.

Finally, make notes about the entry points of plumbing and gas lines, the direction the room's doors swing, and the depth and width of the range hood. Depending on the extent of your remodeling plans, you may also need to check the locations of load-bearing walls and partitions (see page 67). Record the dimensions of any tables, chairs, or desks that are permanent features in your kitchen.

Measuring for elevations. Elevations, or straight-on views of each wall, show the visual pattern created by all the elements against that wall. To create such drawings, you'll need to know the height and width of each element.

You've already measured the width of the fixtures, appliances, windows, and doors on each wall; now you'll need to measure the height of those elements and the height of each wall. Follow a sequence similar to the one you used in measuring a wall's length. Remember to measure the kickspace (the space between the base cabinet and floor) and the thickness of the countertops. Add all the figures and check the total against the overall floor-to-ceiling measurement. Also, note heights of the range hood, light fixtures, window trim, and any valances.

Scale plans

The keys to drawing neat, readable floor plans and elevations are well-prepared sketches with accurate measurements; you also need a reasonable degree of skill at converting measurements to scale. Kitchen designers generally use a scale of ½ inch to 1 foot.

Drawing a floor plan. With masking tape, attach the corners of your graph paper to a smooth surface or drawing board. Use a ruler or T-square to draw horizontal lines, a triangle to draw vertical lines at right angles to horizontal lines, and a compass for drawing the doors' direction of swing.

Complete the floor plan, using your sketch as a model. To guide you, architectural symbols and a sample floor plan are shown below. Be sure to indicate the thickness of the walls and the shape of the sink (square or rectangular). Use dotted lines to show appliances in open positions.

Drawing elevations. Next, complete the elevations. Keeping your sketch handy for reference, start by drawing the perimeter of each wall; then fill in the appropriate features of all of the elements against the wall. Be sure to indicate the location of appliance handles and cabinet hardware.

EXISTING FLOOR PLAN

BREAKFAST AREA

KITCHEN

Poor planning makes this relatively spacious kitchen and breakfast area a difficult place in which to work. The counter that partially separates the breakfast and kitchen areas sticks out into the middle of what would be a straight traffic path from the back door to the hallway. Counter space is practically nonexistent, and the only storage area lies across the room from the sink and range. Three ceiling fixtures are the only sources of artificial light in the kitchen.

For a look at a new design for this same space, see page 52.

ARCHITECTURAL SYMBOLS

ARCHITECTURAL SYMBOLS

▬▬▬	Wall	⊖	Duplex wall outlet
▬▬▬	Window	⊛	Range outlet
▬▬⌐	Door swing	⊢	Wall switch
		⊢³	Three-way switch
⊙	Gas, sewer,	⊕	Ceiling fixture
⊛	or water		
⊚	connections	⊢⊕	Wall fixture

Architects and designers use a set of standard symbols to indicate certain features on floor plans; some of the most common ones are shown at left. It's a good idea to become familiar with these symbols, since you'll want to use them on your own plans. Also, knowing them will help you communicate more effectively with your building department, contractor, or professional designer.

Basic layouts

An ideal floor plan eases the cook's work and enables others to enjoy the kitchen's warmth and fragrance without getting in the way. The floor plans shown below and on the facing page have become classics—they're practical both for utilizing space and for incorporating an efficient work triangle (facing page). However, you should let the dimensions of your room and your particular needs determine the final plan.

When space permits, don't hesitate to consider taking out walls or relocating or closing off a door or window. If the result is a more efficient and pleasant kitchen, it may be well worth the extra expense. Besides, at this stage you're simply brainstorming—you can always scale back your ideas later.

Experimenting with your ideas

Begin by tracing the scale floor plan of your existing kitchen and any adjoining space you're thinking of "borrowing." If you're considering removing or relocating walls, eliminate the existing partitions. Now, try different arrangements on the tracing. As you experiment, set aside the plans that you like and start fresh with another tracing of the kitchen's perimeter in its future form.

In looking at your available space, imagine where you'd like to perform what activities. If a window offers a pleasant view, would you rather enjoy it while eating or while washing dishes? Would you like to prepare food on an island or peninsula? Imagine all the possibilities and then draw circles on the plan to represent the locations of different work areas.

Even though you'll be determining the details of storage and counter space later, you need to begin outlining general storage areas now. If your current plan doesn't give you enough storage and work space, try different configurations. Could you make room for a walk-in pantry or a wine cellar?

The layout of appliances and the lengths of work surfaces affect storage possibilities. Any space beneath counters that's not taken up by an appliance, such as a dishwasher, will be available for base cabinet or drawer storage. A garbage disposer limits storage beneath the sink; a drop-in cooktop opens up additional storage underneath.

Consider major or minor structural changes that would increase your options for locating activity centers. If your present window offers only a view of the neighbor's wall, could you close it and open another wall for light and view? Would pushing out the wall a few feet allow you to add a sunny breakfast area or a baking center?

Concentrate only on overall space planning for now, taking into account the traffic pattern through the kitchen at different times of day; you can work out the specifics of each work area later.

SAMPLE LAYOUTS & WORK TRIANGLES

ONE-WALL KITCHEN

L-SHAPED KITCHEN

CORRIDOR KITCHEN

U-SHAPED KITCHEN

Consider the work triangle

Ever since kitchen layout studies in the 1950s introduced the term, designers have been evaluating kitchen efficiency by means of the work triangle. The three legs of the triangle connect the refrigerator, sink, and range (or cooktop). An efficient work triangle greatly reduces the steps a cook must take during meal preparation; the ideal sum of the three legs is between 12 and 23 feet. Whenever possible, the work triangle should not be interrupted by the traffic flow through the kitchen.

Today, the reign of the work triangle is being challenged by two-cook layouts, elaborate island work centers, peninsulas, and specialized appliances, such as modular cooktops, built-in grills, and microwave and convection ovens. Adding a second sink can also alter the traditional work triangle by taking pressure off the main work area. How much entertaining is done will help determine the location of the second sink and which satellite appliances are grouped around it.

New studies are under way to bring kitchen theory current with the latest designs. Nevertheless, the work triangle is still a valuable starting point for planning kitchen efficiency. One hint: Sometimes it's useful to sketch in multiple triangles to cover different requirements. If you follow the countertop guidelines described on pages 44–45, your basic triangle, or triangles, should fall into place.

Locating eating areas

To plan an efficient eating area in the kitchen, think first about how you'll use the space. For quick breakfasts or occasional meals, all you need is an eating counter on the outside of a peninsula or island with some stools or chairs that tuck underneath. But for regular meals, you'll probably want a separate table, located out of the main traffic flow.

If you don't think you'll have enough clearance for individual chairs, consider fixed, upholstered seats. Adding a bay window or large greenhouse section can create more dining space.

Planning special work or hobby areas

Though a dining table or eating counter can double as an office/menu-planning center, especially if you include nearby storage areas, having a space set aside for a work center is far more practical. You'll have a place to stack mail, pay bills, store cook books, and enjoy hobbies—and you won't have to clean up the table when it's time to serve dinner.

If there's a gourmet cook in your family, you might choose to add a specialized area for entertaining, baking, barbecuing, pasta-making, or the like. Locating this entertaining/cooking center away from the work triangle enables two people to work together comfortably at the same time.

GREAT ROOM

L-SHAPED KITCHEN WITH ISLAND

U-SHAPED KITCHEN WITH ISLAND

PENINSULA KITCHEN

KITCHEN PLANNING AT A GLANCE

SINK/CLEANUP CENTER
24" on one side, 36" on other

RANGE/COOKING CENTER
12" minimum on both sides of range or cooktop
15" minimum on one or both sides of wall ovens

REFRIGERATOR/ FOOD STORAGE CENTER
15" minimum on handle side of refrigerator

Angled corner cabinet

Appliance garage

Dishwasher to left of sink for right-handed user

Built-in microwave

Pantry pack

Tall cabinets and appliances at end of counter run

Refrigerator opens out from room

Island

Lazy susan for maximum storage

SERVING CENTER (optional)
36" to 84" between cooktop and sink; may share space with cleanup and cooking centers

FOOD PREPARATION/MIXING CENTER
42" to 84" between refrigerator and sink

The five work centers

The key to planning an efficient kitchen layout is to design around the five principal work centers, allowing for both adequate countertop space and storage in each area.

Listed below (and illustrated on the facing page) are guidelines for planning each center. Keep in mind, however, that these rules aren't absolute—in very small or oddly shaped spaces, you'll need to compromise. Adjacent centers may share space. Corners don't count, since you can't stand in front of them.

As a rule, items should be stored in the *area of first use*. The one exception? Everyday dishes and flatware: store them near the *point of last use*—the dishwasher or sink.

As you're working out storage details, be sure to leave enough space for future purchases. If you fill every available inch with what you now have, you may soon run into the old problems of clutter and inaccessibility.

Refrigerator/food storage center

Allow at least 15 inches of countertop space on the handle side of the refrigerator as a landing area for groceries. Ideally, the refrigerator is located at the end of a cabinet run, near the kitchen access door, with that door rotating out of the room. If you need to place the refrigerator inside a cabinet run, consider a built-in, side-by-side model: the narrower doors require less clearance when open.

Make room, if possible, for an 18 or 21-inch drawer unit in this area. A smaller unit is too narrow to be useful, and 24-inch or larger drawers will almost inevitably fill up with junk.

An over-the-refrigerator cabinet is a good place to stow infrequently used items. Floor-to-ceiling open shelving or a stock "pantry pack" are perfect for the tall, narrow spot flanking the refrigerator.

Sink/cleanup center

Figure on a minimum of 24 inches of counter space on one side of the sink and 36 inches on the other. (If you're planning a second, smaller sink elsewhere, you can reduce those clearances.) It's best to locate the sink and cleanup center between the refrigerator and range or cooktop.

Traditionally, designers place the dishwasher for a right-handed person to the left of the sink area and to the right for a lefty. But do whatever makes you comfortable. Consider the location in relation to your serving center (see at right).

Plan to store cleaning supplies in the sink area. A large variety of bins and pull-outs—both built-ins and retrofits—are available for undersink storage. Tilt-down fronts for sponges and other supplies come on many sink base cabinets.

Range/cooking center

You'll need at least 12 inches of countertop area on each side of the range or cooktop as a landing area for hot pots and casseroles, and to allow pot handles to be turned to the sides while pots are on the burners. If the cooktop is on an island or peninsula, the same rule applies.

You also should allow 15 inches of countertop on one or both sides of a wall oven. Typically, stacked wall ovens are placed at the end of a cabinet run; if they're in the middle, allow 15 inches on both sides. Remember that the area above the oven may get hot while the oven is on, so plan storage accordingly.

Though a microwave oven is thought of as part of the cooking center, many people prefer it near the refrigerator/freezer or in the serving center. Depending on the model, microwave ovens can be mounted inside an oven cabinet, on the underside of a wall cabinet, or just below the countertop in a base cabinet run. The microwave can always sit on the counter if you have sufficient space.

Plan to store frequently used pots and pans in base cabinet pull-out drawers mounted on heavy-duty, full-extension drawer guides.

Food preparation/mixing centers

This auxiliary center is ideally located between the refrigerator and sink; allow a minimum of 42 inches of countertop, a maximum of 84 inches. Though it may not be a good idea to raise or lower countertop heights (it can affect the resale value of your home), the food preparation area is a good place to customize, as some tasks may require lower than standard-height countertops. A marble counter insert is a boon for the serious pastry chef.

Appliance garages with tambour or paneled doors neatly hide a collection of small appliances, such as a can opener, a coffee grinder, and a blender. Place the garage in a deep corner to provide maximum storage space. (If you place an electrical outlet in the recess, all you have to do is pull the appliance to the front of the garage, and it's ready for use.) For immediate access to spices or staples, consider an open shelf or backsplash rack.

Serving center

If you have space, locate this optional work center between the range and sink; size it between 36 and 84 inches (remember, you can share space here with both cleanup and cooking centers).

Everyday dishes, glassware, flatware, serving plates, and bowls, as well as napkins and placemats, belong in this area. The dishwasher should be nearby; some models even have integral trays that can be placed right into the flatware drawer.

Heights & clearances

STANDARD KITCHEN DIMENSIONS

42" minimum clearance

20" clearance for dishwasher loading

26" minimum

Traffic pattern

36" minimum

Breakfast table

Ceiling 96"

Soffit

Top of wall cabinet 84"

Highest shelf 72"

Bottom of wall cabinet 54"

Switches and outlets 44"

42" eating counter
36" eating counter
30" desk/table height

Countertop 36"

3"

18" chair height

4"

24"

30"–32" stool height

24" stool height

Once you've decided on a basic layout and blocked out the various work centers in your kitchen, it's time to fine-tune your floor plan. You'll need to mark all the details of the design you've worked out onto a scale drawing of your kitchen's perimeter.

It's also time to turn your attention to the walls. To do this, you'll want to draw elevations of each wall, indicating the location and dimensions of all the elements in your kitchen.

If the layout of your kitchen is changing significantly, you may need to make adjustments in the room's heating, electrical, or plumbing systems, rerouting lines or adding new ones. Indicate on your plan where plumbing, gas, and electrical lines enter the room and how they'll reach the appliances.

Also, mark the tentative locations of electrical outlets, switches, and light fixtures (see pages 50–51 for more on lighting). Every countertop longer than 12 inches should have at least one two-plug outlet; most should have an outlet every 12 feet—or at least one outlet per wall, regardless of size. In an area where you'll be storing and using small appliances, you'll want to increase the number of outlets.

If your first kitchen measurements were in feet and inches, you may now wish to convert them to inches—you'll find it simpler when working with professionals or shopping for cabinets and appliances.

Checking clearances

As shown above left, standard minimum clearances have been established for kitchens. These dimensions ensure enough space for both a busy cook and occasional foot traffic; enough door clearance for unhindered access to cabinets, dishwasher, and refrigerator; and enough traffic lanes for diners to comfortably enter and exit a breakfast nook.

To visualize possible problems, it's a good idea to make cardboard cutouts to scale of both cabinets and major and minor appliances you'd like in your kitchen. For planning purposes, allow a width of 36 inches for a refrigerator or a double-bowl sink, 24 inches for a dishwasher or a single-bowl sink, and 30 inches for a range or built-in cooktop. Place the cutouts on a tracing of your floor plan and draw the shapes onto the plan. Check to see that your design meets the minimum clearances outlined in the drawing.

As you're fine-tuning, think about the traffic pattern through the kitchen at different times of day and during parties. Trace the work triangle and door openings on a separate sheet of paper, indicating the traffic flow with arrows. If traffic must intersect the work triangle at any point, it's best to have it cross the path to the refrigerator.

To redirect traffic, try moving a door, angling a peninsula, or adding an island. Also check whether any appliance doors interfere with traffic. Now's the time to make the necessary changes on your plan.

A SAMPLE ELEVATION

Elevation drawings are actually previews of the new arrangement of structural elements, appliances, and storage units. Because this preview is on paper, you can iron out the placement and proportions of various elements before you spend a penny.

Mapping elevations

To complete your elevation drawings, you'll need exact dimensions of all doors, windows, and appliances. It will also be necessary to work out storage details for each work center and decide on the heights of work surfaces, wall ovens, and hoods. For help, consult the drawing on the facing page, which gives standard heights and depths for base and wall cabinets and shelves, plus recommended heights for counters, stools, chairs, and desks and tables.

The height of a work surface affects the height of the storage units above and below it. Depending on your height, a standard 36-inch-high counter may or may not be comfortable for you. If your elbow height (measuring from the floor) is less than the average 40 inches, you may want your countertops to be only 34 inches high; if your elbow height is more, consider making your counters higher. Though most appliances are manufactured to fit beneath or along a 36-inch-high counter, sinks and drop-in cooktops can be positioned at any height.

Even if you opt for standard cabinet heights, you may want to plan at least one lower or higher work surface. A pull-out board or an island that's at a different height from the rest of your counters would solve the problem; or perhaps all you need is a roll-around butcherblock-top table.

Most modular base and wall cabinets come in 3-inch increments (see pages 54–55 for detailed information on cabinetry). Exact measurements are essential, so it's a good idea to have your supplier check your final measurements on the site before you order your cabinets. If you run into a problem of fit, filler strips can be used between units or alongside a wall. You'll have to use filler strips in the corner if you choose cabinets without faceframes that show (those that have full overlay doors, for example). To keep costs down, you may want to buy a few wide cabinets rather than many narrow ones.

Corners are the number one problem when planning cabinet runs. Two cabinets that simply butt together in a corner waste valuable storage area: on a base run, this adds up to a 24 by 24-inch waste; above, it's a 12 by 12-inch waste. Angled cabinets, blind cabinets, corner sinks, and lazy susans all offer corner solutions.

You'll also have to decide what to do with the soffit area, the space between a typical wall cabinet (84 inches top line) and the ceiling (96 inches or higher). If you like, you can simply leave the space open and use it to display china and collectibles, mounting them on the wall or protecting them behind a rail attached to the top of the cabinets. Or you can close in the space with framing pieces and wallboard. Another choice is to build a box soffit out over the wall cabinets for downlights, good for task lighting on countertops.

Unless you're planning a downventing exhaust system, you need to install a hood over the cooktop or range. Local codes as well as manufacturers of hoods can give you the required hood width (based on the size of the cooktop) and height above the burners. Generally, a hood should extend 3 inches on either side of the cooktop and be placed 21 to 30 inches above it. (For information on your options, see page 59.) Check to see if the hood fits your cabinet run.

Form & color

The lines, shapes, proportions, and arrangement of storage units and appliances affect the visual space and design of your kitchen. You'll need to consider each of these elements—plus color, texture, and pattern—to achieve the overall look you want.

Looking at lines

Most kitchens incorporate many different types of lines—vertical, horizontal, diagonal, curved, and angular—but often, one predominates and characterizes the design. Vertical lines give a sense of height, horizontal lines add width, diagonals suggest movement, and curved and angular lines impart a feeling of grace and dynamism.

Continuity of lines gives a sense of unity to a design. Look at one of your elevation sketches. How do the vertical lines created by the base cabinets, windows, doors, wall cabinets, and appliances fit together? It's not necessary for them to align perfectly, but you should consider such changes as varying the width of a wall cabinet (without sacrificing storage) to line it up with the range, sink, or corresponding base cabinet below.

You can follow a similar process to smooth out horizontal lines. Does the top of the window align with the top of the wall cabinets? If the window is just a few inches higher, you can either raise the cabinets or add trim and a soffit on top. If you're including a wall oven, align its bottom with the counter or its top with the bottom of the adjacent wall cabinet.

Studying shapes

Continuity and harmony of shapes are also important in achieving a unified design. This doesn't mean exact repetition, which can be monotonous when carried too far. It means, instead, that even when the sizes of objects are different, their shapes can be similar or their arrangement balanced for an overall effect.

Study the shapes created by doorways, windows, cabinets, appliances, peninsulas, islands, and other elements in your kitchen. Are these shapes different or is there a basic sense of harmony? If you have an arch over a cooking niche, for example, you may want to repeat that shape in a doorway or in the trim of an open shelf. To complement a curved island, consider adding a gentle curve to the base cabinets on the opposite wall.

Keeping to scale

When the scale of kitchen elements is proportionate to the overall scale of the kitchen, the design appears harmonious. A small kitchen will seem even smaller if it's fitted with oversize appliances and expanses of closed wall and base cabinets. Open shelves, large windows, and a simple overall design will visually enlarge such a room.

Think about the proportions of adjacent elements as well. Smaller objects arranged in a group help balance a larger item, making it less obtrusive. Trace fresh ideas on top of your existing elevations.

Bright, spacious kitchen works hard, thanks to lacquered European cabinets and an organized layout. Angled, multi-use island plays off main L; granite countertops and backsplashes link areas visually. Wall cabinets run to ceiling, simplifying shapes and adding "lift." Note how cabinet fronts, appliances, and work areas blend seamlessly.

Scheming with color

The size and orientation of your kitchen, your personal preferences, and the mood you want to create all affect the selection of your color scheme. But as you plan, let the following basic principles guide you.

A color's visual temperature can alter the sense of space in a room. Oranges, yellows, and other colors with a red tone impart a feeling of warmth, but they also contract space. Blues, greens, and other colors with a blue tone make an area seem cool—and larger.

Intensity and value also play a role in altering the perception of room size. More intense colors, whether warm or cool, make a room seem smaller. Low-intensity colors visually increase the sense of space. Light values (shades) of all colors reflect light, making walls recede and opening up space. Darker values absorb light and appear to bring objects closer, diminishing room size or visually lowering a ceiling.

In a small kitchen, too much contrast has the same effect as a dark color—it reduces the sense of space. Contrasting colors do work well for adding accents or drawing attention to interesting structural elements. If you want to conceal a problem feature, it's best to use one color throughout the area.

A light, monochromatic color scheme (one that uses different shades of one color) is usually restful and serene. Contrasting colors, on the other hand, add vibrancy and excitement to a design; note, however, that a color scheme built on contrasting colors can be overpowering unless the tones of the colors are varied.

If in doubt, you might include bright, intense colors as accents for furnishings and accessories that can be changed without too much trouble or cost.

Note, also, that the placement of light fixtures, and the kinds of bulbs used in them, will have an effect on overall color rendition in your kitchen; for details, see page 50.

Texture & pattern—for definition

Texture and pattern work like color in defining a room's space and style. The surface materials in a kitchen may include many different textures—from a shiny tiled backsplash to rough oak cabinets, from matte wallpaper to a glossy enameled sink, from coarse quarry tile flooring to smooth plastic laminate countertops.

Rough textures absorb light, dull colors, and lend a feeling of informality. Smooth textures reflect light and suggest elegance or modernity. Using similar textures helps unify a design and create a mood.

Pattern choices must also harmonize with the predominant style of the room. Though pattern is usually associated with wallpaper or some flooring, natural substances such as wood, brick, and stone also create patterns. Nevertheless, natural products generally work well with all textures and colors.

Though variety in texture and pattern adds design interest, too much variety can be overwhelming. It's best to allow a strong feature or predominant pattern to act as the focus of your design and choose other surfaces to complement rather than compete with it.

DESIGNER: LOU ANN BAUER / BAUER INTERIOR DESIGN

Clear-finished, vertical-grain base cabinets contrast with blue-dyed wall cabinets; backsplash tiles bridge area vertically and contribute striking color and texture. Stainless steel vent hood and white solid-surface countertops provide a clean, quiet counterpoint.

Lighting guidelines

No matter how efficient its layout and how interesting its design, a kitchen with poor lighting will be an unpleasant and tiring place to work. A good lighting plan provides shadowless, glarefree illumination for the entire room as well as bright, uniform light for specific tasks. If you plan to dine and entertain in the kitchen, you'll also want to be able to vary the levels of lighting for a softer, more dramatic mood.

You've probably already considered how to bring in natural light and where to locate light fixtures. These additional details will help you finalize your design.

Natural light

Natural light can enter a kitchen through windows, doors, skylights, or all three. Though eminently desirable, natural light may illuminate your kitchen unevenly; a single window in the middle of a wall often creates such a strong contrast with the surrounding area that it causes glare. For more even light, consider using two windows on adjacent walls, adding a skylight, or compensating for the glare by illuminating the surrounding area with artificial light.

Artificial light

Today's designers separate lighting into three categories: task, ambient, and accent. Task lighting illuminates a particular area where a visual activity—such as slicing vegetables—takes place. Ambient, or general, lighting fills the undefined areas of a room with a soft level of light—enough, say, for munching a midnight snack. Primarily decorative, accent lighting is used to highlight architectural features, to set a mood, or to provide drama.

Which fixtures are best? Generally speaking, *small* and *discreet* are the bywords in kitchen light fixtures; consequently, recessed downlights are the most popular choice in today's kitchens. Fitted with the right baffle or shield, these fixtures alone can handle ambient, task, and accent needs. Typically, downlights follow countertops or shine on the sink or island. Track lights or mono-spots also offer pinpoint task lighting or can be aimed at a wall to provide a wash of ambient light. In addition, designers frequently tuck task lighting behind a valance under wall cabinets.

Surface-mounted fixtures, once a kitchen mainstay, are now used specifically to draw attention. Hanging pendants are especially popular: place them over a breakfast nook or an island—or anywhere else they won't present a hazard.

Dimmers (also called rheostats) enable you to set a fixture at any level from a soft glow to a radiant brightness. They're also energy savers. It's easy and inexpensive to put incandescent bulbs on dimmers; the initial cost of dimmers for fluorescents is greater, and the variety of fixtures is limited.

Light bulbs and tubes. Light sources can be grouped in categories according to the way they produce light.

Incandescent lights, the kind used most frequently in homes, is produced by a tungsten thread that burns slowly inside a glass tube. A-bulbs are the old standbys; R and PAR bulbs produce a more controlled beam; silvered-bowl types diffuse light. Decorative bulbs are also available.

Low-voltage incandescent lighting is especially useful for accent lighting. Operating on 12 or 24 volts, these lights require transformers (often built into the fixtures) to step down the voltage from standard 120-volt household circuits.

Fluorescent tubes are unrivaled for energy efficiency; they also last far longer than incandescent bulbs. In some energy-conscious areas, general lighting for new kitchens *must* be fluorescent.

Older fluorescent tubes have been criticized for noise, flicker, and poor color rendition. Electronic ballasts and better fixture shielding against glare have remedied the first two problems; as for the last one, manufacturers have developed fluorescents in a wide spectrum of colors, from very warm to very cool.

Bright white *quartz halogen* bulbs are excellent for task lighting, pinpoint accenting, and other dramatic accents. Halogen is usually low-voltage but may be standard line current. The popular MR-16 bulb creates the tightest beam; for a longer reach and wider coverage, choose a PAR bulb. You'll find many shapes and sizes for pendants and undercabinet strip lights.

Halogen has two disadvantages: high initial cost and very high heat. Shop carefully, as some fixtures on the market are not UL-approved.

Fixture placement. For best illumination, tracks or downlights should be installed at least 2 feet away from a wall (almost the width of a standard counter). To avoid shadows on the work surface, point lamps directly over the counters or place them so light comes from the side. Place recessed fixtures sufficiently close to each other that their light patterns overlap.

For lighting under wall cabinets, choose fluorescent tubes or long, narrow incandescent strips especially designed for this job (shown on facing page, bottom right). Add shielding strips, or valances, to cabinet fronts to hide fixtures and prevent glare.

If you choose a pendant light, the fixture should be positioned 30 to 36 inches above the table. For an eating counter, place it at least 6 feet above the floor.

On your plan, show which switch operates which light source and indicate whether it's a single or multiple switch or a dimmer. Plan to add a three or four-way switch if your kitchen has more than one entrance. Switches are usually placed 44 inches above the floor on the open (or latch) side of doorways.

DESIGNER: THE MINIMAL SPACE

DESIGNER: KALEIDOSCOPE INTERIOR DESIGN / LEDOUX DESIGN ASSOCIATES

DESIGNER: RICK SAMBOL / DESIGN CONSULTANTS

Kitchen lighting falls into three categories: ambient, task, and accent. Trim track lights (top) perform all three functions. Custom overhead unit (left) combines indirect fluorescent uplighting with directional incandescent downlights. Low-voltage strip (above), tucked behind a valance, provides task lighting for countertop; reflections add decorative touch to polished stone backsplash.

Finalizing your plan

Once you've worked out an efficient layout, planned your storage requirements, and decided on color and lighting schemes, it's time to draw up your revised floor plan. Have you made your final decisions regarding new appliances, cabinets and countertops, flooring, and so on? (For help, see pages 54–63.) And don't forget such finishing touches as doorknobs and drawer pulls, hinges and moldings, curtains and blinds—all the details that pull a design together.

Depending on the extent of your project, you may need one or more building permits before you can start work. If so, you must submit clear and complete drawings of your existing floor plan and the new one to the building department.

Drawing a floor plan

Draw your new floor plan, or working drawing, the same way you did the existing plan (see page 41). On the new plan, include existing features you want to preserve and all the changes you're planning to make. If you prefer, you can hire a designer, drafter, or contractor to draw the final plan for you.

For more complicated projects, the building department may require additional or more detailed drawings of structural, plumbing, and wiring changes. You may also need to show areas adjacent to the kitchen so building officials can determine how the project will affect the rest of your house. Elevation sketches are not required, but they'll prove helpful in planning the work.

If you do the ordering of materials for your remodeling project, you'll need to compile a detailed master list. Not only will this launch your work, but it will also help you keep track of purchases and deliveries. For each item, specify the following information: name and model or serial number, manufacturer, source of material, date of order, expected delivery date, color, size or dimensions, quantity, price (including tax and delivery charge), and a second choice.

Building permits

To discover which building codes may affect your remodeling project and whether a building permit is required, check with your city or county building department.

You probably won't need a building permit for simple jobs, such as replacing a window with one of the same size, installing a garbage disposer, or changing flooring or wall coverings. But for more substantial changes, you may need to apply for one or more permits: structural, plumbing, mechanical heating or cooling, reroofing, or electrical. More complicated projects sometimes require that the design and the working drawings be executed by an architect, designer, or state-licensed contractor.

For your permit you'll be charged either a flat fee or a percentage of the estimated cost of materials and labor. You may also have to pay a fee to have someone check the plans.

If you're acting as your own contractor, it's your responsibility to ask the building department to inspect the work as it progresses. Failure to obtain a permit or an inspection may result in your having to dismantle completed work.

NEW FLOOR PLAN

Removing the old partition between the kitchen and breakfast area and adding a large island in the center of the room have greatly improved the old design (see page 41).

For the most part, the major appliances remain in their original positions. The sink is now flanked by a dishwasher, and the existing range becomes a cooktop with cabinets below. The refrigerator moves from its original position to the far side of the sink, permitting a bank of wall ovens and a landing zone near the new cooktop. The island-housed utility sink sets up a second preparation area.

Storage capacity increases dramatically: wall cabinets are added over base cabinets, a pantry pack flanks the refrigerator, and closed doors mask a large utility closet. Recessed downlights provide flexible lighting for varied activities, beaming down on work areas as well as an office alcove, island seating, and a dining area.

WORKING WITH PROFESSIONALS

Major kitchen remodeling projects are not easy work. If you know how to draw plans but dislike physical labor, you'll need someone else to perform the actual construction. If you're able to wield a saw and hammer but can't draw a straight line, you may need professional help only to prepare working drawings. Or you can let professionals handle all the tasks, from drawing plans through applying the finishing touches.

Hiring the right professional for the job need not be daunting. No matter whom you consult, be as precise as possible about what you want. Collect photographs from magazines, brochures, and advertisements. Describe exactly what materials you want to use. Provide your preliminary plans and some idea of your budget. If you have questions, write them down as you think of them. The more information you can supply, the better job a professional will be able to do.

Remember, too, that your home is an expression of your family's identity. A kitchen remodel is more than just a construction project; it's a personal project. In choosing a professional, look not only for someone who is technically and artistically skilled but also for someone with whom you and your family feel comfortable.

Architect or designer?

Either an architect or a designer can draw plans acceptable to building department officials; each can send out bids, help you select a contractor, and supervise the contractor's performance to ensure that your plans and time schedule are being followed. Some architects and designers even double as their own contractors.

Most states do not require designers to be licensed, as architects must be; designers may charge less for their labor. If stress calculations must be made, designers need state-licensed engineers to design the structure and sign the working drawings; architects can do their own calculations.

Many architects are members of the American Institute of Architects (AIA), and many designers belong to the American Institute of Building Designers (AIBD). If you're working with kitchen designers, look for members of the National Kitchen & Bath Association (NKBA) or a Certified Kitchen Designer (CKD). Each organization has a code of ethics and a continuing program to inform members about the latest building materials and techniques.

You may also wish to call on the services of an interior designer for finishing touches. These experts specialize in the decorating and furnishing of rooms. They can offer fresh, innovative ideas and advice. Through their contacts, you have access to materials not available at the retail level. Many designers belong to the American Society of Interior Designers (ASID).

Architects and designers may or may not charge for time spent in an exploratory interview. For plans, you'll probably be charged on an hourly basis. If you want an architect or designer to select the contractor and keep an eye on construction, plan to pay either an hourly rate or a percentage of the cost of materials and labor—15 to 25 percent is typical. Descriptions of the services and amount of the charges should be stated in advance in writing to prevent later expensive misunderstandings.

Choosing a contractor

Contractors do more than construction. Often, they're skilled drafters, able to draw plans acceptable to building department officials; they also can obtain the necessary building permits. A contractor's experience and technical know-how may even end up saving you money.

If you decide to use a contractor, ask architects, designers, and friends for recommendations. To compare bids for the actual construction, contact at least three state-licensed contractors; give each one either an exact description and sketches of the desired remodeling, or plans and specifications prepared by an architect or designer. Include a detailed account of who will be responsible for what work.

Don't be tempted to make price your only criterion for selection; reliability, quality of work, and on-time performance are also important. Ask the contractors for the names and phone numbers of their clients. Call several and ask them about the contractor's performance; if you can, inspect the contractor's work. Check bank and credit references to determine the contractor's financial responsibility.

Though some contractors may want a fee based on a percentage of the cost of materials and labor, it's usually wiser to insist on a fixed-price bid. This protects you against both a rise in the cost of materials (assuming that the contractor does the buying) and the chance that the work will take more time, adding to your labor costs. Many states limit the amount of "good faith" money that contractors can require before work begins.

Hiring subcontractors

When you act as your own general contractor and put various parts of your project out to bid with subcontractors, you must use the same care you'd exercise in hiring a general contractor.

You'll need to check references, financial resources, and insurance coverage of a number of subcontractors. Once you've received bids and chosen your subcontractors, work out a detailed contract for each specific job and carefully supervise all the work.

Kitchen showcase

Choosing appliances and materials can be an exciting—but time-consuming—part of designing and remodeling your kitchen. On these pages we present an illustrated guide to simplify your shopping experience. This mini-showcase offers an overview of styles, functions, installation techniques, and other variables that will form the basis of your selections. The showcase concludes with listings of materials commonly used in the kitchen for countertops and floors.

Tour our showcase before you shop. Though it's by no means exhaustive, it offers basic information to help you plan your new kitchen.

CABINETS

Cabinets determine a kitchen's "personality." The wide range of available styles and sizes allows you great freedom to create your choice of decor. Whether you select sleek plastic or warm wood, though, careful attention to construction and materials should be your first consideration. Check on such details as interior finish, joints, drawer guides, shelving, hinges, catches, and pulls. Make sure laminate and edge banding are thick enough not to peel at the corners and edges.

Traditional American cabinets mask the raw front edges of each box with a 1 by 2 faceframe. On European, or frameless, cabinets, a simple narrow trim strip covers raw edges; doors and drawers usually fit to within ¼ inch of each other, revealing a thin sliver of the trim. Door hinges are invisible. Thanks to absolute standardization of every component, frameless cabinets are unsurpassed in versatility.

You can buy stock, custom, or modular cabinets. Mass-produced, standard-size units are least expensive and can be an excellent choice if you clearly understand your needs. Though it's generally a more expensive approach, custom shops can match old cabinets, build to odd configurations, and accommodate details that can't be handled by stock cabinets. A new hybrid, the custom modular cabinet, is manufactured but offers more design flexibility than stock. Not surprisingly, modular cabinets cost more, too; you place an order and wait.

Style

Base

Sink base

Base with drawers

Base with drawer and door

Pullout shelves

Divider unit

Double cabinet

Characteristics

Base cabinets do double duty combining storage space with working surface. Though usually equipped with only one top drawer, some base cabinets have three or four drawers, making them particularly useful near sink, range, or refrigerator. "Sink" units have a false drawer front at the top.

Standard dimensions are 24 inches deep by 34½ inches high; the addition of a countertop raises them to 36 inches. In width, base cabinets range from 9 to 60 inches, increasing in increments of 3 inches from 9 to 36 inches and in increments of 6 inches after that.

Style	Characteristics

Wall

Usually mounted on walls, these cabinets can also be hung from the ceiling for peninsula and island installation. Wall cabinets come in singles, doubles, and various specialty configurations. Typically 12 or 15 inches deep, cabinets can vary in width from 9 to 60 inches. Though the most frequently used heights are 15, 18, and 30 inches, units range from 12 to 36 inches high or more. The shorter cabinets are typically mounted above refrigerators, ranges, and sinks.

Single door

Double door

Over refrigerator or sink

Double set of doors

Curved end cabinet

Appliance garage

Bottle rack

Open shelves

Special use

Manufacturers produce a variety of special-purpose cabinets. You can buy cabinets with cutouts for sinks, built-in ranges, and microwave or slide-in ovens. Island and pantry units also fall into this category. Before purchasing expensive custom cabinets, look into stock cabinets that can be modified with pull-out boards, turn-around or slide-out shelves, and storage for small appliances.

Oven cabinet

Two-sided (island or peninsula) cabinet

Lazy susan

Pantry pack

Refrigerator cabinet

SINKS & ACCESSORIES

Commercially available sinks have one, two, or three bowls with or without attached drainboards. Most have predrilled holes for faucets, sprayers, soap or hot water dispensers, or air gaps. Self-rimming sinks with molded overlaps are supported by the edge of the countertop cutout; flush deck-mounted sinks have surrounding metal strips to hold the basin to the countertop; unrimmed sinks are recessed under the countertop opening and held in place by metal clips. Integral-bowl sinks are also available.

Common sink materials include stainless steel, enameled cast iron or steel, brass, and copper.

Stainless steel is relatively noisy; look for a sink with an undercoating. Matte-finish 18-gauge chromium/nickel blends are the most durable and easiest to keep clean. Enameled cast-iron sinks have a heavier layer of baked-on enamel than enameled steel, making them quieter and less likely to chip. Beautiful brass or copper finishes require zealous maintenance.

Among the newcomers is a composite, or "quartz," sink, an expensive import from Europe that looks similar to enamel but stands up better to abuse and is easier to clean. Porcelain is also emerging in elegant, though costly, designs.

Style	Characteristics

Single bowl

Self-rimming

Flush-mount

Self-rimming with disposer

Bar sink

Single-bowl sinks range from 12 to 33 inches long by 15 to 22 inches wide. Smaller models are large enough for soaking pans, yet don't waste counter space. Some have a small, elevated disposer compartment. Small bar, or hospitality, sinks come with either a 2-inch or a 3½-inch drain opening; if you're planning to add a disposer, you'll want the larger opening.

Multiple bowls

Integral-bowl sink

Corner sink

Triple sink with cutting board

Double sink with steel deck

Larger than single-bowl units, typical multiple-bowl sinks measure 33 inches from side to side and 22 inches from front to back, and offer two or more basins for handling meal preparation and dishwashing simultaneously. In triple-bowl models, the disposer rests in a separate center well. Accessories such as cutting boards and built-in drainers abound.

Faucets

Single-lever

Single-lever with pull-out sprayer

Gooseneck with individual handles

Today's faucets fall into one of two camps: Euro-sophistication or traditional. Enameled single-lever fixtures with pull-out sprayers and interchangeable attachments are fashionable, but traditional brass or chrome gooseneck styles with individual handles remain popular, too. Whatever you choose, most kitchen professionals agree that solid-brass construction is the way to go.

COOKTOPS

Before confronting the bewildering array of cooktops on the market, you'll need to make some decisions. First, which type of energy do you prefer? Gas units heat and cool quickly, and the flame is visible and easy to control. Electric units provide low, even heat. Unless you buy a downventing model, the cooktop will require an overhead hood (see page 59).

Typically, cooktop units have four burners, though some models have more. The majority of cooktops come in 30 or 36-inch widths; they're all at least 2 to 3 inches shallower than the standard 24-inch cabinet depth. Drop-in cooktops with no venting run from about 2½ to 8 inches high (figure about 16½ inches for downventing models).

Style	Characteristics
Conventional Electric coil Solid-element electric Downventing gas with heavy-duty burner	A conventional gas or electric cooktop is built into a counter like a sink, with connections underneath. The standard electric coil heats up fairly quickly and is more forgiving than some other elements. Newer solid-element electric burners are basically cast-iron disks with resistance coils below. The disks produce more even heat than standard coils, and they're easier to clean. Some gas units have three standard burners that each give off 8,000 BTUs and one heavy-duty burner that gives off 12,000. Stylish sealed gas burners are fused to the cooktop: they're easier to clean than conventional burners and just as efficient. All gas units have pilotless ignition now, and some manufacturers offer an instant reignition feature. Note that white grates may turn brown over time. Downventing cooktops have built-in ventilators that pull out smoke and odors through ducting below.
Modular Downventing electric Modular "hobs"	Convertible gas or electric cooktops are similar to conventional models but offer interchangeable and reversible modules that let you replace burners with a grill, a griddle, and other specialty items. Popular mix-and-match cooktop modules (often called "hobs") go one step beyond: they can be grouped together with connecting hardware or, if you choose, embedded separately. Typical module width is 12 inches.
Smoothtop Smoothtop Halogen	Electric cooktops with ceramic glass over the coils heat and cool slowly, retaining heat for up to an hour after shutoff. They require flat-bottomed pans for cooking, as well as special products for cleaning. Newer formulations are more durable than earlier models, which scratched and cracked. Halogen is the latest technological kitchen marvel. Though more expensive to operate than gas, halogen is the most efficient electric source. One drawback: Halogen cooktops are costly.
Commercial gas Commercial Commercial with griddle	Commercial gas units are made of heavy-duty cast iron or fabricated metal finished in stainless steel, black enamel, or silver gray. Available with as few as one or as many as eight burners, cooktops often come with hot plates or griddles. Simmering is difficult; a cast-iron simmer top may be available as an accessory. Commercial gas cooktops are usually 6 to 7 inches high with short legs for installing on a base of tile, brick, or other noncombustible material.

WALL OVENS

In ovens, as with cooktops, you have several choices: conventional gas or electric, microwave, and convection. Most are built-in units, saving precious counter space. Double ovens can be installed one above the other (the more common configuration) or side by side; combining a conventional radiant-heat oven with a microwave or energy-saving convection oven is a popular choice. Oven features include built-in warmer shelves, rotisseries, attached meat thermometers, variable-speed broilers, and interchangeable door panels. The interior may be "easy-off" (old-fashioned elbow grease required), continuous cleaning (a steady, slow process), or self-cleaning (the most effective method).

Style	Characteristics

Radiant

30" single with window

Single with window and rotisserie

Conventional radiant-heat ovens are available in single or double units. Single ovens range from 25 to 32 inches high and 23 to 28½ inches deep. The most common width is 27 inches, though many space-efficient European imports are 24 inches; recently, the 30-inch oven has also caught on. Even one 36-inch unit is available. So-called built-under ovens provide a range effect without interrupting the countertop; add the cooktop of your choice.

Oven options include continuous or self-cleaning, door window, removable door, clock and timing device, rotisserie, and automatic temperature probe (the oven turns off when food reaches a preset temperature).

Microwave

Built-in

Countertop

In a microwave, foods cook quickly but seldom brown. Some models offer a separate browning element; other units combine microwave with radiant or convection cooking. Sizes range from 13 to 17 inches high, 22 to 27 inches wide, and 17 to 22 inches deep. Units can be placed on a counter, built into cabinetry, or purchased as part of a double wall oven or double-oven range.

Some microwaves, specially designed to be installed above a range (underneath wall cabinets), incorporate a vent and cooking lights; these are wider (30 inches) and shallower (13 to 17 inches deep). Most units open from the right. Features include dial, button, or touch controls, as well as memory bank, programmable cooking, timers, temperature probe, rotisserie, and electronic sensors.

Convection

Convection with meat probe

Microwave and radiant/convection

Gas or electric convection ovens circulate hot air around the oven cavity (you can tell them by the fan). More energy-efficient than radiant ovens, they reduce cooking time by 30 percent and use lower temperatures. Unlike food cooked in a microwave, food cooked in a convection oven does brown, and nicely at that. Convection cooking is good for roasting and baking (it first caught on in commercial bakeries) but is less effective for foods cooked in deep or covered dishes, such as stews and casseroles. Sizes vary from microwave size to standard radiant-heat size.

RANGES & HOODS

Ranges combine cooktop and oven in a single unit; model choices and finishes are as varied as those offered in separate units. Additional features include bottom drawers or broilers and easy-to-clean backsplashes. Take your choice of three types of ranges: freestanding, slide-in (freestanding without side panels to fit between cabinets), and built-in (drop-in). Gas ranges are available with pilot lights or electronic ignition.

Unless your range is downventing, you'll need a hood over the cooktop. Ducted hoods channel odors, smoke, excess heat, and moisture from the kitchen to the outside; if exterior venting is impossible, ductless hoods draw out some smoke and grease through charcoal filters. Effectiveness depends on the hood's holding capacity, the power of the fan or blower (blowers are quieter and more efficient), and the ductwork routing. See page 111 for ducting logistics.

Style

Characteristics

Ranges

Electric single oven

Built-in gas

Residential/commercial gas

A freestanding range rests on the floor, with burners above the oven; some slide in between cabinets. A few units offer a microwave oven above, with a built-in ventilator or downventing cooktop. Electric ranges may have coil or smooth cooktops and radiant or convection/radiant ovens. Gas ranges have either radiant or convection ovens; lower ovens may be self-cleaning. Some ranges feature interchangeable modules. Normal width is 30 inches; some 24 and 36-inch models are also available.

Commercial gas ranges offer from four to twelve burners, one or two radiant and/or convection ovens, and sometimes a high shelf or broiler at the top. They perform well, but they're not as well insulated as residential units and are potentially dangerous for young children. Such ranges are also tough to clean and may be too heavy for your floor. So-called residential/commercial units have the look and high-BTU output of commercial units but are better insulated; they also offer additional niceties, such as self-cleaning ovens.

Built-in, or drop-in, ranges have a cooktop with oven below. Permanently installed in specially designed kitchen cabinets, the counter-height units rest on a wood base. Models are generally 30 inches wide. Built-in ranges are particularly useful for peninsula or island installation. Though these units have no bottom drawer, the broiler is raised to a convenient height. Both gas and electric built-ins offer a choice of finishes, interchangeable cooktop modules, and standard oven accessories.

Hoods

Low-profile

Freestanding

Installed beneath cabinet

A hood should cover the entire cooking area and extend 3 to 6 inches on each side; its bottom edge should be 21 to 30 inches above the cooking surface. The power of a fan or blower is rated in cubic feet per minute (CFM), the loudness in sones; quality hoods handle a minimum of 300 CFM, with a noise level of less than 8 sones. Powerful units with variable-speed controls perform quietly; units with ventilators or blowers installed on the roof or exterior wall are the most quiet.

REFRIGERATORS & FREEZERS

For efficiency's sake, base your selection of a refrigerator, refrigerator/freezer, or freezer on the size of your family, your shopping habits, and your life-style. Eight cubic feet of refrigerator space is the minimum recommended for two people; add a cubic foot for each additional family member and 2 extra feet if you entertain frequently. Two cubic feet per person is the rule for a freezer compartment.

Standard refrigerators measure from 27 to 32 inches deep, so they project from standard 24-inch-deep base cabinets; however, several manufacturers offer relatively expensive 24-inch built-in refrigerators (one side-by-side model measures 48 inches wide and has a 30.5 cubic-foot capacity). Finishes include standard appliance colors (enameled or textured), brushed chrome, wood grain, and black glass; some models offer interchangeable door panels.

Consider these features: number and adjustability of shelves, humidity drawers, meat storage compartments, location and range of temperature controls, icemaker and defrost options, and energy-saving devices such as a power-saver switch. Some models use heat generated by the condenser to eliminate excess moisture, further cutting operating costs.

Style	Characteristics

Refrigerators

Side-by-side

Top-mount

Under-counter

Popular two and three-door side-by-side refrigerators permit easy visibility and access to food, but relatively narrow shelves make it difficult to store bulky items. Many such models offer ice and water dispensers in the door. Standard sizes range from 64½ to 69 inches high and 30½ to 36 inches wide, with an overall capacity of 18.7 to 27.6 cubic feet.

Double-door refrigerators have the freezer positioned at the unit's bottom or top. The bottom-mount makes it easier to reach the more frequently used refrigerator section; the popular top-mount provides easy storage for large or bulky items and offers the greatest number of choices in size and design. Top-mount sizes are 56 to 58 inches high and 28 to 33 inches wide, with an overall capacity of 12 to 32 cubic feet. Bottom-mount units are 66 to 68 inches high and 28 to 32 inches wide. Overall capacity is 16.2 to 22 cubic feet.

Though single-door refrigerators are smaller and more economical, their lower cubic-foot capacity (10.6 to 13.9) limits the amount of food that can be stored. Many of these units must be defrosted manually. Sizes range from 56 to 57½ inches high and 24 to 28 inches wide. Under-counter refrigerators are 33 to 34 inches high, 18 to 57 inches wide, and 25 to 32 inches deep, with a 2.5 to 6 cubic-foot capacity.

Freezers

Chest

Built-in, commercial

Top-opening chest freezers are usually less expensive to operate than uprights, but many require manual defrosting. Freezer options include power lights, food organizers, and door locks. Chest freezers are 34 to 37 inches high, 25 to 71 inches wide, and 23 to 31 inches deep; their cubic-foot capacity ranges from 5.1 to 28. Uprights are 51 to 70 inches high, 24 to 33 inches wide, and 25 to 32 inches deep, with cubic-foot capacity of 10.1 to 31.1.

DISHWASHERS

Whether portable or built-in, most dishwashers are one standard size: roughly 24 inches wide, 24 inches deep, and 34 inches high. One manufacturer offers a compact 18-inch-wide unit. Improved insulation has led to operating levels as low as 50dB.

Look for such energy-saving devices as a booster heater that raises the water temperature of the dishwasher only, separate cycles for lightly and heavily soiled dishes, an air-drying option, and a delay start that allows you to wash dishes at a preset time (during the night instead of at peak-energy hours). Other features to consider are prerinse and pot-scrubbing cycles, strainer filtering systems, adjustable racks, and rinse-agent dispensers.

Style	Characteristics
Dishwashers	Most built-in dishwashers are installed between two base cabinets or at the end of a cabinet run. Side panels can be added to the latter to match cabinetry. Standard finishes include enameled steel, brushed stainless, and ¼-inch wood or plastic front panels.

Portable units come with casters and hoses for attaching to sinks. Some have wood cutting-board tops or a hookup system that allows use of the faucet while the dishwasher is in operation. Most newer models, designed for later conversion to a built-in unit, are front-loading.

Portable

Built-in with decorative panel

COMPACTORS

Compactors quickly reduce bulky trash to a fraction of its original size. A normal compacted load—a week's worth of trash from a family of four—will weigh 20 to 28 pounds. Some models use standard 30-gallon trash bags that can be stored inside the door; others require special bags from the manufacturer.

Look for such features as a toe-operated door latch and a key-activated safety switch. Some machines may operate more quickly and quietly than others.

Standard appliance colors are available for all compactor models; finish options include black glass with stainless steel and custom wood panels with or without trim kits. Sizes vary from 12 to 18 inches wide (15 inches is standard), 18 to 24½ inches deep, and 34 to 36 inches high.

Style	Characteristics
Compactors	Compactors can be freestanding, installed between base cabinets (often near the sink), or added to the end of a cabinet run (similar to a dishwasher). Their height and adjustable kickspace (3 to 4 inches) allow them to blend with existing cabinetry. Features include reversible manual or automatic doors, separate top-bin doors for loading small items (even while the unit is operating), drop-down or tilt-out drawers for easy bag removal, and charcoal-activated filters or deodorizers to control odor.

Freestanding compactors have the same dimensions and features as built-in models. Freestanding units also offer an optional cutting-board top.

Built-in

Freestanding with cutting top

COUNTERTOPS

Plastic laminate, ceramic tile, solid-surface acrylics, wood, stainless steel, and stone: these are the major countertop choices for kitchens. Any one of these six surfaces can be installed throughout your kitchen. But you may want to consider a combination, placing heat-resistant materials near the stove, easy-cleanup surfaces near the sink, and a cool stone insert where it's handy for dough preparation.

Style	Characteristics
Plastic laminate	Laminate comes in a wide range of colors, textures, and patterns. It's durable, easy to clean, water-resistant, and relatively inexpensive. It does have drawbacks, however. It can scratch, scorch, and chip. Also, smooth, reflective surfaces tend to show dirt and water marks. Most laminate has a dark backing that shows at its seams; new solid-color laminate, designed to avoid this, is somewhat brittle and more expensive. Post-formed tops, premolded and prefabricated, are the least expensive option; a custom top with a built-up lip and backsplash looks best but is more costly.
Ceramic tile	Good-looking ceramic tile comes in many colors, textures, and patterns. Installed correctly, it's heatproof, scratch-resistant, and water-resistant. Grout is also available in numerous colors. On the other hand, grout may be hard to keep clean, even when a grout sealer is used. Also, tile's hard, irregular surface can chip glassware. High-gloss tiles show every smudge. Prices range from modest to extravagant, depending on style, accents, and accessory pieces. Nonporous glazed tiles won't soak up spills and stains.
Solid-surface	Durable, water-resistant, nonporous, and easy to clean, this marblelike material allows for a variety of edge details and sink installations, including integral units. Blemishes and scratches can be sanded out. Solid-surface countertops are expensive and require firm support from below. Until recently, color selection was limited to white, beige, and almond; now, imitation stone and pastels are readily available. Costs go up for wood inlays and other fancy edge details.
Wood	Wood is handsome, natural, easily installed, and easy on glassware and china. However, wood can scorch and scratch, and may blacken when near a source of moisture. Mineral oil can be used as a sealant (both sides must be sealed or the top will warp). Polyurethane, a permanent protective sealer, can also be used, but then you can't cut on the counter. Maple butcherblock, the most popular choice, is sold in 24, 30, and 36-inch widths; installed price is comparable to ceramic or top-of-the-line laminate. Smaller pieces are available for inserts. Oak, sugar pine, and birch are also used for counters.
Stainless steel	Stainless is waterproof, heat-resistant, easy to clean, and durable. Countertops are available with integrated sinks. Stainless is good for areas where you'll be using water a lot. It can't be used for cutting. Fabrication is expensive; you can, however, reduce the cost by using flat sheeting and a wood edge. Typical detailing includes sink cutouts, faucet holes, and bends and welds for edges and backsplashes. Custom touches and high-chromium stainless increase the price.
Stone	Granite and marble are beautiful natural materials for countertops. Their cool surfaces are very helpful for working with dough or making candy. They're heatproof, water-resistant, easy to clean, and very durable. Oil, alcohol, and any acid (such as those in lemons or wine) will stain marble or damage its high-gloss finish; granite can stand up to all of these. Solid stone slabs are very expensive; stone tiles, including slate and limestone, are less expensive alternatives.

FLOORING

The vast array of kitchen flooring materials provides a palette that would please an artist. But beyond esthetic considerations, you need to weigh the physical characteristics of the various flooring materials. Will installation involve preparing the subfloor? Can you do the work yourself? Kitchen floors take a lot of wear and tear: is your choice water-resistant, durable, and easy to clean? Is the material hard to walk on or noisy underfoot?

Resilient flooring, ceramic tile, and properly sealed wood and stone are all good choices for kitchens. Resilient flooring is the simplest (and often the least expensive) of the four to install; the other three are trickier.

Style	Characteristics
Resilient	Generally made of solid vinyl, rubber, or polyurethane, resilients are flexible, moisture and stain-resistant, easy to install, and simple to maintain. A seemingly endless variety of colors, textures, patterns, and styles is available. Resilient is vulnerable to dents and tears but can be repaired; tiles can collect moisture between seams if improperly installed.
	Sheets run up to 12 feet wide, eliminating the need for seaming in some kitchens; tiles are generally 12 inches square. Vinyl and rubber are comfortable to walk on. Polyurethane finish eliminates the need for waxing. Some vinyl comes with a photographically applied pattern, but most is inlaid; the latter is more expensive but wears much better.
Ceramic tile	Made of hard-fired slabs of clay, tiles are usually classified as *quarry* tile, commonly unglazed (unfinished) red-clay tiles that are rough and water-resistant; *pavers*, rugged unglazed tiles in earth-tone shades; and *glazed* tile, available in glossy, matte, or textured finishes and in many colors. Tile sizes and colors can be creatively mixed to produce a wide range of border treatments and field accents.
	Tile can be cold, noisy, and, if glazed, slippery underfoot. If not properly grouted, tiles can leak moisture. They can also crack and chip. Grouting can be tough to keep clean and can come loose.
	Cost varies widely; three-dimensional patterns and multicolored glazes can easily double costs. Purer clays fired at higher temperatures generally make costlier but better-wearing tiles.
Wood	Wood feels good underfoot, resists wear, and can be refinished. The three basic types of wood flooring are *strip*, narrow tongue-and-groove boards in random lengths; *plank*, tongue-and-groove boards in various widths and random lengths; and *wood tile*, often laid in blocks or squares in parquet fashion. "Floating" floor systems have several veneered strips atop each tongue-and-groove backing board. Wood flooring may be factory-prefinished or unfinished; if the latter, it's sanded and finished in place. Wood is moderate to expensive in cost, depending on quality, finish, and installation. Floating systems are generally the most expensive.
	Moisture will damage wood flooring; also, an adequate substructure is crucial. Some surfaces can be mopped; some cannot. Bleaching and some staining processes may wear unevenly and are difficult to repair. Beware of softwoods such as pine and fir: they dent easily.
Stone	Natural stone, such as slate, flagstone, marble, granite, and limestone, has been used for flooring for centuries. Today, its use is even more practical, thanks to the development of sealers and finishes. Easy to maintain, stone flooring is also virtually indestructible.
	Stone can be used in its natural shape or cut into uniform pieces—rectangular blocks or more formal tiles. Generally, uniform pieces are butted together; irregular flagstones have grouted joints. The cost of most stone flooring is high. Moreover, it requires a strong, well-supported subfloor. Some stone is cold and slippery underfoot. Careful sealing is a must; limestone and marble absorb stains and dirt.

REMODELING BASICS

Installation ▪ Removal ▪ Tools ▪ Techniques

Remodeling a kitchen means different things to different people. A minor task, such as adding a row of track lights to illuminate a dark area or brightening your walls with new coverings, can transform the whole space and satisfy you with the fresh new look. Perhaps, though, you're ready to begin a major overhaul—relocate the sink, install a dishwasher and garbage disposer, move a wall, lay a tile floor, or open the ceiling with a skylight.

This chapter touches on all aspects of kitchen remodeling; you'll find information on dismantling as well as installing everything from appliances to windows. If you're planning only a few improvements, turn directly to the sections in which you're interested. Instructions for replacing wall cabinets or countertops, for example, can be found under "Cabinets & countertops" on pages 92–97. Do you need new wall coverings to complement those cabinets? Turn to the section "Walls & ceilings," pages 86–91.

Can you do the job yourself? Our directions assume that you have some knowledge of basic tools, building terms, and techniques—how to hammer a nail, use a straightedge, and handle an adjustable wrench. If you need more detailed information on step-by-step procedures, take a look at the *Sunset* books *Basic Carpentry Illustrated*, *Basic Plumbing Illustrated*, and *Basic Home Wiring Illustrated*.

Resilient tiles are an ideal flooring product for do-it-yourselfers. Some tiles are self-sticking; others, like those shown at left, require a thin bed of adhesive. Standard 12-inch squares go together quickly; color options allow you to add accents as desired. For installation details, see page 99.

Before work begins

Are you ready to remodel? Before plunging into a project, you should form a clear idea of the sequence of steps necessary to complete the job, obtain any necessary permits from your local building department, and evaluate your own ability to perform each of the tasks. To do the work yourself, you'll also need to provide yourself with the proper materials and tools.

After you have a clear understanding of what's involved, you're ready to begin.

Can I do the work myself?

The level of skill required to remodel your kitchen depends on the scale of the improvements. Surface treatments—such as painting, wallpapering, replacing light fixtures, hanging cabinets, or laying resilient flooring—are within the realm of any homeowner with the rudiments of do-it-yourself ability. Some projects may require a few specialized tools, generally available from a building supply or home improvement center.

Complex remodeling tasks—such as moving bearing walls, running new drain and vent pipes, or wiring new electrical circuits and service panels—are often best handled by professionals. Many smaller jobs within the structural, plumbing, and electrical areas, though, are within the skills of a homeowner with basic experience.

Even if there's little you can build, you may discover a talent for demolition—and save money in the process; note, however, that some contractors may not want to relinquish this task. If you take it on, be sure you're finished by the time the remodeling crew is ready to begin.

Planning your attack

As the scale of your remodeling project increases, the need for careful planning becomes more critical. Before work begins, doublecheck the priorities listed below.

■ Establish the sequence of jobs to be performed, and estimate the time required to complete each one.

■ If you're getting professional assistance, make sure you have firm contracts and schedules with contractors, subcontractors, or other hired workers.

■ Obtain all required building permits (see page 52).

■ Arrange for delivery of materials; be sure you have all the necessary tools on hand.

■ If electricity, gas, or water must be shut off by the utility company, arrange for it before work is scheduled to begin.

■ Find out where you can dispose of refuse, and secure any necessary dumping permits.

■ Be sure there is a storage area available for temporarily relocating fixtures or appliances.

■ Measure fixtures and appliances for clearance through doorways and up and down staircases.

Remodels can be inconvenient at best and totally disruptive at worst. Consider setting up a temporary kitchen equipped with a refrigerator, hot plate, and toaster oven somewhere away from the fray.

How to use this chapter

The sections in this chapter are arranged in the order in which you'd proceed if you were installing an entirely new kitchen. Read consecutively, they'll give you an overview of the scope and sequence of kitchen improvements.

The first three sections survey the relatively complex subjects of structural, plumbing, and electrical systems. Whether or not you plan to do the work yourself, you'd be wise to review these sections for background information. A knowledge of your home's inner workings enables you to plan changes more effectively and to understand the reasons for seemingly arbitrary code restrictions affecting your plans.

Some of your most difficult re-modeling hours may be spent tearing out old work. To minimize the effort, we've included removal procedures within the appropriate installation sections.

If you're planning only one or two simple projects, turn directly to the applicable sections for step-by-step instructions. Special features within the chapter present additional ideas and information for maximum improvement with minimum work and expense.

STEPS IN REMODELING

You can use this chart to plan the basic sequence of tasks involved in dismantling your old kitchen and installing the new one. Depending on the scale of your job and the specific materials you select, you may need to alter the suggested order. Manufacturers' instructions offer additional guidelines.

Removal sequence

1. Accessories, decorative elements
2. Furniture
3. Contents of cabinets, closets, shelves
4. Fixtures, appliances
5. Countertops, backsplashes
6. Base cabinets, wall cabinets, shelves
7. Floor materials
8. Light fixtures
9. Wall coverings

Installation sequence

1. Structural changes: walls, doors, windows, skylights
2. Rough plumbing changes
3. Electrical wiring
4. Wall and ceiling coverings
5. Light fixtures
6. Wall cabinets, base cabinets, kitchen islands, shelves
7. Countertops, backsplashes
8. Floor materials
9. Fixtures, appliances
10. Furniture
11. Decorative elements

Structural basics

Acquiring a basic understanding of your kitchen's structural shell is required homework for many kitchen improvements. Your kitchen's framework probably will conform to the pattern of the "typical kitchen," shown in the illustration below.

Starting at the base of the drawing, you'll notice the following framing members: a wooden sill resting on a foundation wall; a series of horizontal, evenly spaced floor joists; and a subfloor (usually plywood sheets) laid atop the joists. This platform supports the first-floor walls, both interior and exterior. The walls are formed by vertical, evenly spaced studs that run between a horizontal sole plate and parallel top plate. The primary wall coverings are fastened directly to the studs.

Depending upon the design of the house, one of several types of construction may be used above the kitchen walls. If there's a second story, a layer of ceiling joists rests on the walls; these joists support both the floor above and the kitchen ceiling below. A one-story house will have either an "open-beamed" ceiling—flat or pitched—or a "finished" ceiling. In simple terms, a finished ceiling covers the roof rafters and sheathing which, if exposed, would constitute an open-beamed ceiling. With a flat roof, the finished ceiling is attached directly to the rafters. The ceiling below a pitched roof is attached to joists or to a metal or wooden frame.

Removing a partition wall

Often a major kitchen remodeling means removing all or part of an interior wall to enlarge the space.

Walls that define your kitchen may be bearing or nonbearing. A bearing wall helps support the weight of the house; a nonbearing wall does not. An interior nonbearing wall, often called a partition wall, may be removed without special precautions. The procedure outlined in this section applies to partitions only. If you're considering a remodeling project that involves moving a bearing wall or any wall beneath a second story, consult an architect or contractor about problems and procedures.

How can you tell the difference in walls? All exterior walls running perpendicular to ceiling and floor joists are bearing. Normally, at least one main interior wall is also a bearing wall. If possible, climb up into the attic or crawlspace and check the ceiling joists. If they are joined over any wall, that wall is bearing. Even if joists span the entire width of the house, their midsections may be resting on a bearing wall at the point of maximum allowable span. If you have any doubts about the wall, consult an architect, contractor, or building inspector.

Bearing walls (in black)

Nonbearing walls (in white)

Direction of rafters, floor joists, and ceiling joists

Though removing a partition wall is not complicated, it can be quite messy. Cover the floors and furnishings, and wear a dust mask, safety glasses, and gloves. NOTE: Check the wall for signs of electrical wiring, water and drainpipes, or heating and ventilation ducts. Any of these obstructions must be carefully rerouted before you remove the wall.

Removing wall covering. First, if there's a door in the wall, remove it from its hinges. Pry off any door trim, ceiling molding, and base molding.

The most common wall covering is gypsum wallboard nailed to wall studs. To remove it, knock holes in the wallboard with a hammer, then pull it away from the studs with a pry bar. After one surface is re-

BASIC STRUCTURAL ANATOMY

Rafters

Ceiling joists

Top plate

Header

Wall studs

Rough sill

Subfloor

Floor joists

Sole plate

Joist header

Foundation wall

Sill

■Structural basics

HOW TO REMOVE WALL FRAMING

Saw through the middle of the wall studs; bend the studs sideways to free the nails from the top and sole plates.

Cut gaps through the sole plate with a saw and chisel; insert a pry bar in each gap to free the sole plate.

Strip ceiling materials back from the top plate, cut gaps in the plate, and pry out sections of plate.

moved, you can hit the other side from behind to knock it free.

If the wall covering is plaster and lath, chisel away the plaster until the lath backing—wood strips or metal—is exposed. You'll have to cut through the lath to break it up; then pry the lath and plaster away from the studs.

Dismantling the framing. Remove studs by sawing through the middle of each one; then push and pull them sideways to free the nails. To get at end studs (attached to studs or nailing blocks in adjacent walls), first strip wall coverings back to the bordering studs; then saw and pry as required.

To remove the sole plate, saw a small section out of the middle down to the finished floor level, chisel through the remaining thickness, and insert a pry bar in the gap.

To remove a top plate that lies parallel to the joists, cut ceiling materials back to adjacent joists, and pry off the plate. If the top plate is perpendicular to the joists, cut an even 2-foot strip in the ceiling materials, making certain that you don't cut into joists; remove the plate.

Patching walls, ceilings, and floors. Wallboard and plaster aren't difficult to patch (see page 94); the real challenge lies in matching a

special texture, wallpaper, shade of paint, or well-aged floor. This is not a problem if your remodeling plans call for new wall coverings, ceiling, or flooring. In either case, see the sections "Walls & ceilings" (pages 86–91) and "Flooring" (pages 98–103) for techniques and tips.

Framing a new wall

To separate a kitchen from an adjoining living area or to subdivide

space within the kitchen, you may need to build a new partition wall.

Framing a wall is a straightforward task, but you must measure carefully and continue to check the alignment as work progresses. The basic steps are listed below. To install a doorway, see page 70.

Plotting the location. The new wall must be anchored securely to the floor, ceiling joists, and, if possible, to wall framing on one side.

WALL FRAMING COMPONENTS

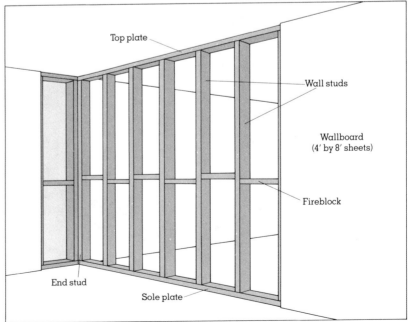

To locate the studs, try knocking with your fist along the wall until the sound changes from hollow to solid. If you have wallboard, you can use an inexpensive stud finder; often, though, the nails that hold wallboard to the studs are visible on close inspection.

To locate ceiling joists, use the same methods or, from the attic or crawlspace, drive small nails down through the ceiling on both sides of a joist to serve as reference points below. Adjacent joists and studs should be evenly spaced, usually 16 or 24 inches away from those you've located.

A wall running perpendicular to the joists will demand least effort to attach. If wall and joists will run parallel, though, try to center the wall under a single joist; otherwise, you'll need to install nailing blocks every 2 feet between two parallel joists (see illustration above right). If the side of the new wall falls between existing studs you'll need to install additional nailing blocks.

On the ceiling, mark both ends of the center line of the new wall. Measure 1¾ inches (half the width of a 2 by 4 top plate) on both sides of each mark; snap parallel lines between corresponding marks with a chalkline; the top plate will occupy the space between the lines.

Positioning the sole plate. Hang a plumb bob from each end of the lines you just marked and mark these new points on the floor. Snap two more chalklines to connect the floor points.

Cut both sole plate and top plate to the desired length. Lay the sole

HOW TO ANCHOR A TOP PLATE

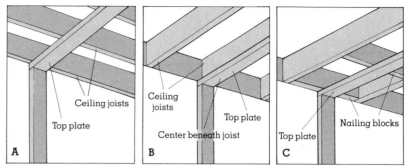

To anchor a top plate, nail to perpendicular joists (A), to the bottom of the parallel joist (B), or install nailing blocks between the parallel joists (C).

plate between the lines on the floor and nail it in place with 10-penny nails spaced every 2 feet. (If you have a masonry floor, use a masonry bit to drill holes through the sole plate every 2 or 3 feet. Then insert expansion bolts.)

If you're planning a doorway (see "Framing a doorway," page 70), don't nail through that section of the plate; it will be cut out later.

Marking stud positions. Lay the top plate against the sole plate, as shown in the illustration below. Beginning at the end that will be attached to an existing stud or to nailing blocks, measure in 1½ inches—the thickness of a 2 by 4 stud—and draw a line across both plates with a combination square. Starting once more from that end, measure and draw lines at 15¼ and 16¾ inches. From these lines, advance 16 inches at a time, drawing new lines, until the far end of both plates is reached. Each set of lines will outline the placement of a stud, with all studs

evenly spaced 16 inches "on center" (O.C.). Don't worry if the spacing at the far end is less than 16 inches. (If local codes permit, consider a 24-inch spacing—you'll save lumber—and adjust the initial placement of lines to 23¼ and 24¾ inches.)

Fastening the top plate. With two helpers, lift the top plate into position between the lines (marked on the ceiling); nail it to perpendicular joists, to one parallel joist, or to nailing blocks, as shown above.

Attaching the studs. Measure and cut the studs to exact length. Attach one end stud (or both) to existing studs or to nailing blocks between studs. Lift the remaining studs into place one at a time; line them up on the marks, and check plumb with a carpenter's level. Toenail the studs to both top plate and sole plate with 8-penny nails.

Many building codes require horizontal fireblocks between studs. The number of rows depends on the code; if permitted, position blocks to provide an extra nailing surface for wall materials.

Finishing. After the studs are installed, it's time to add electrical outlets and switches (see pages 80–82), as well as new plumbing (see pages 74–76). It's also time for the building inspector to check your work. Following the inspection, you can apply your wall coverings (see pages 86–91), patch the ceiling, and add base moldings.

(Continued on next page)

HOW TO MARK STUD POSITIONS

■Structural basics

HOW TO FRAME A DOORWAY

Mark and cut studs within the opening, even with the top of the new header.

Nail the new header to the king studs; nail into ends of the new cripple studs.

Nail trimmer studs to the king studs; block out a third trimmer, if needed.

Framing a doorway

Relocating kitchen appliances, cabinets, or counters or simply redirecting traffic flow may involve moving a door opening. Covering an existing door is relatively easy (see below). To create a new opening, it's necessary to remove wall materials, add door framing, and possibly hang a new door. Be sure the wall you plan to cut into is a non-bearing wall (see "Removing a partition wall," page 67). If the wall contains electrical wires, pipes, or ductwork, they must be rerouted.

Positioning the opening. Are you planning an open doorway, or a frame for a bifold, sliding, or standard prehung door? Determine the door type before starting work, and check the manufacturer's "rough opening" dimensions—the exact wall opening required after the new framing is in place.

You'll need to plan an opening large enough to accommodate both the rough opening and the rough door framing—an additional 1½ inches on top and sides. If you're recycling an old door or your new unit did not come with rough opening dimensions, add an additional ⅜ inch all around for shimming (adjusting level and plumb) the typical door frame.

Often it's simpler to remove the wallboard from floor to ceiling be-tween two bordering studs (the new king studs) that will remain in place. (This is the method illustrated.) In any case, you'll save work later if you can use at least one existing stud as part of the rough framing.

Regardless of the method you choose, use a carpenter's level for a straightedge, and mark the outline of the opening on the wall.

Removing wall covering and studs. First remove any base molding. Cut along the door outline with a reciprocating or keyhole saw, being careful to sever only the wallboard, not the studs beneath. Pry the wall-board away from the framing. To remove plaster and lath, chisel through the plaster to expose the lath; then cut the lath and pry it loose.

Cut the studs inside the opening to the height required for the header (see drawing above). Using a combination square, mark these studs on the face and one side, then cut carefully with a reciprocating or crosscut saw. Pry the cut studs loose from the sole plate.

Framing the opening. With wall covering and studs removed, you're ready to frame the opening. Measure and cut the header (for a partition wall you can use a 2 by 4 laid flat), and toenail it to the king studs with 8-penny nails. Nail the header to the bottoms of the cripple studs.

Cut the sole plate within the opening, and pry it away from the subfloor.

Cut trimmer studs and nail them to the king studs with 10-penny nails in a staggered pattern. You'll probably need to adjust the width by blocking out a third trimmer from one side, as shown above right.

Hanging the door. Bifold, swinging, or sliding pocket doors are most commonly used in kitchens. Methods of hanging doors vary considerably, depending on type. Check the manufacturer's instructions carefully before you plan the wall opening.

Even if you're not hanging a door, you'll probably want to install a preassembled door frame—consisting of a top jamb and two side jambs—to cover the rough framing.

Installing trim. When the framing is completed and the door is hung, patch the wallboard (see page 94) and install new trim (casing) around the opening. Some prehung doors have casing attached.

Closing a doorway

It's easy to eliminate an existing doorway. Simply add new studs within the opening and attach new wall coverings. The only trick is to match the present wall surface.

First, remove the casing around the opening. Then remove the door from its hinges or guide track and pry any jambs or tracks away from the rough framing.

Next, measure the gap on the floor between the existing trimmer studs; cut a length of 2 by 4 to serve as a new sole plate. Nail it to the floor with 10-penny nails. (If you have a masonry floor, attach the 2 by 4 with expansion bolts.)

Measure and cut new 2 by 4 studs to fill the space; position studs at 16-inch intervals. Toenail the studs to the new sole plate and the header with 8-penny nails. Add fireblocks between studs if required by the local code.

Strip the wall coverings back far enough to give yourself a firm nailing surface and an even edge. Then add new coverings to match the existing ones (see pages 86–87), or resurface the entire wall. Match or replace the baseboard molding.

Window basics

Framing and hanging a window is similar to installing a door (see page 70), though in addition you must cut into the exterior siding and sheathing of the house. But the most important factor to consider is the possibility that you may be dealing with a bearing wall (see page 67). Removing studs from a bearing wall means constructing a temporary support wall before you start work and using more rigid framing than that required for partition wall openings.

An outline of basic installation follows. For details about tools and help with step-by-step techniques, consult the manufacturer's instructions or your window dealer.

Removing an existing window. First, remove any interior and exterior trim that's not an integral part of the unit. Take out the sash, if possible (see drawing above); then remove the frame. The window may have been nailed directly to the rough framing materials or secured by flanges or brackets.

BASIC WINDOW COMPONENTS

Basic window framing. Unlike rough door framing, window framing includes cripple studs at the top and bottom. The rough sill—a length of 2 by 4 or 2 by 6 lumber laid flat and sometimes doubled for strength—lies at the bottom edge of the opening. The top edge is bounded by the header. The header for a bearing wall opening and (depending on local codes) for any exterior wall is typically composed of matching lengths of "2-by" framing lumber turned on edge, with ½-inch-thick plywood spacers sandwiched between them. The exact size of 2-by material required depends on both the width of the window opening and your local building code.

Cutting a new opening. You should receive a rough opening size for your new window from the manufacturer. (If not, measure the unit and add an extra ⅜ inch on all sides for leveling and plumbing the window.) The actual opening will be somewhat larger: add to the rough opening size the dimensions of the king studs, trimmer studs, header, and sill. Work from the inside of the house outward. If possible, complete the rough framing before opening the exterior.

Installing a prehung window. A prehung window arrives with the sash already installed inside the window frame—and frequently with the exterior casing (trim) attached. To simply replace an existing window with another of the same size, first remove the interior trim and measure the rough opening; then order the new window to fit.

Using wood shims or blocks, center, level, and plumb the new window in the opening; then fasten it to the rough framing. Depending on window type, you'll either nail through a flange into the outside sheathing, screw the jambs to the header and trimmer studs, or nail through preassembled exterior trim.

Finishing touches. Your new window may need exterior casing and a drip cap. Or you may be required to install metal flashing over the unit's top edge. Thoroughly caulk the joints between the siding and the new window.

Cover the top and sides of the inside opening with casing and install a finished stool over the rough sill. Finally, add one last strip of casing (called an apron).

(Continued on page 73)

AN INTRODUCTION TO GREENHOUSE WINDOWS

Like its full-scale counterpart, a greenhouse window addition will nurture as well as showcase your favorite plants. The greenhouse window also provides a unique decorating tool: plant-laden shelves reach beyond a wall and seemingly expand an enclosed room into the open space beyond. Extending a kitchen countertop into the window unit heightens this illusion; it also can bring within reach an herb garden to inspire a cook.

Greenhouse window details

Greenhouse windows range from 3 feet square to 10 feet wide and 5 feet tall. (Units wider than 5 feet may require special framing and installation.) Standard depth is 12 to 16 inches. Preassembled units include glazing, framing, and adjustable shelving.

Choose either glass or acrylic glazing; both offer a variety of finishes. Though acrylic is shatter-resistant, glass is more durable and less prone to scratching. Aluminum structural sections are lightweight and maintenance-free; wood-framed units, though bulkier, offer you greater possibility in the choice of finish.

Options in greenhouse units include weatherstripping along vents to decrease cold air infiltration, screening inside vents to keep insects out, and double glazing to slow heat loss.

Other means of controlling heat loss through a greenhouse window include interior shutters and quilted window covers that isolate the unit from heated living space. For further information on insulating and shading greenhouse windows, consult a window covering specialist.

Installing the window unit

Installation techniques differ, depending on local building codes, the exterior siding of your house, type of window unit, and whether or not you're replacing an existing window with a unit of the same size. Greenhouse windows can be attached to the wall around an existing opening or to an existing wooden frame.

Before purchasing a window unit, it's a good idea to study various manufacturers' specifications and installation instructions.

Adding furring strips. If your home has a wood-finished exterior such as beveled siding or shingles, you'll need to add 1 by 4 furring strips around the window frame. (For masonry, masonry veneer, or stucco, follow the manufacturers' instructions or consult a contractor.)

To attach the strips, cut the siding back to the underlying sheathing so that the furring can lie flat. If building paper covers the sheathing, leave the paper intact.

Apply a generous bed of caulking to the sheathing or building paper. Then secure the furring with nails long enough to penetrate furring, building paper, and sheathing. Nails should extend into the studs or header a distance equal to twice the thickness of the furring. Set the nail heads below the furring surface.

Mounting the greenhouse window. With helpers holding the unit in place, level the window. Temporarily nail the unit in place and check the level again. Attach the window unit with screws long enough to penetrate the mounting flange, furring, sheathing, building paper, and at least an inch into the studs and header.

Finishing details. For units wider than 5 feet, bracing between the base and wall is recommended. Caulk the seams between the flange and furring and between the furring and siding. If you like, you can cover the base of the window with tile or finish it to match an adjacent countertop.

Insect screen

Vents

Furring strips

Building paper

Sheathing

Jamb

Studs

Sill

Siding

Mounting flange

Adjustable plant shelf

■Structural basics

Skylight basics

Installing a skylight in a pitched roof with asphalt or wood shingles is a two-part process: you cut and frame openings in both roof and ceiling, and connect the two openings with a vertical or angled light shaft. (You don't even need a light shaft for a flat roof or open-beamed ceiling, which requires only a single opening.) Here is a brief description of the installation sequence; for complete information on the tools and techniques required for the job, consult the manufacturer's instructions or your skylight dealer.

Marking the openings. Using the rough opening measurements supplied by the manufacturer, mark the location of the ceiling opening; then drive nails up through the four corners and center so they'll be visible in the attic or crawlspace. From the attic, check for obstructions, shifting the location if necessary. You'll save work if you can use one or two ceiling joists as the edges of your opening.

With a plumb bob, transfer the ceiling marks to the underside of the roof; again, drive nails up through the roofing materials to mark the location. If you run into obstructions on the roof, change the position slightly and use an angled light shaft to connect the two openings.

Framing the roof opening. On a day with zero probability of rain, cut and frame the roof opening. Exercise extreme caution when working on the roof; if the pitch is steep or if you have a tile or slate roof, you might consider leaving this part to professionals.

When you work with a skylight designed to be mounted on a curb frame, build the curb first; 2 by 6 lumber is commonly used. (If your skylight has an integral curb or is self-flashing, you can skip this step.)

To determine the actual size of the opening you need to cut, add the dimensions of any framing materials (see below) to the rough opening size marked by the nails. You may need to remove some extra shingles

BASIC SKYLIGHT COMPONENTS

Skylight

Step flashing

Curb

Apron flashing

Sheathing

2 by 4 studs

Wallboard in light shaft

Rafter

Header

Header

Joist hanger

Ceiling joists

or roofing materials down to the sheathing to accommodate the flashing of a curb-mounted unit or the flange of a self-flashing unit.

Cut the roof opening in successive layers: roofing materials first; sheathing next, and finally any necessary rafters. Before cutting the rafters, support them by 2 by 4s nailed to the ceiling joists below.

To frame the opening, you'll need double headers and possibly trimmers. Install the headers with double joist hangers.

If you're installing a curb-mounted unit, position and flash the curb. Toenail the curb to the rafters or trimmers and to the headers. Pay special attention to the manufacturer's instructions concerning directions for flashing.

Mounting the skylight. For a curb-mounted unit, secure the skylight to the top of the curb with nails and a sealant. Set a self-flashing unit in roofing cement, then nail through the flange directly to the roof sheathing. Coat the joints and nail holes with more roofing cement.

Opening the ceiling. Double-check your original ceiling marks against the roof opening and the intended angle of the light shaft. Cut through the ceiling materials and then sever the joists. Support joists to be cut—do this by bracing them against adjacent joists. Frame the opening in the same manner used for the roof opening.

Building a light shaft. Measure the distance between the ceiling headers and roof headers at each corner and at 16-inch intervals between the corners. Cut studs to fit the measurements and install them as illustrated above. This provides a nailing surface for wall coverings.

Final touches. Insulate the spaces between studs in the light shaft before fastening wall coverings to the studs. Painting wallboard white maximizes reflected light.

Trim the ceiling opening as required. Adding a plastic ceiling panel (one that's either manufactured or cut to size) helps diffuse light evenly.

Plumbing basics

Do you know how your plumbing system works? If not, the kitchen is a good place to start learning, for the plumbing here is much less complicated than in other areas—bathrooms, for instance.

A plumbing overview

Three complementary sets of pipes work together to fill your home's plumbing needs: the drain-waste and vent (DWV) systems, and the water supply system. In the typical kitchen, these pipes serve the "sink complex"—the sink and related appliances, such as the dishwasher and garbage disposer.

The supply system. Water that eventually arrives at your kitchen faucet enters the house from the public water main or from a source on the property. At the water service entrance, the main supply line divides in two—one line branching off to be heated by the water heater,

the other remaining as cold water. The two pipes usually run parallel below the first-floor level until they reach the vicinity of a group of fixtures, then head up through the wall or floor. Sometimes the water supply—hot, cold, or both—passes through a water softener or filter (see drawing below) before reaching the fixtures.

Drain-waste and vent systems. The drain-waste pipes channel waste water and solid wastes to the sewer line. Vent pipes carry away sewer gas and maintain atmospheric pressure in drainpipes and fixture traps.

Every house has a main soil stack that serves a dual function: below the level of the fixtures, it is your home's primary drainpipe; at its upper end, which protrudes through the roof, the stack becomes a vent. Drainpipes from individual fixtures, as well as larger branch drains, connect to the main stack. A

fixture or fixture group located on a branch drain far from the main stack will have a secondary vent stack of its own rising to the roof.

The sink complex. Generally, a single set of vertical supply pipes and one drainpipe serve the entire kitchen. For both convenience and economy, fixtures and appliances that require water usually are adjacent to the sink. Supply pipes for a dishwasher, hot water dispenser, and automatic ice maker branch off the main hot and cold supply lines leading to the sink faucet. Similarly, the dishwasher and disposer share the sink's trap and drainpipe. The hot water dispenser discharges directly into the sink.

Roughing in new plumbing

You will need to add new plumbing to your kitchen if you move your present sink and related appliances, plumb a sink into a new

A PLUMBING OVERVIEW

Your kitchen's plumbing is part of a coordinated system of hot and cold supply pipes leading water to fixtures and appliances, and drain-waste and vent pipes carrying wastes and gases away (A). Kitchen plumbing is commonly concentrated in the "sink complex" area (B).

kitchen island, or add a new fixture—such as a second sink.

If you have some pipefitting experience from previous plumbing projects, you may be able to handle these jobs yourself. But if you're not confident of your abilities, consider hiring a professional plumber to rough in the new pipes. When that work is finished, you can then hook up the fixtures or appliances yourself; refer to pages 104–111.

Mapping your present system. If you're considering a plumbing change, you'll first need a detailed map of the present plumbing. Begin your investigation from an unfinished basement or crawlspace or, if necessary, from the attic or roof. Locate the main stack, branch drains, and any secondary stacks. Positioning yourself directly below or above the kitchen, try to determine whether the sink complex is tied directly into the main stack or connected to a branch drain with its own vent. Find the spot where vertical supply lines branch off from horizontal lines and head up into a wall or the floor.

Extending DWV pipes. Your plans to relocate a sink or add a new fixture depend on the feasibility of extending present DWV pipes. Plumbing codes, both national and local, are quite specific about the following: the size of the drainpipe or branch drain serving the kitchen sink complex or any new fixture requiring drainage; the distance (called the "critical distance") from the traps to the main stack, secondary stack, or other vent; and the point where a new drainpipe or branch drain ties into the branch drain or main stack.

A proposed fixture located within a few feet of the main stack (check local codes for the exact distance) usually can be drained and vented directly by the stack. New fixtures distant from the stack probably will require a new branch drain beneath the floor, running either to the stack or to an existing cleanout in the main drain (see drawing below); you'll also need to run a new secondary stack up to the roof.

The drainpipe required for a kitchen sink complex normally has a diameter of at least 1½ inches (2 inches if you also plan to vent directly into the stack). Minimum vent size for a secondary stack is commonly 1¼ inches, unless a dishwasher installed without a separate air gap necessitates a larger pipe.

Older DWV pipes probably are made of cast iron, with "hub" or "bell-and-spigot" ends joined by molten lead and oakum. To extend the system, you may substitute "hubless" fittings (consisting of neoprene gaskets and stainless steel clamps), which are simpler to install.

Since plastic is considerably lighter than cast iron and is easily joined with solvent cement, you may want to use ABS (acrylonitrile-butadiene-styrene) or PVC (polyvinyl chloride) pipe in your extension. First check the local code; some areas prohibit the use of plastic pipe.

Extending supply pipes. Because no venting is required, extending sup-

PIPES & FITTINGS

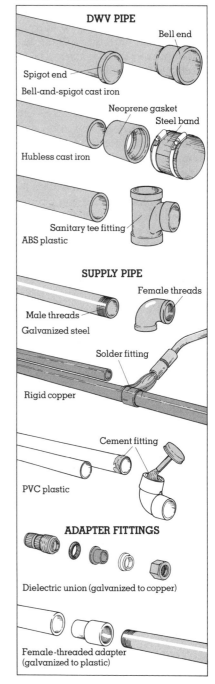

HOW TO EXTEND YOUR PLUMBING SYSTEM

To drain kitchen plumbing additions, you can either (A) tap into the present main stack, if nearby, or (B) install a new branch drain and secondary vent stack.

■Plumbing basics

ply pipes is a much easier task than extending the DWV system. The selection of correctly sized pipes, as outlined in detail by local codes, depends equally on the type of fixture to be added, the volume of water it demands, and the length of the new pipe.

Your home's supply pipes most likely are either galvanized steel (referred to as "galvanized" or "iron" pipe) connected by threaded fittings, or rigid copper joined with soldered fittings. Some local codes permit the use of plastic supply lines; special adapters will enable you to convert from one material to another (see page 75).

Routing new pipes. Ideally, new drainpipes should be routed below the kitchen floor. They can be suspended from floor joists by pipe hangers, inserted in the space between parallel joists, or threaded through notches or holes drilled in perpendicular joists. If you have a finished basement, you'll need to cut into the ceiling to thread pipes between or through joists, hide the pipes with a dropped ceiling, or box them in.

Drainpipes must slope away from fixtures; a minimum slope of ¼ inch per foot is usually required.

A new vent stack must be installed inside an existing wall (a big job), built into a new or "thickened" wall (see "Building a wet wall," below), or concealed in a closet or cabinet. In mild climates, an enclosed vent may also run up the exterior of the house, within a box.

Supply pipes normally follow drainpipes, but for convenience, can be routed directly up through the wall or floor from main horizontal lines below. Supply pipes should run parallel to each other, at least 6 inches apart.

Building a wet wall. The main soil stack, and often a secondary stack, are commonly hidden inside an oversize house wall called a "wet wall."

Unlike an ordinary 2 by 4 stud wall (shown on page 68), a wet wall has a sole plate and top plate built from 2 by 6 or 2 by 8 lumber. Additionally, the 2 by 4 studs are set in pairs, on edge, as shown below. This construction creates maximum space inside the wall for large DWV pipes, which often are wider than a standard wall, and for the fittings, which are wider yet.

You can also "fur out" an existing wall to hide added pipes—attach new 2 by 4s to the old ones, then add new wall coverings (see above right). Similarly, a new branch drain that can't run below the floor may be hidden by furring strips laid beside the pipe and covered with

new flooring materials. (For flooring details, see pages 98–103.)

Gas system basics

When you convert from electricity to gas or simply relocate a gas appliance, keep in mind a few basic guidelines.

Materials approved for gas supply vary with the area and the type of gas. The most universally accepted materials are threaded pipe of galvanized steel, and "black pipe" (steel pipe without galvanizing). Heavier grades of copper pipe used for plumbing systems (types K and L) are also permitted in some areas.

The plumbing code, or separate gas code, will specify pipe size according to cubic foot capacity and the length of pipe between the meter or storage tank and the appliance. All gas appliances should have a numerical rating in BTUs per hour stamped on the nameplate. To convert BTUs to cubic feet, figure 1,000 BTUs to 1 cubic foot; for example, 65,000 BTUs = 65 cubic feet.

Each appliance must have a nearby code-approved shutoff valve with a straight handle, to turn off gas in an emergency.

There's no room for error when installing a gas system. It's advisable to have a professional make the installation. You must, in any case, have the work inspected and tested before the gas is turned on.

Electrical basics

What may appear to be a hopelessly tangled maze of wires running through the walls and ceiling of your home is actually a well-organized system of circuits. In your kitchen, those circuits serve the light fixtures, switches, and power outlets. Some circuits run directly to large appliances.

In this section you'll find an explanation of your home's electrical system as it relates to kitchen lighting and appliances. Outlined are the techniques necessary to make basic electrical improvements. If you're replacing or adding light fixtures, refer to pages 83–85 for help in installing them.

Should you do your own electrical work? It's not always permitted. Local building departments restrict the extent and type of new wiring a homeowner may undertake. In some areas, for example, you may not be permitted to add a new circuit to the service panel. Or if the wiring inside the walls of an older home is the knob-and-tube variety, local regulations may require that new hookups be made by licensed electricians. When restrictions don't apply, problems can still crop up. If you have any doubt about how to proceed, it's best to hire a professional.

Before you do any of the work yourself, talk with your building department's electrical inspector about local codes, the National Electrical Code (NEC), and your area's requirements concerning permits and inspections.

Understanding your system

Today most homes have what's called "three-wire" service. The utility company connects three wires to your service entrance panel. Each of two "hot" wires supplies electricity at approximately 120 volts. During normal operation, the third—or "neutral"—wire is maintained at zero volts. (Don't be misled, though, by the harmless sound of "neutral"; all three wires are "live.")

Three-wire service provides both 120-volt and 240-volt capabilities. One hot wire and the neutral wire combine to supply 120 volts, used for most household applications such as lights and small appliances. Both hot wires and the neutral wire can complete a 120/240-volt circuit for such needs as an electric range or clothes dryer.

Many older homes have only two-wire service, with one hot wire at 120 volts and one neutral wire. Two-wire service does not have 240-volt capability.

Service entrance panel. This panel is the control center for your electrical system. Inside you'll find the main disconnect (main fuses or main circuit breaker), the fuses or circuit breakers protecting individual circuits, and the grounding connection for the entire system.

After entering the panel and passing through the main disconnect, each hot wire connects to one of two "bus bars," as shown below. These bars accept the amount of current permitted by the main disconnect and allow you to divide that current into smaller branch circuits. The neutral wire is attached to a neutral bus bar, which is in direct contact with the earth through the grounding electrode conductor.

Your home may also have one or more subpanels from which branch circuits originate. A subpanel is an extension of the service entrance panel; the two are connected by hot and neutral "subfeeds."

Simple circuitry. The word "circuit" represents the course that electric current travels; carried by the hot wire, it passes from the service entrance panel or subpanel to one or more devices using electricity (such as a group of light fixtures), then returns to the panel by way of the neutral wire. The devices are normally connected by parallel wiring, as shown below. The hot and neutral wires run continuously from one fixture or outlet box to another; separate wires branch off to individual devices.

Each 120-volt branch circuit consists of one hot wire and one neutral wire. The hot wire originates at a branch circuit fuse or circuit breaker connected to one of the hot bus bars. A 120/240-volt circuit, which requires both hot wires, is connected through the fuse or breaker to both hot bus bars. All neutral conductors originate at the neutral bus bar inside the panel.

Grounding prevents shock. The NEC requires that every circuit have a grounding system. Grounding ensures that all metal parts of a wiring system will be maintained at zero volts. In the event of a short circuit, a grounding wire carries current back to the service entrance panel and ensures that the fuse or circuit breaker will open, shutting off the flow of current.

The grounding wire for each circuit is attached to the neutral bus bar and then is run with the hot and neutral wires; individual "jumper" wires branch off to ground individual metal devices and boxes as required.

(Continued on next page)

■Electrical basics

Planning electrical improvements

Before you start daydreaming about new track lighting, a dishwasher, or a disposer, you'll need to know whether your present system can handle an additional load.

Service type and rating. First, determine your present type of electrical service. Looking through the window of your meter, you'll see several numbers on the faceplate: 120V indicates two-wire service; 240V indicates three-wire service that provides both 120-volt and 240-volt capabilities.

Your electrical system is also rated for the maximum amount of current (measured in amperes—or "amps") it can carry. This "service rating," determined by the size of the service entrance equipment, should be stamped on the main fuses or circuit breaker. If your system doesn't have a main disconnect, call your utility company or building department for the rating.

Codes. Requirements for electrical circuits serving a modern kitchen and dining area are clearly prescribed by the NEC. Plug-in outlets and switches for small appliances

and the refrigerator must be served by a minimum of two 20-amp circuits. Light fixtures are not connected to these circuits, but they share one or more 15-amp circuits. Any outlet within 6 feet of a sink should be protected with a ground fault circuit interrupter (GFCI).

If you're installing a dishwasher and/or disposer, you'll need a separate 20-amp circuit for each. Most electric ranges use an individual 50-amp, 120/240-volt major appliance circuit. Wall ovens and a separate cooktop may share a 50-amp circuit.

Tapping into a present circuit. A circuit can be tapped wherever there's an accessible housing box (see "Selecting a power source," page 79). Because of code restrictions, though, you must tap the correct type of circuit.

It's also very important to determine that the circuit you're planning to tap doesn't already carry the maximum load allowed. For help in mapping your circuits, consult an electrician or your local building department.

Adding a new circuit. When an existing circuit can't handle a new load

or when a new appliance requires its own circuit, you can often add a new circuit or a subpanel. However, your present house load combined with the proposed addition still must not exceed your service rating.

To help calculate the house load, the NEC has established representative values and formulas based on typical electrical usage. For further aid check with your building department's electrical inspector.

Older homes with two-wire service of less than 100 amps simply can't support many major improvements. To add a new oven or dishwasher you may need to increase your service type and rating, which means replacing the service entrance equipment.

Working with wire

To wire basic extensions to your present electrical circuits, you'll need a few tools and materials, a knack for making wire splices, and the patience to route new wire from box to box and then patch wall and ceiling materials. For work on this scale, an electrical permit will probably be required.

Here's the most important rule for all do-it-yourself electricians:

TYPICAL KITCHEN CIRCUITS

Dimmer switch

Overhead lights

Plug-in outlet for small appliances

120/240-volt, 50-amp circuit for range

MAIN

120-volt, 20-amp circuit for small appliances

120-volt, 15-amp circuit for lighting

Refrigerator

Range

120-volt, 20-amp circuit for refrigerator/small appliances

Plug-in outlet for refrigerator

120-volt, 20-amp circuit for dishwasher

Dishwasher

Never work on any "live" circuit, fixture, plug-in outlet, or switch. Your life may depend on it.

Before starting to work, you must disconnect the circuit at its source, either in the service entrance panel or in a separate subpanel. If fuses protect your circuits, remove the appropriate fuse. In a panel or subpanel equipped with circuit breakers, switch the breaker to the *OFF* position to disconnect the circuit, then tape over the switch for extra safety.

Selecting a power source. A circuit can be extended from a present outlet box, fixture box, switch box, or junction box. The one exception is a switch box without a neutral wire (see page 82).

Before deciding which box to tap, consider how you'll route wire to the new switch, outlet, or fixture. Look for the easiest paths behind walls, above ceilings, and under floors. Then choose the most convenient power source.

The box tapped must be large enough to accommodate the new wires (minimum box sizes are specified by the NEC) and must have a knockout hole through which you can thread the cable. If your box doesn't meet these requirements, replace it with one that does.

Preparing for new boxes. Housing boxes—capped with fixture canopies, outlet plates, or switch plates—come in many shapes and sizes. For outlets, switches, and fixtures weighing 5 pounds or less, choose "cut-in" boxes, which need not be secured to studs or joists. (If wall or ceiling coverings haven't been in-

stalled, you can nail a "flange" box to studs or joists.) Unless codes prohibit the use of plastic, you may select either plastic or metal boxes. Metal boxes, though sturdier, must be grounded; plastic boxes cost less and need not be grounded.

Plain box (for wood or plaster walls)
Fixture box with hanger bar
Flange box (nailed to stud or joist)
Cut-in box (for wallboard)

Position the box between studs or joists in an area free of pipes and other wires. To find a suitable location, first cut off power to all circuits that might run behind the wall or ceiling where you're placing the box. Drill a small test hole, and probe behind the surface with a length of stiff wire until you find a space.

Trace the outline of the box on the wall or ceiling, omitting any protruding brackets. Drill a starter hole in one corner, then make the cutout with a keyhole or saber saw.

Routing new cable. Your new "wires" actually will be self-contained lengths of nonmetallic sheathed ca-

ble. A single cable contains either one or two hot wires, a neutral wire, and a grounding wire, each wrapped in its own insulation. To ensure the best splices, use only cable containing all-copper wire. Check local codes for the correct cable size.

After cutting the holes but before mounting the boxes, you must run cable from the power source to each new box location. Access from an unfinished basement, an unfloored attic, or a garage adjacent to the kitchen makes it easy to run cable either on top of joists and studs or through holes drilled in them.

If walls and ceilings are covered on both sides, you'll have to "fish" the cable (see drawing below). Use a fish tape (buy it at a plumbing supply or hardware store—or you may find one to rent) or a length of stiff wire.

Attaching new boxes. After you've routed the new cable, secure each housing box to the ceiling or wall. Slip a cable connector onto the end of the cable and insert it through a knockout in the box. Fasten the connector to the box, leaving 6 to 8 inches of cable free for making the connections. Then mount the box.

(Continued on next page)

HOW TO ROUTE CABLE TO FIXTURES

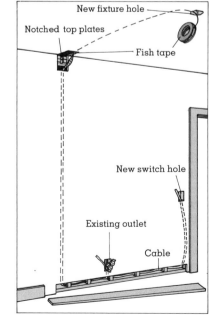

New fixture hole
Notched top plates
Fish tape
New switch hole
Existing outlet
Cable

HOW TO ROUTE CABLE TO OUTLETS

Original box
Cut wall covering
Wall studs
Box hole
Drill ¾" holes, or notch studs
Box hole
Cable

■Electrical basics

HOW TO WIRE INTO THE POWER SOURCE

FIXTURE BOX AS POWER SOURCE

From service panel

Grounding wires

To existing switch

Hot wires (white wire should be painted black near splice)

Neutral wires

To new boxes

OUTLET BOX AS POWER SOURCE

From service panel

Hot wires

Grounding wires

Neutral wires

To new boxes

SWITCH BOX AS POWER SOURCE

From service panel

Hot wires

Grounding wires

To new boxes

Neutral wires

To existing light

Wiring into the power source. Connections to three types of boxes used as power sources are illustrated above. A fourth option is a junction box, where wires are simply joined.

Wirenuts join and protect the stripped ends of spliced wires within housing boxes. The correct wirenut size depends on the number and size of wires you'll be joining.

To join wires with a wirenut, follow this sequence: strip 1 inch of

NOTE: For simplicity's sake, the wires illustrated on these pages are color-coded as follows:

■ **Hot wires: thick black or gold**

■ **Neutral wires: thick white**

■ **Grounding wires: narrow black**

Actual hot wires are usually black or red, but may be any color other than white;, gray, or green. Actual neutral wires are white or gray; grounding wires are bare copper or aluminum, green, or, in rare cases, black.

Occasionally a white wire will be used as a hot wire, in which case it should be taped or painted black near terminals and splices for easy identification.

insulation from the wire ends and twist the ends clockwise at least 1½ turns (A); snip ⅜ to ½ inch off the twisted wires (B); then screw the wirenut clockwise onto the wires (C).

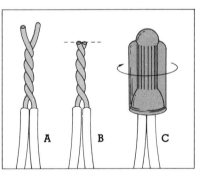

Wiring plug-in outlets

Plug-in outlets can be wired in several ways. You may want to keep one or both halves electrically live at all times so that appliances can be controlled by their own switches. Or you may wish to turn one or both halves on and off with wall switches—for example, to control a garbage disposer.

Outlets should be evenly distributed between small appliance circuits in the kitchen area. For example, if there are two small appliance circuits and eight outlets in the area, each circuit should serve four outlets.

All outlets for 15 or 20-amp circuits must be of the grounding type shown at the top of page 81. Outlets are rated for a specific amperage and voltage; be sure to buy the type you need.

If you want to add a grounded outlet to a circuit that does not contain a grounding wire, you'll have to run a separate wire from the new outlet to a nearby cold water pipe (see page 83).

Most outlets have three different-colored screw terminals. The brass ones are hot, the white or silver ones are neutral, and the green one is the grounding terminal.

The drawings at the top of page 81 show two common ways to wire new outlets. The first, the usual arrangement, has both halves always hot. In the second, the two halves operate independently of each other, with one half controlled by a wall switch (use pliers to remove the break-off ear that connects the outlet's two hot terminals).

The housing boxes are assumed to be metal; if you choose plastic, there's no need to ground the boxes, but you'll have to attach a grounding wire to each outlet. Simply loop the end of the wire under the grounding screw.

After you've made the wire attachments, fold the wires back into

HOW TO WIRE PLUG-IN OUTLETS

BOTH HALVES ALWAYS HOT

From service panel

Neutral wires

Grounding wires

Hot wires

To fixture or next outlet

BOTTOM HALF ALWAYS HOT; TOP HALF CONTROLLED BY WALL SWITCH

To wall switch

Neutral wire

Break off ear

Grounding wires

Hot white wire (should be painted black near splice)

From service panel

the box and screw the outlet to the box. Adjust the screws in the mounting slots until the outlet is straight. If necessary, shim it out, using either the break-off portions of the outlet's mounting brackets or washers. Finally, add the cover plate.

Wiring 240-volt outlets

Because a straight 240-volt circuit has two hot wires, a grounding wire, and no separate neutral wire, you'll need a two-pole, three-wire outlet of

the correct amperage. Most models feature push-in terminals, as shown below. Using the outlet's strip gauge as a guide, strip insulation from the ends of the wires, push the wires onto the correct terminals, and tighten the screws.

Circuits rated for 120/240 volts have two hot wires and a neutral wire but, depending on whether the circuit originates at the service entrance panel or at a subpanel, may or may not have a grounding wire.

If the circuit originates at the

service entrance panel, some codes permit you to ground the device connected to it through the neutral wire, which lets you use a three-pole, three-wire outlet. However, if your circuit runs from a subpanel, you must include a separate grounding wire and use a three-pole, four-wire outlet. The drawing below left shows both situations.

Built-in protection: the GFCI

The ground fault circuit interrupter (GFCI) is a device designed to protect you from electric shocks. The protection value of a GFCI has made it standard equipment in new construction; the NEC requires that all kitchen outlets within 6 feet of a water source (such as a sink) be equipped with one. Depending on the model, the GFCI may also protect all other outlets downstream (away from the source) from it, but it will not protect any outlets upstream (toward the source).

A GFCI receptacle is wired like an ordinary plug-in outlet. If yours comes with short wires instead of terminals, use wirenuts to splice their free ends to the wires in the box. A typical hookup is shown below.

(Continued on next page)

A LOOK AT 240-VOLT OUTLETS

3-POLE, 3-WIRE RECEPTACLE

Hot wires

Neutral wire

3-POLE, 4-WIRE RECEPTACLE

Grounding wire

Hot wires

Neutral wire

HOW TO WIRE A GFCI

Incoming wires

Outgoing wires

Grounding wires

■Electrical basics

HOW TO WIRE SINGLE-POLE SWITCHES

Wiring new switches

Both "single-pole" and "three-way" switches are used in homes. A single-pole switch may control one or more light fixtures or outlets; two three-way switches may also control one or more devices.

Like outlets, each switch must have the same amp and voltage rating as the circuit. Remember when wiring that switches are installed only along hot wires.

The switches shown on this page have no grounding wires. Because the plastic toggles used on most home switches are shockproof, these switches don't need to be grounded. If switches are housed inside metal boxes, the boxes do need to be grounded.

Single-pole switches. These switches have two screw terminals of the same color (usually brass) for wire connections, and a definite vertical orientation. You should be able to read the words ON and OFF embossed on the toggle. It makes no difference which hot wire goes to which terminal. Because of wiring logistics, the cable sometimes will run to the fixture first and at other times to the switch. Both situations are shown at left.

Three-way switches. These switches have two screw terminals of the same color (brass or silver) and one of a darker color, identified by the word "common." Either end of a three-way switch can go up. It's important to observe, though, which terminal is the odd-colored one; it may be located differently than in the drawing below.

To wire a pair of three-way switches, first connect the hot wire from the service entrance panel or subpanel to the odd-colored terminal of one switch; then connect the hot wire from the fixture or outlet to the odd-colored terminal of the other switch. Wire the remaining terminals by running hot wires from the two same-colored terminals on one switch to the two same-colored terminals on the other.

Installing dimmer switches

Most dimmer switches can be wired into existing circuits in the same way as the switches they replace. The exception is a dimmer for a fluorescent fixture: if available, this type may require extra steps and hardware.

A single-pole switch must be replaced with a single-pole dimmer. If the dimmer comes with short wires instead of terminals, use wirenuts to splice their free ends to the wires in the switch box (for details on using wirenuts, see page 80).

Likewise, if you wish to add a dimmer to a three-way system, replace the three-way switch most frequently used with a three-way dimmer. The wire attached to the common terminal on the switch must be reattached to the common terminal on the dimmer.

TWO WAYS TO WIRE THREE-WAY SWITCHES

Light fixtures

Kitchen lighting needs fall into two categories—general and task lighting. Both incandescent and fluorescent lights can be used to satisfy either need. You'll probably implement lighting with one or more of the three popular types of fixtures: surface-mounted, track, and recessed downlight or panel.

Replacing an existing light fixture with one of the same type usually is a minor operation; you simply unscrew the fixture from its housing box, disconnect the wires of the old fixture, and hook up new wires. Adding a new fixture where there was none is a more complex process. After running new cable from a power source, you must install a housing box and a switch to control the fixture. Do you feel that's out of your league? For help, see "Electrical basics" on pages 77–82.

Installing surface-mounted fixtures

Surface-mounted fixtures are either attached directly to a fixture box in the wall or ceiling or suspended from the box by chains or cord. New fixtures usually come with their own mounting hardware, adaptable to any existing fixture box. Sometimes, though, the weight of the new fixture or the wiring necessary for proper grounding requires that you replace the box before installing the fixture.

Attaching fixtures. The weight of the fixture determines how it will be attached. Boxes for fixtures weighing more than 5 pounds must be nailed to a joist or hung on a box between joists. If the fixture weighs more than 30 pounds, the fixture should be connected to the box's metallic stud with a hickey or reducing nut.

Grounding metal fixtures. The National Electrical Code requires that all incandescent and fluorescent fixtures with exposed metal parts be grounded.

If the fixture box is not grounded (as is the case when your present house wiring includes no grounding wire), you'll have to extend a grounding wire from the box to the nearest cold water pipe. The pipe must be metal and unbroken by plastic fittings or runs along its length. Bypass a problem spot or your water meter with a "jumper" wire.

Replacing fixtures. Whether you're replacing an old fixture with the same type or with a new fluorescent unit, the steps are the same.

First, disconnect the circuit by removing the fuse or switching the circuit breaker to OFF. Carefully remove any shade from the old fixture. Unscrew the canopy from the fixture box; detach the mounting bar if there is one. Have a helper hold the fixture to keep it from falling.

Now, make a sketch of how the wires are connected. If they're spliced with wirenuts, unscrew them and untwist the wires. If the wires are spliced only with electrician's tape, simply unwind the tape. New splices will be covered with wirenuts. Lay the old fixture aside.

As your helper holds up the new fixture, match its wires to the old wires as shown in your sketch. Splice with wirenuts (see page 80).

Secure the new fixture by reversing the steps you took to loosen the original, using any new hardware included with the fixture. If you need to patch the wall or ceiling, see page 94.

Adding new fixtures. Installing a new surface-mounted fixture is

SURFACE-MOUNTED FIXTURES

Neutral wires
Hot wires
Mounting bar
Nipple
Canopy
Nut
Tube holder
Hot wires
Neutral wires
Pivot bar
Cap nut
CEILING-MOUNTED FLUORESCENT FIXTURE
Grounding bar
Ballast
WALL SCONCE
Hanger bar
Grounding jumper
Neutral wires
Canopy
Hanger pole
Hot wires
CEILING FAN & LIGHT

■Light fixtures

TRACK SYSTEMS

much like replacing one, once the cable has been routed from a power source and the fixture box and switch installed.

New nonmetallic cable routed to the box should include a grounding wire, which is attached to the box's grounding screw. If more than one cable enters the box (for example, a separate cable may be connected to the switch box), you'll need to attach the end of a short length of #12 wire (a "jumper") to the grounding screw and splice its other end to the ends of the grounding wires in the cables. Cap the splice with a wirenut.

ONE CABLE

To switch   Grounding wire

TWO CABLES

From service panel

Grounding wires

To switch

A cord or chain-hung fixture must also have a grounding wire run from the socket to the box. Most new fixtures are prewired with a grounding wire.

Match the box's wires to those of the new fixture—black wire to black, white to white, as shown on page 83. Cap all splices with wirenuts. Then mount the fixture with the hardware specified by the manufacturer.

Installing track systems

Track systems are mounted, either directly or with mounting clips, to the wall or ceiling. Power is provided from a fixture box or through a cord plugged into an existing outlet. Tracks are often wired into two separate circuits controlled by two switches or dimmers.

Low-voltage track fixtures with integral transformers or adapters can be plugged into a standard 120-volt track. Other systems require an external transformer to step down power to the track itself. In this case, you'll need to mount the transformer and then route wire to the track location.

Connecting the system. A plug-in connector, which includes a 12-foot cord and a lamp plug, lets you place a track wherever the cord will reach an outlet. Plug-in connectors

are available only with single-circuit tracks.

A track system with a wire-in connector is hooked up directly to a fixture box. You may be able to use an existing box, or you may have to install a new one (see pages 78–79). In either case, you'll need as many wall switches as your track has circuits. By using a special connector available with some track systems, you can bring in power along a track run rather than at the end.

To install a wire-in connector, position the fixture box saddle and then splice the connector's wires to the incoming cable wires. Cap each splice with a wirenut. Some connectors attach to the fixture box cover; others are simply held in place by the track.

Mounting the track. To attach a track or mounting clips to the ceiling or wall, you'll use screws or toggle bolts in predrilled holes. To lay out and drill the necessary holes, line up a chalkline or the edge of a yardstick with the center slot of the connector; snap or draw a line to the proposed end of the track.

Setting a length of track beside the line, mark along the line the positions of the knockout holes in the roof of the track. These marks show you where to drill.

Because most connectors lie flush against the wall or ceiling surface, you can usually attach the track directly to the surface. Slip the two bare wire ends of the first length of track into the connector receptacles; secure the track with screws or toggle bolts. Proceed in a similar manner with the remaining lengths of track.

Some connectors hold the ends of the track ¼ to ½ inch away from the mounting surface. In this case, you'll need special clips to hold the track at the same level. Once clips are screwed or bolted to the ceiling or wall, slip the first length of track into the connector; press it, and succeeding lengths, into the clips.

Installing recessed fixtures

Common recessed fixtures include incandescent circular or square downlights and larger fluorescent ceiling, or "troffer," panels. You'll need to cut a hole in the ceiling between the joists, or remove tiles or panels from a suspended ceiling, to install either type. Larger troffer panels may also require 2 by 4 blocking between joists for support.

Recessed fixtures need several inches of clearance above the fin-ished ceiling. They're most easily installed below an unfinished attic or crawlspace. Because of the heat generated by many downlights, you must either buy a special zero-clearance model (type ICT), or plan to remove insulation within 3 inch-es of the fixture and make sure that no other combustible materials come within ½ inch.

Most low-voltage downlights come with an integral transformer attached to the frame; if yours doesn't, you'll first need to mount an external transformer nearby and then route wire to the fixture.

Cutting the ceiling hole. If there's no crawlspace above the ceiling, find the joists (see page 69).

Once you've determined the proper location for the fixture hous-ing, trace its outline on the ceiling with a pencil; use a keyhole saw or saber saw to cut the hole (don't for-get to shut off power to any circuits that might be wired behind the ceil-ing before cutting). Brace a plaster ceiling as you cut.

Mounting the fixture. If you don't have access from above, look for a remodeling fixture. The version shown below, at left, slips through the ceiling hole and clips onto the edge of the ceiling. The fixture trim then snaps onto the housing from below. (Hook up the wires to the circuit before securing the fixture and trim.)

So-called new-work or rough-in downlights with adjustable hanger bars (shown at right) are easy to in-stall from above. Simply nail the ends of the bars to joists on either side; then clip the trim or baffle into place from below.

Adding under-cabinet fixtures

One of the most common types of under-cabinet lighting, and one of the easiest to install, is an integral fluorescent unit composed of one or two tubes and a ballast. These lights can be permanently wired to a switch or plugged into nearby outlets. For greatest efficiency, the fixture should span at least two-thirds of the area to be lighted and should be mounted as close as pos-sible to the front of the cabinet.

You can also buy lengths of in-candescent or halogen strip lights, mounted on metal strips or inside clear plastic tubing. Installation is similar to that for fluorescent units, though you may need to add a low-voltage transformer. These fixtures emit clean, warm light and are easy to place on a dimmer switch.

Adding a wood or metal valance to a fixture mounted at eye level hides the unit and eliminates glare (see below). Some wall cabinets in-clude this trim; otherwise, measure the required space and cut a piece of cardboard to use as a mockup.

RECESSED DOWNLIGHTS

FOR REMODELING
Housing box
Housing box
Clips (anchor fixture to existing ceiling)
Incandescent bulb
Baffle or reflector
Fixture trim

FOR NEW CONSTRUCTION
Compact fluorescent tubes
Adjustable hanger bars (fasten to joists)
Fixture trim

Cabinet
Fluorescent fixture
Valance

Walls & ceilings

Installing new wallboard or a suspended ceiling can change the entire appearance of your room. Or you can give your kitchen a completely new look simply by splashing on a coat of colorful paint or by applying a complementary wall covering.

Fortunately, these improvements are among the easiest projects for the average homeowner to tackle—many of the new products on the market require little or no experience to apply.

Installing gypsum wallboard

Cutting and installing gypsum wallboard is a straightforward procedure, but concealing the joints between panels and in the corners demands patience and care. And the weight of full panels can be awkward to negotiate. Wallboard is easily damaged; take care not to bend or break the corners or tear the paper covers.

Standard wallboard panels are 4 feet wide and from 8 feet to 16 feet long. Common thicknesses are ⅜ inch for a backing material for other wall coverings, ½ inch for final wall coverings, and ⅝ inch where the walls border a garage space. Water-resistant wallboard, identified by green or blue paper covers, is designed for areas where heavy moisture might collect.

Cutting wallboard. To make a straight cut, first mark the cut line on the front paper layer with a pencil and straightedge, or snap a line with a chalkline. Cut through the front paper with a utility knife as shown below.

INSTALLING WALLBOARD ON A WALL

Lift each wallboard panel into position and center the edges over wall studs. Then nail the panel to the studs, dimpling the wallboard surface slightly with the hammer. Stagger panels in adjacent rows so that ends don't line up.

Turn the wallboard over and break the gypsum core by bending it toward the back. Finally, cut the back paper along the bend. Smooth the edge of the cut with a perforated rasp.

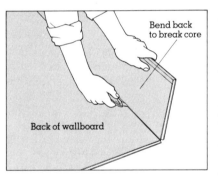

For openings within a panel, drill a pilot hole and make the cutout with a keyhole or wallboard saw. Larger edge cutouts should also be made with a keyhole or wallboard saw.

When laying out openings or fitting wallboard around obstructions such as doorways, carefully measure from the edge of an adjacent wallboard panel or reference point to the obstruction. Transfer the measurements to a new panel, and cut out the correct area.

Basic wall application. Wall panels may be positioned either vertically or horizontally—that is, with the long edges either parallel or perpendicular to wall studs. Most professionals prefer the latter method because it helps bridge irregularities between studs and results in a stronger wall. But if your wall is higher than 8 feet, you may not want to use this method, since the extra height requires more cutting and creates too many joints.

Before installing wall panels, mark the stud locations on the floor and ceiling.

Starting at a corner, place the first panel tight against the ceiling and secure it with nails, drywall screws, or construction adhesive supplemented by nails. Drive in nails with a hammer, dimpling the wallboard surface without puncturing the paper. Fastener spacings are subject to local codes, but typical nail spacing is every 8 inches along panel ends and edges and along intermediate supports (called "in the field").

INSTALLING WALLBOARD ON A CEILING

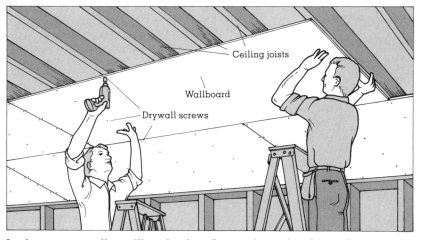

It takes two to install a wallboard ceiling. Prop each panel in place with your heads; screw or nail first in the center and then where it will take the weight off your heads.

Apply additional panels in the same manner (if you're applying wallboard horizontally, stagger the end joints in the bottom row so they don't line up with the joints in the top row).

Basic ceiling application. Methods for installing a wallboard ceiling are basically the same as those for walls. If you're covering both surfaces, do the ceiling first.

Fasten panels perpendicular to joists with annular ring nails, drywall screws, or a combination of nails and construction adhesive. Screws are quick and strong, but you'll need a power screw gun or a drill with adjustable clutch to drive them. Typical screw spacing is every 7 inches along panel ends and at intermediate joists.

Taping joints and corners. To finish wallboard neatly, you'll need wallboard tape (buy tape that's precreased) and taping compound.

The taping process is done in stages. To tape a joint between panels, first apply a smooth layer of taping compound over the joint with a 6-inch taping knife. Before the compound dries, embed wallboard tape into it and apply a sec-

ond thin coat of compound over the tape, smoothing it with a knife.

To tape an inside corner, apply a smooth layer of compound to the wallboard on each side of the corner. Measure and tear the tape, fold it in half vertically along the crease, and press it into the corner with a taping knife or corner tool. Apply a thin layer of compound over the tape and smooth it out.

Exterior corners are covered with a protective metal cornerbead and finished with compound.

Continue taping all the joints. Then, using smooth, even strokes with the 6-inch knife, cover the inside nail dimples with compound.

Allow the taping compound to dry for at least 24 hours before sanding lightly to get a smooth surface. (NOTE: Wear a face mask and goggles while sanding.)

Using a 10-inch knife, apply a second coat of compound, feathering out the edges past each side of the taped joint.

Let the second coat dry. Then sand it and apply a final coat. Use a 10-inch or an even wider knife to smooth out and feather the edges, covering all dimples and joints. After the compound dries, sand it again to remove even minor imperfections.

Textured versus smooth finish. Though many people prefer the smooth look, texture can hide a less-than-perfect taping job—and add some visual interest to an uninterrupted wall. Some joint compounds double as texturing compounds; other effects may require special texturing materials. Ask your dealer for recommendations.

Professionals often apply texturing with a spray gun, but others achieve good results by daubing, swirling, or splattering the compound with a sponge, paint roller, or stiff brush—whatever tool produces the desired appearance.

Let the compound set up until slightly stiff; then even it out as required with a wide float or trowel. Allow the finished surface to dry for at least 24 hours before painting.

HOW TO TAPE WALLBOARD JOINTS

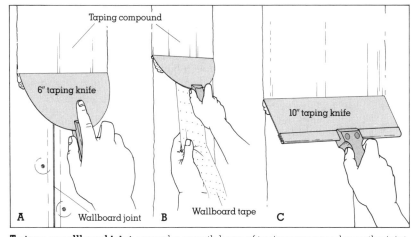

To tape a wallboard joint, spread a smooth layer of taping compound over the joint (A), embed paper tape in compound (B), and apply a second, thinner layer of compound. When it's dry, sand smooth and apply a wider layer (C), feathering the edges.

∎ Walls & ceilings

MOLDING JOINTS

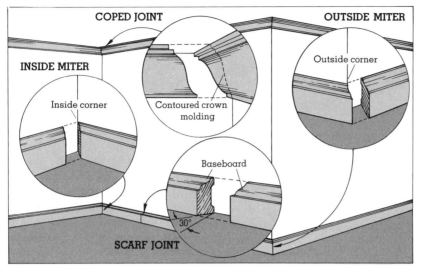

Moldings & trim

The absence of moldings, it's often said, is a sign of good craftsmanship. Even in the most basic wallboard-paneled room, though, moldings have their place along the base of walls and around door and window frames; in fact, many traditional architectural styles make extensive use of moldings.

Measuring and cutting. Traditionally, a miter box and backsaw are the tools for neatly cutting trim. But if you're making lots of cuts or working with unusual angles, you may want to borrow or rent a power miter saw. The precision miter saw allows you to cut the trim a bit long and then nibble fine bits of wood until the joint is perfect.

When you're measuring for miters—to frame a window, for example—measure the inside dimensions and cut your material accordingly (that is, adding on the mitered part). Remember that you must reverse the cuts on the ends of each piece of molding.

Contoured moldings may require a coped joint at inside corners for a smooth fit. To form a coped joint, cut the first piece of molding square and butt it into the corner. Then cut the end of the second piece back at a 45° angle, as shown at right. Next, using a coping saw, follow the exposed curvature of the

molding's front edge while reinstating the 90° angle.

Fastening moldings. Unless your molding calls for special adhesive or color-matched fasteners, nail it in place with finishing nails and recess the heads with a nailset. Choose a nail that's at least twice

COPING A JOINT

For a coped joint, first miter end at a 45° angle, using a power miter saw (A) or a backsaw and miter box. Then follow shape of exposed edge with a coping saw while reinstating original 90° angle (B).

as long as your molding's thickness.

If you'll be painting the trim, fill the holes with wood putty; if you're staining or varnishing, apply a color-matched filler after finishing.

Painting your kitchen

A fresh coat of paint provides the fastest way to "remodel" your kitchen. Here are some guidelines.

Choosing the paint. Your basic choices are latex and alkyd paint. Latex is easy to work with, and best of all, you can clean up wet paint with soap and water. Alkyd paint (often called oil-base paint) provides high gloss and will hang on a little harder than latex; however, alkyds are trickier to apply and require cleanup with mineral spirits.

Tools of the trade. Choosing the correct brushes is almost as important as selecting the paint. Natural bristles (hog hairs) are traditionally used to apply oil-base paints. They should not be used with latex paint; the bristles soak up water from the paint and quickly become soggy and useless. Synthetic bristles, nylon or nylonlike, are best for applying latex, but most can also be used with oil-base paints.

For window sashes, shutters, and trim, choose a 1½ or 2-inch angled sash brush. For woodwork and other medium-size surfaces, a 2 or 3-inch brush is best—if brushing is your choice.

When you want to paint a large flat area quickly and easily, though, a roller is the answer. A 9-inch roller will handle all interior paint jobs. A handle threaded to accommodate an extension pole will allow you to reach high walls and ceilings without a ladder. The roller's cover is important—choose a nylon blend for latex, lambskin for oil-base paint, or mohair for use with both. A well-designed roller tray is also essential.

Preparing the surface. A key factor in preventing cracking and peeling after the paint dries is preparing the

TOOLS OF THE PAINTING TRADE

Putty knife

9″ roller

Paint guide

Corner roller

1½″ angled trim brush

Paint scraper

2″ woodwork brush

4″ brush

Roller tray

surface correctly. It's *essential* to the bonding and durability of any latex paint application.

Start by removing light fixtures and faceplates. Then inspect the area you're painting for small holes as well as more extensive damage, and make all necessary repairs.

If an old paint finish is flaking, you must sand it smooth. And when you paint over a glossy surface, you must first roughen the old finish with sandpaper so the new paint will adhere. Use a sponge soaked with paint thinner on any spots that are very greasy. Then an overall dusting, a sponging with an abrasive cleanser, and rinsing (complete a small area at a time) will finish off the surface preparation. Allow about 24 hours for all washed areas to dry completely.

Sometimes an old finish is in such poor condition that the paint must be removed entirely. The easiest method of stripping old paint is to apply a commercial liquid paint remover, then scrape off the softened paint with a broad knife or paint scraper. Finish the surface by sanding lightly until it's clean and smooth.

It's possible to paint over wallpaper that's smooth and attached firmly to the wall. Apply a sealing primer such as pigmented shellac or a flat oil-base enamel undercoat. Let the sealer dry completely before you paint.

It's often safer, though, to re-move the wallpaper, especially if it's tearing and flaking. See "Hanging new wallpaper" for details.

Unpainted plaster or wallboard should be primed with latex paint or latex primer-sealer. Prime unpainted wood with oil-base paint whether you plan to finish with oil-base or latex.

Painting tips. If you're painting both walls and ceiling, start with the ceiling. Paint the entire ceiling without stopping. You'll want to paint in rectangles, approximately 2 feet by 3 feet, starting in a corner and working across the ceiling in the direction of the shortest distance.

Begin the first section by using a brush, pad applicator, or special corner roller to paint a narrow strip next to the wall line and around any fixtures. Then finish the section with a roller, overlapping any brush marks. Continue painting, one section at a time, from one end of the ceiling to the other and back again.

Then it's on to the walls. Mentally divide a wall into 3-foot-square sections, starting from a corner at the ceiling line and working down the wall. As with ceilings, use a brush, pad applicator, or corner roller along the ceiling line, corners, fixtures, or edges of openings. Finish each section with a roller, overlapping any brush marks.

At the bottom edge along the floor or baseboard, or along the edges of cabinets and counters, use

a brush and paint guide; as before, overlap the brush strokes with a roller. Return to the ceiling line and again work down in 3-foot sections.

Hanging new wallpaper

Next to paint, wallpaper is the most popular covering for kitchen walls. Easier than ever to install, wallpaper is available in a kaleidoscope of colors and patterns.

Choices for the kitchen. A wallpaper for the kitchen should be scrubbable, durable, and stain resistant. *Solid vinyl* wallpapers, available in a wide variety of colors and textures, fill the bill. *Vinyl coatings* also give wallpaper a washable surface but aren't notably durable or grease resistant.

If you're a beginner, you may want to consider prepasted and pretrimmed paper.

To find an adhesive suitable for your material, check the manufacturer's instructions or ask your dealer.

Preparing the surface. To prepare for papering, you'll need to remove all light fixtures and faceplates. Thoroughly clean and rinse the surface. Most manufacturers recommend that you completely remove any old wallpaper before hanging a nonporous covering like solid vinyl.

If the existing paper is strippable, it will come off easily when you pull it up at a corner or seam. To remove nonstrippable wallpaper, use either a steamer (available for rent from your dealer) or a spray bottle filled with very hot water. Before steaming, break the surface of the old paper by sanding it with very coarse sandpaper or by pulling a sawblade sideways across the wall.

Within a few minutes of steaming (wait longer if it's a nonporous material), you can begin to remove the old paper. Using a broad knife, work down from the top of the wall, scraping off the old wallpaper.

If yours is a new gypsum wallboard surface, tape all joints between panels (see page 87) before papering. When dry, sand the wall

■Walls & ceilings

smooth and apply a coat of flat, oil-base primer-sealer.

If you want to apply wallpaper over previously painted surfaces that are in good condition, simply clean off all the dirt, grease, and oil, and let it dry. If latex paint was used, or if you can't determine the type, you must apply an oil-base undercoat over the old paint.

Ready to start? Plan the best place to hang your first strip. If you're papering all four walls with a patterned paper, the last strip you hang probably won't match the first, so plan to start and finish in the least conspicuous place—usually a corner, door casing, or window casing.

Most house walls are not straight and plumb, so you'll need to establish a plumb line. Figure the width of your first strip of wallpaper minus ½ inch (which will overlap the corner or casing); measure that distance from your starting point, and mark the wall. Using a carpenter's level as a straightedge, draw a line through your mark that's perfectly plumb. Extend the line until it reaches from floor to ceiling.

It's a good idea to measure the wall height before cutting each strip of wallpaper. Allow 2 inches extra at the top and bottom. Be sure also to allow for pattern match.

Using a razor knife, cut the strips. Number them on the back at the top edge so you can apply them in the proper sequence.

With some wallpapers, you'll need to spread adhesive on the backing with a wide, soft paint roller or pasting brush; other papers are prepasted—all you have to do is soak them in water before hanging.

After pasting or soaking, strips should be "booked," as shown below, until ready to hang.

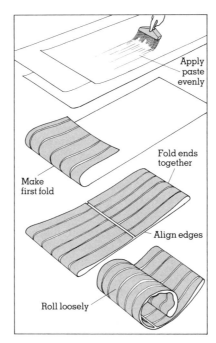

Apply paste evenly

Make first fold

Fold ends together

Align edges

Roll loosely

Trim the edges of the wallpaper at this stage, if necessary. You're now ready to hang the paper.

Hanging the wallpaper. First, position a stepladder next to the plumb line you've marked. Open the top fold of the first booked strip, raising it so that it overlaps the ceiling line by 2 inches. Carefully align the strip's edge with the plumb line.

Using a smoothing brush, press the strip against the wall. Smooth out all wrinkles and air bubbles. Then release the lower portion of the strip and smooth it into place.

Carefully roll the edges flat, if necessary, with a seam roller. To trim along the ceiling and baseboard, use a broad knife and a very sharp razor knife. With a sponge dipped in lukewarm water, remove any excess adhesive before it dries.

Unfold your second strip on the wall in the same way you did the first. Gently butt the second strip against the first, aligning the pattern as you move down the wall. Continue around the room with the remaining paper.

Dealing with corners. Because few rooms have perfectly straight corners, you'll have to measure from the edge of the preceding strip to the corner; do this at three heights.

HANGING THE FIRST STRIP

To hang wallpaper, first open the top fold of the strip, overlap the ceiling line, and align the strip's edge with the plumb line (A); press the strip against the wall with a smoothing brush (B). Release the lower fold and smooth into place; roll the edges flat with a seam roller (C). Trim the strip along the ceiling and baseboard with a broad knife and a razor knife (D). Remove excess adhesive with a sponge dipped in lukewarm water (E).

Cut a strip ½ inch wider than the widest measurement. Butting the strip to the preceding strip, brush it firmly into and around the corner. At the top and bottom corners, cut the overlap so the strip will lie flat.

Next, measure the width of the leftover piece of wallpaper. On the adjacent wall, measure the same distance from the corner and make a plumb line at that point.

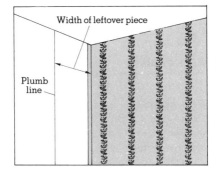

Position one edge of the strip along the plumb line; the other edge will cover the ½-inch overlap. (If you're hanging vinyl wallpaper, you should apply a vinyl-to-vinyl adhesive on top of the overlap.)

Cutouts. It's easy to cut around electrical switches and plug-in outlets. Be sure all faceplates have been removed before hanging the wallpaper; then before making the cutout, shut off the electricity.

Hang the paper as described above. Then use a razor knife to make an X-shaped cut over the opening, extending the cuts to each corner. Trim the excess along the edges of the opening with the razor knife and a broad knife.

Installing a suspended ceiling

Easy-to-install suspended ceilings consist of a metal grid suspended from above with wire or spring-type hangers. The grid holds acoustic or decorative fiberboard panels.

The most common panel size is 2 feet by 4 feet, though panels are available in a variety of sizes. Transparent and translucent panels and egg-crate grilles are made to fit the gridwork to admit light from

HOW TO INSTALL A SUSPENDED CEILING

To hang a suspended ceiling, snap a chalkline around the room and install L-shaped molding with its base on the chalkline (A). Set the main runners on the molding at each end, attach them to the joists with #12 wire (B), lock 4-foot cross tees to the main runners (C), and push the panels into place (D).

above. Recessed lighting panels that exactly replace one panel also are available from some manufacturers. All components are replaceable, and the panels can be raised for access to the area above.

Figuring your needs. Here is the easiest way to determine the number of panels you'll need: Measure your wall lengths at the proposed ceiling height. Draw the ceiling area to scale on graph paper, using one square per foot of ceiling size. Block in the panel size you'll be using. Finally, count the blocked areas and parts of areas to get the number of panels you'll need.

For a professional-looking job, plan equal borders on the opposite sides of the room. To determine the nonstandard width of panels needed for perimeter rows, measure the extra space from the last full row of panels to one wall and divide by two. This final figure will be the

dimension of border tiles against that wall and the opposite wall. Repeat this procedure for the other room dimensions.

Installing the ceiling. First, figure the ceiling height—at least 3 inches below plumbing, 5 inches below lights (minimum ceiling height is 7 feet 6 inches). Snap a chalkline around the room at that level and install L-shaped angle molding with its base on the chalkline.

Next, install the main runners perpendicular to the ceiling joists, (see above). Cut the runners to length with tinsnips. Setting them on the molding at each end, support them every 4 feet with #12 wire attached to small eyebolts screwed into joists above. Lock 4-foot cross tees to the main runners by bending the tabs in the runner spots.

Set the panels into place and install any recessed lighting panels. Cut border panels as necessary.

Cabinets & countertops

Installing new cabinets and dressing them up with the countertops of your choice can be the passport to a whole new world of kitchen style and efficiency.

Removing and installing cabinets and countertops is not difficult and requires only basic hand tools. But the work must be done carefully to ensure a professional-looking fit.

Removing old cabinets

If you remove base cabinets first, you'll have room to get underneath wall cabinets without strain, and you'll avoid damaging walls or cabinets.

Base cabinets. First, pry away any vinyl wall base, floor covering, or molding from the base cabinet's kickspace or sides, as shown above. Next, disconnect plumbing supply lines and the drain trap from the kitchen sink (see page 105). Also disconnect plumbing and electrical lines to a dishwasher or garbage disposer (see page 106), electric or gas range, wall ovens, or cooktop (see page 109). Be sure plumbing and gas lines and electrical circuits are properly shut off before disconnecting them. Remove the sink, fixtures, and appliances from the area.

Old base cabinets are usually attached to wall studs with screws or nails through nailing strips at the back of each unit. Sometimes they're also fastened to the floor with nails through the kickspace trim or cabinet sides. Screws are easy to remove unless they're old and stripped. To remove nails, you may need to pry the cabinet away from the wall or floor with a pry bar (use a wood scrap between the pry bar and the wall or floor to prevent damaging those surfaces).

Several base units may be fastened together and covered with a single countertop. If you can remove the entire assembly intact, you'll save time and labor. Otherwise, unscrew or pry the units apart—they're fastened either through adjacent sides or face frames—and remove the countertop.

CABINET ANATOMY

BASE CABINET — Corner gusset, Nailing strip, Screws or nails, Vinyl wall base, Nails driven into subfloor, Shoe molding

WALL CABINET — Soffit, Screws or nails, Nailing strip, Molding

Countertops typically are anchored to the cabinet frame from below, through rails or corner gussets. Plastic laminate, hardwood butcherblock, and the backing for ceramic tile countertops are normally fastened with screws; masonry and synthetic marble are attached with adhesive.

Wall cabinets. Once the base cabinets are out of the way, you're ready to remove the wall cabinets. They're either screwed, bolted, or nailed through nailing strips at the back of the cabinets to wall studs behind each unit. They might also be fastened to the ceiling or an overhead soffit.

If the cabinets are screwed or bolted to the wall, recruit some helpers to hold them in place while you unfasten them. Then remove the cabinets from the area. If the cabinets are fastened with nails, you'll have to use a pry bar. Again, individual units are probably fastened together. If you have a helper or two, the assembly can often be removed intact.

Installing new cabinets

Both wall and base cabinets are carefully aligned with layout marks previously drawn on the walls. Then they're fastened to studs with screws. In order to give yourself adequate working room and prevent damage to base cabinets, it's usually simpler to install wall cabinets first.

Wall cabinets. Your first task is to locate and mark wall studs in the area of your new cabinets. (For help in finding studs, see page 69.)

Next you'll need to lay out lines on the wall for the top and bottom of the cabinets. Measure up 84 inches from the floor (the standard top height for wall cabinets). Because floors are seldom completely level, measure in several spots and use the highest mark as your reference point. Trace a line from this mark across the wall, using a carpenter's level as a straightedge.

Now subtract the exact height of the new cabinet units from the top line and mark this line on the wall. Screw a temporary ledger strip made from 1 by 4 lumber to the wall studs, with the ledger's top edge exactly flush with the bottom line.

Start your cabinet installation either from a corner of the kitchen or from any full-height cabinet. You can determine the location of the latter from your kitchen plans. Again, mark the wall.

Remove cabinet doors by their hinge pins, if possible. Then, with as much help as you can recruit, lift the first cabinet into place atop the ledger strip. While your helpers hold the cabinet in position, drill pilot holes through the top and bottom nailing strips and into wall studs; loosely fasten the cabinet to the studs with woodscrews long enough to extend 1½ inches into the studs when tight.

CABINET REFERENCE LINES

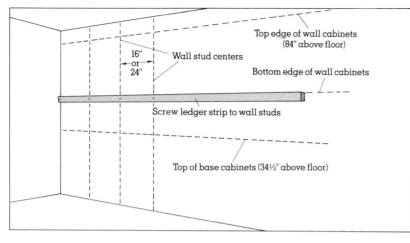

Top edge of wall cabinets
(84" above floor)

16" or 24"

Wall stud centers

Bottom edge of wall cabinets

Screw ledger strip to wall studs

Top of base cabinets (34½" above floor)

At this point, some careful attention to detail will ensure a first-rate installation. Check the cabinet carefully for level and plumb—from top to bottom and from front to back—with your carpenter's level. Because walls seldom are exactly plumb, you may have to make some fine adjustments to enable the cabinet to hang correctly. Bumps and high points on the wall can sometimes be sanded down; low points will need to be shimmed.

Drive shims as needed between the cabinet back and the wall, either down from the top or in from the side. Tap the shims in a little at a time, and keep checking with the level. When all is in order, tighten the woodscrews; then recheck with the level. If the tightening has thrown the cabinet out of plumb, shim again.

Some cabinets are designed with "scribing strips" along the sides. Others come with decorative panels that "finish" the visible end of a cabinet run. Both designs include extra material you can shave down to achieve a perfect fit between the end cabinet and an irregular wall.

To scribe a cabinet, first position it; then run a length of masking tape down the side to be scribed. Setting the points of a compass with pencil to the widest gap between the scribing strip and the wall, run the compass pivot down the wall next to the strip, as shown above right. The wall's irregularities will be marked

on the tape. Remove the cabinet from the wall and use a block plane, file, or power belt sander to trim the scribing strip to the line. Then reinstall the cabinet.

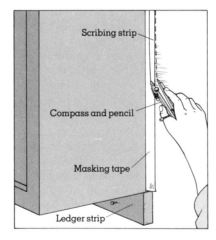

Scribing strip

Compass and pencil

Masking tape

Ledger strip

If your cabinets don't have scribing strips or panels, you can cover any large irregularities with decorative molding or latex caulk.

Adjacent wall cabinets may be joined together on the wall or on the floor; clamp them together with C-clamps, carefully align the front edges, and screw together adjacent cabinet sides or face frames, as shown at right.

Base cabinets. Though base cabinets are less awkward to position than wall cabinets, you must now deal with the vagaries of both wall and floor.

Before you begin, remove any baseboard, moldings, or wall base that might interfere. From the floor, measure up 34½ inches—the height of a standard base cabinet.

Again, take several measurements and use the highest mark for your reference point. Draw a level line through the mark and across the wall.

If you need to cut access holes in a cabinet's back or bottom for plumbing supply and drain pipes, or for electrical wire serving the sink complex, you'll want to do so *before* you install the cabinet.

With helpers, move the cabinet into position, threading any plumbing connections or wiring through the access holes. Measure the cabinet carefully for level and plumb—from side to side and front to back. Then shim the unit as necessary between the cabinet base and floor.

Scribing strips may be included along the sides to allow full alignment with the wall. Both shims and irregularities in the floor can be hidden by baseboard trim, vinyl wall base, or new flooring.

When the cabinet is aligned, drill pilot holes through the nailing strip at the back of the cabinet into the wall studs. Secure the unit with woodscrews or drywall screws.

Once installed, base cabinets are fastened together like wall cabinets: screw together the adjacent sides or faceframes. Now it's time to install the new countertop.

(Continued on page 95)

Align cabinet fronts exactly

Pilot hole

C-clamp

TIPS FOR PATCHING WALLBOARD & PLASTER

Sometimes, all it takes to add new life to kitchen walls are a few repairs and a fresh coat of paint. Gypsum wallboard and plaster, the two most common wall materials, are not difficult to patch, but you'll have to work carefully to match the patch to the surrounding surface.

Patching gypsum wallboard

Cracks, nail holes, or gouge marks can be patched with a putty knife and either spackling compound or patching plaster; cracks may also be filled with a special crack patcher.

To patch holes between wall studs, first cut a neat rectangle around the hole with a sharp utility knife or hacksaw blade. Then, from another piece of wallboard, cut a rectangle 1 inch larger on all sides. Laying the new piece face side down, recut it the same size as the wall rectangle—*without* scoring the paper on the face side. Lift off the inch of cut board around all sides, leaving the paper margins intact (A).

Spread a thin layer of spackling compound around and on the edges of the hole. Position the patch (B) and cover the seams and entire surface with a thin coating of spackle. Let it dry; then smooth carefully with fine sandpaper.

Large holes will often uncover at least one wall stud, which may be used as a nailing surface for the new patch. Or you can enlarge the hole to use two flanking studs as nailing surfaces. For best support, nail the patch to horizontal blocking installed between the studs. Install and finish the patch as if you were installing a brand new panel (see pages 86–87 for techniques).

Patching plaster walls

Small cracks in plaster are treated exactly like those in wallboard, except that extra steps may be required to match the present surface texture (see below).

For holes or wide cracks that go all the way to the lath or wallboard backing, first knock out all loose, cracked plaster with a hammer and chisel. Undercut the edges to strengthen the eventual bond. Using a sponge, dampen the area surrounding the hole.

If the hole is larger than 4 inches square, it will take three layers of patching plaster to fill. The first layer should fill a little more than half the depth and should bond to the backing (A). Before this layer dries (about 4 hours), score it with a nail (B) to provide a "bite" for succeeding layers.

Re-wet the dried patch and apply a second layer. This coat should come within ½ inch to ¼ inch of the surface. Again, let the patching plaster dry; then apply the third coat.

To fill deep holes without backing (for example, where an electrical housing box has been removed), first pry out any cracked material around the hole and dust the area thoroughly. Then loop a length of wire through a piece of rust-resistant screen, as shown below. Push the screen through the hole to be filled, and wind it tightly back against the wall with the wire and a stick (A). Wet the wall adjacent to the hole, and fill the hole with patching plaster to half its depth (B). When the patch is dry, cut off the wire and finish filling the hole.

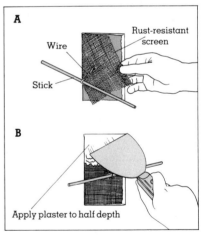

Matching an existing texture requires special treatment of the still-wet plaster. For a smooth surface, pull a wide putty knife or a rubber float across the surface; to achieve an almost glossy smoothness, wipe the plaster with a wet sponge held in one hand, just ahead of the float in the other hand. For a rough surface, scour lightly with a paint brush—either in swirling strokes or jabbed straight at the wall, depending on the texture you're matching.

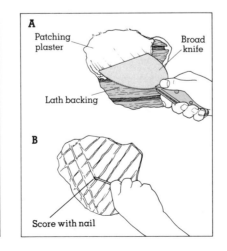

■Cabinets & countertops

Installing plastic laminate countertops

Plastic laminate countertops, the most common countertops used in kitchens, can be divided into two types: post-formed and self-rimmed (for self-rimmed, see page 96).

Post-formed countertops are premolded one-piece tops, from curved backsplash to bullnosed front. They're available in several standard lengths (usually from 6 to 12 feet) and can be cut to the exact length you need. Most types are offered with accessory kits for endsplashes (where the countertop meets a side wall or cabinet) and endcaps.

The term "self-rimmed" simply means that you apply the laminate of your choice over an old countertop or new core material. Though post-formed countertops are simpler to install, building your own enables you to choose from a much greater selection of laminates. You can also tailor the dimensions of the backsplash, endsplash, and overhang to your exact requirements.

Post-formed countertop. Since post-formed countertops come only in standard sizes, you'll normally need to buy one slightly larger than you need and cut it to length. To cut the countertop with a handsaw, mark the cut line on the face. Mark the back if you're using a power saw. Use masking tape to protect the cutting line against chipping (you'll probably have to draw the line again, this time on the tape). Smooth the edge of the cut with a file or sandpaper. Plan to cover that end with an endcap or endsplash.

Exactly what size do you need? The standard overhang on a laminate top varies between ¾ inch and 1 inch in front and on open ends. Add these dimensions to the dimensions of your cabinet. If you plan to include an endsplash at one or both ends, check the endsplash kit: since most endsplashes are assembled directly above the end of the cabinet, you generally *subtract* ¾ inch from the length of the countertop on that side.

POST-FORMED LAMINATE COUNTERTOP

Endsplash Backsplash Scribing strip 1 by 1 batten 1 by 1 batten 1⅛" woodscrew Endcap

Endsplashes are screwed either directly into the edge of the countertop or into "built-down" wood battens previously attached to the edge, as shown above. Apply silicone sealant to the surfaces to be joined. Holding the endsplash in place with C-clamps, drill pilot holes if needed and drive in the screws.

Endcaps (preshaped strips of matching laminate) are glued to an open end with contact cement or, in some cases, pressed into place with a hot iron. Again, you first may need to build down the edge with wood battens. File the edges of the new strip flush with the top and front edges of the countertop, or use an electric router and laminate-trimming bit.

If your cabinets are U-shaped or L-shaped, you'll need to buy mitered countertop sections or have them cut to order. (It's very difficult to cut accurate miters at home.) The mitered sections should have small slots along the bottom edges. They are connected with takeup or draw bolts, as shown below.

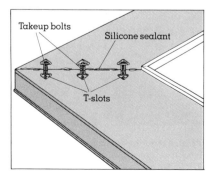

Takeup bolts Silicone sealant T-slots

Coat the edges with silicone sealant, align them carefully, and tighten the bolts. Fasten the backsplashes together with woodscrews.

Countertops, like cabinets, rarely fit uniformly against the back or side walls because the walls rarely are straight. Usually the back edge of a post-formed countertop comes with a scribing strip that can be trimmed to follow the exact contours of the wall. Follow the instructions for scribing cabinets detailed on page 93.

Position the countertop on the cabinet frame. Carefully check with a level—across the front and from front to back. Also make sure you can freely open and close the cabinet doors and top drawers with the countertop overhang in place. You may need to add shims or wood blocks around the perimeter and along cross-members of the cabinet top to level or raise the surface.

Fasten the countertop to the cabinets by running screws from below through the cabinet corner gussets or top frame (see drawing, page 92) and through any shims or wood blocks. Use woodscrews just long enough to penetrate ½ inch into the countertop core. Run a bead of silicone sealant along all exposed seams between the countertop and walls; clean up any excess. If you need to cut a hole in the new countertop for a sink or cooktop, you'll need a keyhole or saber saw and a drill for pilot holes. See page 105 for more details.

(Continued on next page)

■Cabinets & countertops

SELF-RIMMED LAMINATE COUNTERTOP

Laminate top — Backsplash — 2½" woodscrew — Scribing strip — 4" — ¾" plywood or particle board core — Edge strip — 1 by 3 battens — 1⅛" woodscrew

Self-rimmed laminate countertop. To build your own laminate countertop, you'll need to choose the laminate (1/16-inch thickness is the standard) and cut the core material to size from ¾-inch plywood or high-density particle board.

Build down the edges of the core with 1 by 3 battens (see drawing above). Then you can laminate the countertop (do sides and front strips first and then the top surface).

Measure each surface to be laminated, adding at least ¼ inch to all dimensions as a margin for error. Mark the cutting line. Score the line with a sharp utility knife; then cut with a fine-toothed saw (face up with a handsaw or table saw, face down with a circular saw or saber saw). A laminate cutter is ideal.

Apply contact cement to both the laminate back and core surface to be joined, and allow the cement to dry for 20 to 30 minutes. Carefully check alignment before joining the two; once joined, the laminate can't be moved. Press the laminate into place, using a roller or a rolling pin to ensure even contact.

Use a block plane to trim the laminate flush with the core's edges; then dress it with a file. Or trim with an electric router equipped with a laminate-trimming bit.

Backsplashes or endsplashes should be cut from the same core material as the main countertop, then butt-joined to the countertop with sealant and woodscrews.

Installing ceramic tile countertops

Wall tiles, lighter and thinner than floor tiles, are the normal choice for countertops and backsplashes. Standard sizes range from 3 inches by 3 inches to 4½ inches by 8½ inches, with thicknesses varying from ¼ inch to ⅜ inch. Another choice, mosaic tiles, makes your job easier, especially in backsplash areas.

Preparing the base. Before laying tile, remove any old countertops (see page 92); then install ¾-inch exterior plywood, cut flush with the cabinet top, screwing it to the cabinet frame from below. For moisture-tight results, add a waterproof membrane, followed by a layer of cement backerboard on top.

HOW TO SET COUNTERTOP TILES

Sink cap

First, set edge tiles in place, starting from the center line, after buttering the backs with adhesive.

Surfaces may need to be primed or sealed before tile is applied. To determine the best base and preparation for your job, read the information on the adhesive container or ask your tile supplier.

Planning your layout. Before you start laying tile, you must decide how you want to trim the countertop edge and the sink. For ideas, see the drawing below.

Hardwood edge — Cabinet face — Sink cap — Cabinet face — Metal sink rim — Sink cap — Sink — Cabinet face — ¾" plywood — Quarter-round tile — Sink

If you decide to use wood trim, seal the wood and attach it to the cabinet face with finishing nails. When in place, the wood strip's top edge should be positioned at the same height as the finished tile. A recessed sink is also installed at this time (see page 105).

Mastic adhesive — Carpenter's square

Next, install field tiles. Use a square to keep the tiles perpendicular to the edge trim.

On the front edge of your plywood base, locate and mark the point where the center of the sink or the midpoint of a blank countertop will be. Lay the edge tiles out on the countertop, starting from your mark. Some tiles have small ceramic lugs molded onto their edges to keep spacing equal; if your tiles don't, use plastic spacers, available from your tile supplier.

Carefully position the rest of the "field" tiles on the countertop. Observing the layout, make any necessary adjustments to eliminate narrow cuts or difficult fits.

If the countertop will have a backsplash or will turn a corner, be sure to figure the cove or corner tiles into your layout.

Mark reference points of your layout on the plywood base to help you re-create it later; then remove the tile.

Setting the tiles. Set all trim tiles before spreading adhesive for the field tiles. Thinset adhesive, mixed with latex additive, is water-resistant and easy to use.

Butter the back of each front-edge tile and press into place, aligning it with the reference marks. If your edge trim consists of two tile rows, set the vertical piece first.

Next, butter any back cove tiles and set them against the wall. If you've installed a recessed sink, next lay the sink trim. Be sure to caulk

between the sink and the base before setting the trim. If you're using quarter-round trim, you can either miter the corners or use special corner pieces available with some patterns.

Next, spread adhesive over a section of the countertop (for tools and techniques, see page 100). Begin laying the field tiles, working from front to back. Cut tiles to fit as necessary. As you lay the tiles, check the alignment frequently with a carpenter's square.

To set the tiles and level their faces, slide a 1-foot-square scrap of cloth-covered plywood over them and tap the scrap with a hammer.

Now set the backsplash, beginning one grout joint space above the cove tiles or countertop tiles. Cover the backsplash area with adhesive; for a better grip, you can also butter the back of each tile.

Unless you're tiling up to an overhead cabinet or window sill, use bullnose tiles for the last row. If a wall contains electrical switches or plug-in outlets, you can cut tiles in two and use tile nippers to nip out a hole.

Applying the grout. Remove any spacers and clean the tile surface and grout joints until they're free of adhesive. Allow thinset adhesive to set for 24 hours before grouting the joints. For details on grouting tools and techniques, see page 101.

Installing solid-surface countertops

Some solid-surface materials can be cut and joined using woodworking techniques—you'll need power tools and carbide-tipped blades to do the job well. Note, however, that many distributors won't sell solid-surface materials unless they do both the fabrication and the installation.

Blanks used for countertops usually range from ½ inch to ¾ inch thick. The ½-inch thickness must be continuously supported by the cabinet frame or closely spaced plywood blocks. If you're installing a sink, add cross-members to the frame for support.

When you cut the slab, be sure it is firmly supported throughout its length. Mark and cut on the back side. Protect the cutting line with masking tape.

The countertop can be edged with wood trim, strips of solid-surface material, or a combination. If you're skilled with an electric router, you can shape a variety of custom edge treatments.

Run a bead of neoprene adhesive along the top of the frame and on any supports. With helpers, lower the countertop into place, pressing down to seat it in the adhesive. Apply silicone caulk between the countertop and walls.

Installing wood countertops

Handsome and natural, wood countertops are easy to install. Classic wood butcherblock tops, laminated from strips of hardwood laid on edge, are sold in 24, 30, and 36-inch widths and incremental lengths. If required, cut your top to size with a power saw, easing sharp edges and corners with a sander, file, or electric router and roundover bit. Fasten the countertop to cabinets with screws from below. Run a bead of silicone caulk along the seam between the countertop and walls.

You can seal the wood with mineral oil, but seal both sides or the counter may warp.

HOW TO SET BACKSPLASH TILES

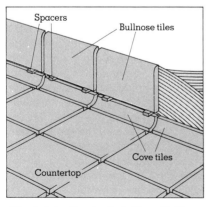

Align joints of backsplash tiles with tiles on the countertop; finish the top with bullnose tiles.

To fit tiles around plug-in outlets, cut a hole in the tile or cut the tile in two and nibble out a hole.

Flooring

Flooring manufacturers are continually revising their wares—improving selection, and making floors easier to care for and easier to install.

Two primary requirements for a kitchen floor are moisture-resistance and durability. Resilient flooring, ceramic tile, and properly sealed hardwood strips are all good choices.

The information in this section applies to floors that are supported by a standard subfloor, with joists or beams below (for an illustration, see page 67). If you're working in a house that's on a concrete slab, you may have to make special preparations to ensure that the slab is perfectly dry.

Resilient sheet flooring

Resilient sheet flooring can be laid in adhesive or placed loosely on the floor like wall-to-wall carpet. Though some types are available in widths up to 12 feet, most sheet flooring is 6 feet wide and may require seaming.

Preparing the subfloor. Both old resilient floors and wood floors make acceptable bases for new resilient sheets, provided their surfaces are completely smooth and level. Old resilient flooring must be the solid, not the cushioned type and firmly bonded to the subfloor. Uneven wood floors may need a rough sanding (see page 103). Both types must be thoroughly cleaned.

Old flooring in poor condition or flooring of ceramic tile or masonry should be removed, if possible, down to the subfloor.

If it is impossible to remove without damaging the subfloor, or if the subfloor is in poor condition, cover the old flooring with ¼-inch underlayment-grade plywood, untempered hardboard, or particle board. Leave a ¹⁄₁₆-inch gap between panels to allow for later expansion. Fasten the panels down with 3-penny ring-shank or 4-penny cement-coated nails spaced 3 inches apart along the edges and 6 inches apart across the face of each panel.

Planning the new floor. Take exact measurements of the kitchen floor and make a scale drawing on graph paper. If your room is very irregular, you may want to make a full-size paper pattern of the floor instead of the scale drawing. To cover a large area, you may need to seam two pieces.

Installing flooring without seams. The most critical step in laying sheet flooring is making the first rough cuts accurately.

Unroll the flooring in a large room or in a clean garage or basement. Transfer the floor plan—or paper pattern—directly onto the top of the flooring, using chalk or a water-soluble felt-tip pen, a carpenter's square, and a long straightedge.

Using a linoleum or utility knife or heavy-duty scissors, cut the flooring roughly 3 inches over-size on all sides. The excess will be trimmed away after the flooring has been positioned.

If adhesive is required with your flooring, it can either be spread over the entire subfloor or, depending on the type of adhesive, spread in steps as the flooring is unrolled. Check the adhesive's "open-time"—the time it takes to dry.

Remove the baseboards and molding from walls and cabinet fronts. Carry the roll of flooring into the kitchen and lay the longest edge against the longest wall, allowing the 3-inch excess to curl up the wall. The flooring should also curl up each adjoining wall. If the entire floor has been covered with adhesive, slowly roll the flooring out across the room.

Cut 3" extra

Actual room size

Take care to set the flooring firmly into the adhesive as you proceed. When you finish, start at the center of the room and work out any air bubbles that may remain. You can use a rolling pin for this, or rent a floor roller.

Installing flooring with seams. Transfer your floor plan or paper pattern to the flooring as described above. On flooring with a decorative pattern, be sure to leave the margins necessary to match the pattern at the seam on adjoining sheets (see below). If your flooring has a simulated grout or mortar joint, plan to cut the seam along the midpoint of the printed joint.

Cut the piece that requires the most intricate fitting first. If using adhesive, spread it on the subfloor as directed, stopping 8 or 9 inches from the seam. Then position the sheet on the floor. If you're not using adhesive, simply put the first sheet in place.

Next, cut the second sheet of flooring and position it to overlap the first sheet by at least 2 inches; make sure the design is perfectly aligned. Again, if using adhesive, stop 8 or 9 inches from the seam; if not, position the second sheet carefully, then secure it to the subfloor with two or three strips of double-faced tape.

When the flooring is in position, trim away excess material at each end of the seam in a half-moon shape so the ends butt against the wall.

Using a steel straightedge and a sharp utility knife, make a straight cut—about ½ to ⅝ inch from the edge of the top sheet—down through both sheets of flooring. Lift up the flooring and spread adhesive under the seam—or if you're not using adhesive, apply a long piece of double-faced tape beneath the seam. Clean the area around the seam, using the appropriate solvent for your adhesive. Fuse the two pieces with a recommended seam sealer.

Trimming to fit. You'll need to make a series of relief cuts at all inside and outside corners to allow the flooring to lie flat on the floor.

At inside corners, gradually trim away the excess with diagonal cuts until the flooring lies flat (see drawing below). At outside corners, start at the top of the lapped-up flooring and cut straight down to the point where the wall and floor meet.

After you cut the corners, remove the material lapped up against the walls. Using an 18 to 24-inch long piece of 2 by 4, press the flooring into a right angle where the floor and wall join.

Lay a heavy metal straightedge along the wall and trim the flooring with a utility knife, leaving a gap of about ⅛ inch between the edge of the flooring and the wall. This will allow the material to expand without buckling; the baseboard and/or shoe molding will cover the gap.

Resilient tile flooring

Resilient tiles come in two standard sizes, 9-inch and 12-inch square. Other sizes and shapes are available, but they often must be specially ordered.

To determine the amount of tile you need, find the area of the floor, subtracting for any large protrusions, such as a peninsula. Add 5 percent so you'll have extra tiles for cutting and later repairs.

If your design uses more than one color or pattern, estimate how many tiles of each kind you'll need

HOW TO TRIM RESILIENT TILES

To lay out a border tile, first place a loose tile on top of the last full tile nearest the wall; then place a second tile over the first, butting it against the wall, and mark it for cutting (A). This same technique can be used to mark L-shaped tiles for outside corners (B). Score tiles with a utility knife (C).

by drawing your design on graph paper with colored pencils.

Placing the tiles. Laying resilient tiles involves three steps: marking the working lines, spreading the adhesive (unless you're using self-stick tiles), and placing the tiles. These steps are similar to those for ceramic tile (for details, see pages 100–101). But unlike ceramic units, resilient tiles are laid tightly against each other, and, because they're made with machine precision, they must be laid out in perfectly straight lines.

Once a tile is in position, press it firmly in place. Lay half a dozen or so, going over them with a rolling pin. If you're using self-stick tiles, take extra care to position them exactly before you press them

into place (they're hard to remove once they're fixed to the floor). Also note the arrows on the back of self-stick tiles—lay the tiles with the arrows going the same way.

Cutting tile. To cut tiles, score them along the mark with a utility knife; then snap the tile along the line. For intricate cuts, use heavy scissors. (The tiles will cut more easily if warmed.)

To mark border and corner tiles for cutting, position a loose tile exactly over one of the tiles in the last row closest to the wall, making sure that the grain or pattern is running correctly. Place another loose tile on top of the first, butting it against the wall. Using this tile as a guide, mark the tile beneath for cutting, as shown at the top of the page.

(Continued on next page)

HOW TO TRIM FLOORING

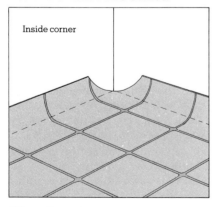

Where flooring turns an inside corner, cut the excess with diagonal cuts.

At outside corner, cut straight down to the point where wall and floor meet.

Trim ⅛" from wall

Utility knife

Straightedge

Trim flooring, leaving a ⅛" gap between the edge and the wall.

■Flooring

Ceramic tile floors

You can install a ceramic tile floor in a three-step operation: lay evenly spaced tiles in a bed of adhesive atop a smooth, dry, and rigid subfloor; fill the joint spaces between tiles with grout; and seal the floor for durability and easy cleaning. Glazed tiles, thinset adhesive with latex additive, and cement-base grout are probably the best materials for the do-it-yourselfer.

Preparing the subfloor. If at all possible, remove old flooring before installing new ceramic tiles. Not only does this enable you to examine the subfloor and make any necessary repairs, but it should also make the new floor level with floors in adjacent rooms. But if your old resilient (solid, not cushioned), ceramic tile, wood, or masonry flooring is level and in good repair, it can be successfully covered with tile. Your tile dealer can recommend the best adhesive and method of application.

To prepare a plywood subfloor, make certain that all panels are securely attached to the joists. If the subfloor is constructed from individual 4 or 6-inch boards, be sure that each board is securely attached. Drive any protruding nails flush with the surface.

To prevent a board subfloor from warping, or if the plywood subfloor is in poor condition, you'll have to install a new layer over the old before laying tile. Use exterior or underlayment-grade plywood or particle board at least ⅜ inch thick, and leave a ¹⁄₁₆-inch gap between adjacent panels. Fasten the panels with 6-penny ring-shank nails spaced 6 inches apart. Where possible, drive nails through the panels into the floor joists.

Regardless of your subfloor material, you may need to use a sealer before applying adhesive. Check your adhesive for instructions.

Establish working lines. The key to laying straight rows of tile is to establish proper working lines. You can begin either at the center of the room or at one wall.

If two adjoining walls meet at an exact right angle, start laying tiles along one wall. This method means that fewer border tiles need to be cut; it also allows you to work without stepping on rows previously set.

To check for square corners and straight walls, place a tile tightly into each corner. Stretch a chalkline between the corners of each pair of tiles; pull the line tight and snap each line. Variations in the distance between chalklines and walls will reveal any irregularities in the walls. You can ignore variations as slight as the width of a grout joint. With a carpenter's square, check the intersection of lines in each corner of the room.

Assuming that your walls are reasonably straight, you can begin laying tile at any straight wall adjoining a straight corner. Snap a new chalkline parallel to the original line and approximately two grout joint widths closer to the center of the room (see drawing above). Lay a similar line, at a right angle to the first, along the adjoining wall. Then nail a batten (wood straightedge) along each of these working lines.

If you can't find a square corner, begin at the center of the room. Locate the center point on each of two opposite walls, and snap a chalkline between the two points. Then find the centers of the other two walls and stretch your chalkline at right angles to the first line; snap the line only after you've used your carpenter's square to determine that the two lines cross at a precise right angle.

Whether you begin at a wall or in the center, it's a good idea to make a dry run before you actually set the tiles in adhesive. Lay the tiles out on the lines, allowing proper spacing for grout joints. Try to determine the best layout while keeping the number of tiles to be cut to a minimum.

Setting the tiles. Using a notched trowel, start spreading a strip of adhesive along one of the battens. Cover about a square yard at first, or the area you can comfortably tile before the adhesive begins to set.

Using a gentle twisting motion, place the first tile in the corner formed by the two battens. With the same motion, place a second tile alongside the first. To establish the proper width for the grout joint, use molded plastic spacers. Continue laying tiles along the batten until the row is complete. Start each new row at the same end as the first. If you're working from the center of the room, follow one of the patterns shown below.

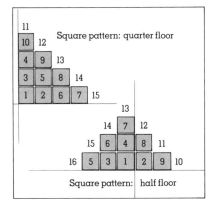

As the tiles are laid, set a piece of carpet-wrapped wood over the tiles; tap it with a mallet or hammer to "beat in" the tiles. Keep checking with a carpenter's square or straightedge to make sure each course is straight. Wiggle any stray tiles back into position while the adhesive is still flexible.

When you're ready to install border tiles, carefully remove the battens. Measure the remaining spaces individually, subtract the width of two grout joints, and mark each tile for any necessary cuts.

HOW TO SET CERAMIC FLOOR TILES

Nail batten boards at right angles, flush with the working lines. Then spread adhesive alongside one batten with a notched trowel.

Begin placing tiles from the corner formed by the battens, using spacers to maintain the width of the grout joint. Continue to the end of the first row.

Start each new row at the same end as the first row. To set tiles in adhesive, slide a beating block (padded wood block) over the tiles while tapping it with a hammer.

You can cut tile with a snap cutter (A) rented from your tile supplier or with a power wet saw. To cut irregular shapes, use a tile nipper (B); first score the cutting lines with a glass cutter. Drill holes in tile with a masonry bit. Smooth any rough edges with an abrasive stone.

After all the tiles are placed, remove any spacers and clean the tile surface so it's completely free of adhesive. Before applying grout, allow the tiles to set properly—about 24 hours with mastic adhesives.

Applying grout. Grout can be applied liberally around glazed tiles. Grouting unglazed tiles requires more care, since the grout may stain the tile's surface. Be sure to read the manufacturer's recommendations.

Using a rubber-faced float or squeegee, apply grout to the surface of the tile. Force the grout into the joints so they're completely filled; make sure no air pockets remain. Scrape off excess grout with the float, working diagonally across the tiles.

Soak a sponge in clear water and wring it out. Wipe the tiles with a circular motion, removing any remaining grout, until the joints are smooth and level with the tiles. Rinse and wring out the sponge frequently.

When the tiles are clean, let the grout dry for about 30 minutes. By then, any film of grout left on the tile will have formed a light haze; immediately polish it off with a soft cloth. Smooth the grout joints with a jointer, striking tool, or toothbrush.

Finishing touches. Most grouts take at least 2 weeks to cure. You'll need to damp-cure a cement-based grout by covering the newly installed floor with plastic. Leave the plastic in place for 24 hours; then remove it and allow the grout to cure thoroughly. Stay off the tile until cured.

Once the grout has fully cured, seal it and the tile with a silicone or lacquer-base sealer recommended by your tile supplier.

Wood strip flooring

Wood strip flooring, the traditional "hardwood" floor, is made up of narrow boards with tongue-and-groove edges and ends, laid in random lengths.

You can buy finished or unfinished wood strips. The latter type is more water-resistant (joints between boards can be sealed), but prefinished flooring is easier to install.

Though widths and thicknesses vary, the most common strip flooring is ¾ inch or $^{25}/_{32}$ inch thick, with a face width of 2¼ inches.

(Continued on next page)

■Flooring

Preparing the subfloor. The sub-floor preparation can be more de-manding than putting in the new flooring. Moisture is the number one enemy of wood floors; you must en-sure that the subfloor is completely dry and will remain dry. Any crawl-space below the floor must also be properly ventilated and protected from moisture.

Though it's possible to lay wood flooring over an old wood floor that's structurally sound and perfectly level, you may need to remove the old flooring to get down to the sub-floor and make necessary repairs or install underlayment. In the long run, this usually provides the most reliable base for your new floor.

Check the exposed subfloor for loose boards or loose plywood pan-els. If planks are badly bowed and cannot be flattened by nailing, give the floor a rough sanding with a floor sander (see page 103) or cover it with ⅜ or ½-inch plywood or parti-cle board. Fasten down ⅜-inch ma-terial with 3-penny ring-shank or cement-coated nails; for ½-inch ma-terial, use 4-penny ring-shank or 5-penny cement-coated nails. Space nails 6 inches apart across the sur-face of the panels.

New or old, the base for the new floor should be cleaned thoroughly, then covered with a layer of 15-pound asphalt-saturated felt (butting seams) or soft resin paper (overlap-ping seams 4 inches).

As you put the felt or paper in place, use a straightedge or a chalkline to mark the center of each joist on the covering. The lines will serve as reference points when you attach the new flooring.

Butt seams together · 15-lb. asphalt felt · Joist marks · Plywood subfloor · Use straightedge to mark joists

Planning the new floor. For a trouble-free installation, the first course you lay must be parallel to the cen-ter of the kitchen.

Measure the width of the room in several spots and locate the cen-ter line as accurately as possible. Snap a chalkline to mark the center, your primary reference point.

Next, measuring from the cen-ter line, lay out and snap another chalkline about ½ inch from the wall you're using as a starting point.

Snap chalkline for starter course · Joist marks · Center line · 15-lb. asphalt felt

In a kitchen that's obviously ir-regular in shape, locate the center line as closely as possible and be-gin laying the first row of flooring from that point. A special wood strip called a *spline* is used to join two back-to-back grooved boards along the center line.

Spline · Groove · Groove · Center line of room · Tongue · Spline

Installing the flooring. When start-ing from the wall, you may need to trim a few boards at the outset. It's

important that your first row of floor-ing line up properly while keeping the ½-inch distance from the wall. If you're starting from the center of an irregular room, the trimming will be done later when you reach the walls.

Tongue-and-groove strip floor-ing is attached by nailing at an an-gle through the tongues, where nail heads won't show. (This is called "blind-nailing.") To ensure a tight floor, install strips perpendicular to joists.

You can make a perfectly ac-ceptable installation using basic hand tools, but a nailer (available from most tool rental companies) will speed the work. Similarly, boards can be neatly cut with a backsaw and miter box, but a radial-arm or power miter saw saves time.

If you're starting along the wall, the first row of boards should be secured by face-nailing; the nails will be covered later with shoe molding. Predrill the boards with holes slightly smaller than the diameter of your nails.

When beginning at the center of an irregularly shaped room, you can start right off by blind-nailing through the tongues—with the nail-er, if you have one.

Stagger end joints so that no joint is closer than 6 inches to a joint in an adjoining row of boards. Leave approximately ½ inch between each end piece and the wall. As a rule, no end piece should be shorter than 8 inches. When laying flooring over plywood or particle board, avoid placing the end joints in the flooring directly over joints in the subfloor.

As you place each row, move a block of wood along the leading edge of the flooring you've just put down, and give it a sharp rap with a mallet or hammer before you drive each nail. To avoid damaging the tongues, cut a groove in the block to accommodate the tongue, or use a short length of flooring.

Since you won't have enough space to use a nailer until you are several rows from the wall, you'll have to nail the first courses by hand. By continuing to predrill holes for the nails, you can keep nails at the

HOW TO LAY WOOD STRIP FLOORING

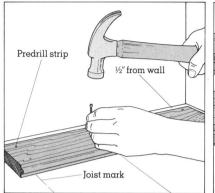

Predrill holes slightly smaller than the nail diameter, then face-nail the first course from the wall.

Nail first few rows by hand—start with a hammer, then drive the nail home with a nailset laid sideways along the tongue.

Once there's working room, drive nails with a nailer and rubber mallet; the nailer automatically drives nails flush.

proper angle—45° to 50° from the floor—and help prevent splitting. Take care not to crush the upper edges of the boards. Instead of using your hammer to drive nails flush, leave the heads exposed; then place a nailset sideways over each nail along the top of the tongue, and tap the nailset with your hammer. Use the nailset's tip to drive the nail flush.

Once you have laid and nailed the first few rows by hand, you can begin to secure the flooring with a nailer, which automatically countersinks all the nails it drives.

When you reach the last few rows, you'll find it difficult to blind-nail the boards. Predrill holes and face-nail them. The final strip of flooring must be placed to leave a ½-inch gap between the flooring and the wall. If you're lucky, a standard board will fit. If not, you'll have to rip several boards down to the proper width.

Finishing touches. An unfinished floor will have to be sanded and finished. Most equipment rental companies offer the necessary heavy-duty equipment.

Typically, three sandings—called "cuts"—using three grades of sandpaper are needed to prepare a floor for finishing. Floor sanding equipment, especially the unwieldy drum sander, must be operated with great care in order to avoid causing irreparable damage to the

new floor. For help with sanding techniques and procedures, ask your flooring supplier for recommendations.

To apply polyurethane, start with a clean brush along the walls and around obstacles. Then use a long-handled paint roller with a mohair cover to apply the finish evenly over the rest of the floor.

At least two (and preferably three) coats of polyurethane are the rule in the kitchen. Between coats, use a floor buffer equipped with #2 steel wool to smooth the surface.

"Floating" wood floors

Preparing a perfectly smooth subfloor and laying strip after strip of hardwood flooring is painstaking work. An easier method is to put

down a "floating floor." Made of several prefinished veneer strips on a tongue-and-grooved shared plywood base, each section is not nailed to the subfloor but joined with adhesive above a cushioned foam layer (see drawing below).

Typical unit size is 8 inches wide by 8 feet long, so the new floor goes down quickly. Start with a dry, even subfloor; then add a layer of polyurethane sheet foam sold for this purpose. The foam masks minor subfloor flaws and helps even out the finish flooring.

Lay out veneer units as you would standard hardwood strips (see page 102), staggering joints and leaving slight gaps along walls (baseboards will cover these later). But don't nail; instead, run a bead of carpenter's glue along each groove as strips are applied.

A LOOK AT FLOATING FLOORS

Fixtures & appliances

Disk faucets, double self-rimmed sinks, built-in dishwashers, microwave ovens—the array of styles, colors, and special features available in kitchen fixtures and appliances can be bewildering. For help in making your selection, see pages 54–63.

Fortunately for the do-it-yourselfer, most variations of the basic fixtures and appliances are installed in a similar manner. The following pages cover the fundamentals. Specific instructions should accompany each unit (check before purchase); follow the manufacturer's instructions if they differ from those below.

Many fixtures and appliances can be easily connected to an existing sink drain or electrical outlet. But before you make any purchase, be sure your home's plumbing and electrical systems can handle the new load. For a discussion of plumbing and electrical systems, their limitations, and applicable codes, see "Plumbing basics," pages 74–76, and "Electrical basics," pages 77–82.

Sometimes the greatest challenge of replacing a major appliance such as a refrigerator, is transporting the old one from the site and bringing in the new one. Always plan your route in advance ("Do we need to remove a door? How will we get it down the steps?"), and have adequate help on hand. An appliance dolly can be indispensable.

Installing a faucet

Most modern kitchen faucets are the deck-mounted type, seated on the rear of the sink and secured from below. When shopping for a replacement, you'll find the selection staggering. You can choose from a lineup of single-lever washerless faucets—valve, disk, ball, and cartridge—and styles ranging from antique reproductions to futuristic compression models. All are interchangeable as long as the new faucet's inlet shanks are spaced to fit the holes on the sink.

If you still have old-fashioned wall-mounted faucets, you face a different decision: either buy an updated style, or switch to a deck-mounted type.

If you decide to use a different type of faucet, you'll be adding several steps to the installation process; at the very minimum, you'll need to reroute pipes from the wall into the kitchen cabinet and patch the wall.

Removing a deck-mounted faucet. Begin by shutting off the water supply, either at the shutoff valves on both hot and cold water supply lines or (if you don't have shutoff valves) at the main house shutoff near the water meter. Then drain the pipes by opening the faucet or faucets.

Use a wrench to unfasten the couplings that attach the supply tubing to the shutoff valves. If space is cramped under the sink, use a basin wrench to loosen and remove the locknuts and washers on both faucet inlet shanks.

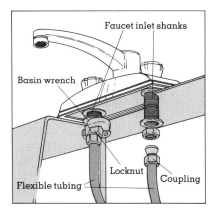

On a kitchen sink equipped with a spray hose attachment, undo the locknuts connecting the hose to the faucet body and the hose nipple. Then lift the faucet away from the sink.

Installing the new faucet. Clean the surface of the sink where the new faucet will sit. Some faucets come with a rubber gasket on the bottom; if yours doesn't, apply plumber's putty or silicone caulk to the base.

Set the faucet in position, simultaneously feeding the flexible supply tubing, if attached, down through the middle sink hole. (If your new faucet has no tubing included, buy two lengths of tubing and attach them at this point.) Press the

HOW TO INSTALL FAUCETS

Apply plumber's putty to the bottom edge of the faucet body if there's no gasket to seal it to the sink's surface.

Set the faucet in place, threading supply tubes through the sink hole; then tighten the locknuts.

Attach flexible tubing to the shutoff valves, using appropriate compression fittings.

faucet onto the sink's surface. Install any required washers and locknuts from below; tighten them with a wrench. Attach a spray hose according to the manufacturer's instructions.

Run the flexible tubing to the shutoff valves, gently bending the tubing as necessary, and connect it using compression fittings. (If you don't have shutoff vales and want to install them in your system, consult a plumber.)

Installing a sink

A deck-mounted kitchen sink fits into a specially cut hole in the countertop. If you're simply replacing a sink, you can choose any model the same size as the present sink, or *larger*; if it's a new installation, you'll have to make the sink cutout first.

Three basic sink types prevail: self-rimmed, frame-rimmed, and re-

cessed, or unrimmed. Most new sinks are self-rimmed; these have a molded overlap that's supported by the countertop cutout. A frame-rimmed sink has a surrounding channel that holds the sink to the countertop. A recessed sink is held in place beneath the countertop by metal clips.

A fourth type, the integral sink, is part of the countertop and comes in both solid-surface and stainless steel versions.

Removing an old sink. First shut off the water supply at the shutoff valves on both hot and cold water supply pipes; if you don't have shutoff valves, turn off the water at the main house shutoff. Then drain the pipes by opening the faucet, and disconnect the supply pipes as described on page 104. You'll also need to disconnect the drain trap from the sink's strainer assembly. Loosen the couplings that hold the tailpiece to the strainer assembly, and the tailpiece to the trap. Push the tailpiece down into the trap.

From below the sink, remove any clamps or lugs holding it to the countertop. If necessary, break the putty seal by forcing the sink free.

Making a sink cutout. For a new installation, trace either a template (included with the new sink) or the bottom edge of the frame onto the exact spot where the sink will sit. Typically, 1½ to 2 inches is left between the edge of the cutout and the front edge of the countertop. Drill pilot holes in each corner of the outline, and insert a saber saw into one of the holes to make the cutout.

Installing the new sink. It's best to mount the fauct and hook up the strainer assembly before installing the new sink in the countertop.

To install a strainer assembly, first apply a bead of plumber's putty to the underlip of the strainer body, then press it down into the sink opening. If the strainer is held in place by a locknut, place the rubber gasket and metal washer over the strainer body, and tighten by hand. Hold the strainer from above while you snug up the locknut, preferably with a spud wrench. If the strainer is held in place by a retainer, fit the retainer over the strainer body and tighten all three screws. Attach the tailpiece with a coupling.

Some self-rimmed sinks include a rubber gasket below the lip. In any case, apply a ½-inch-wide strip of putty or silicone caulk along the edge of the countertop opening. Set the sink into the cutout, pressing it down. Smooth excess putty.

For a frame-rimmed sink, apply a ring of plumber's putty around the top edge of the sink. Fasten the frame to the sink, following the manufacturer's instructions; some frames attach with metal corner clamps, others with metal extension tabs that bend around the sink lip. Wipe off excess putty.

Anchor a recessed sink from below at 6 or 8-inch intervals, using any clamps or lugs provided. You may also need to drill separate holes in the countertop for the faucet or accessories.

Finally, hook up the supply pipes and drain trap. Turn on the water and check for leaks.

SINK DRAIN ELEMENTS

Strainer

Strainer body

Putty

Rubber gasket

Metal washer

Locknut

Strainer sleeve

Tailpiece

Couplings

Washers

Trap

Cleanout plug

Saber saw

Pilot holes

Countertop

■Fixtures & appliances

Installing a garbage disposer

Installing a disposer takes a few hours, but the basic connection is not difficult. Most units fit the standard 3½ or 4-inch drain outlets of kitchen sinks and mount somewhat like a sink strainer (see page 105).

Plumbing a disposer involves altering the sink trap to fit the unit. If your model has direct wiring, you must run electrical cable to a nearby junction box or other power source (see pages 77–82 for information). Plug-in disposers require a 120-volt grounded (three-prong) outlet under the sink and a separate wall switch adjacent to the sink.

Before installing a disposer, check plumbing codes for any restrictions.

Removing a strainer or disposer.

If you're adding a disposer for the first time, first disconnect the sink strainer assembly. Start by removing the tailpiece and trap (see page 105); then disassemble the strainer components and lift them out of the sink. Clean away any old putty or sealing gaskets around the opening.

If you're replacing a disposer, first turn off the electricity; then unplug the unit or disconnect the wiring. Loosen the screws on the mounting ring assembly and re-move the parts; finally, remove the sink flange from above.

Mounting the disposer. The disposer comes with its own sink flange and mounting assembly. Run a bead of plumber's putty around the sink opening and seat the flange. Then, working from below, slip the gasket, mounting rings, and snap ring up onto the neck of the flange. The snap ring should fit firmly into a groove on the sink flange to hold things in place temporarily.

Uniformly tighten the slotted screws in the mounting rings until the gasket fits snugly against the bottom of the flange. Remove any excess putty from around the flange.

Attach the drain elbow to the disposer. Lift the disposer into place, aligning the holes in the disposer's flange with the slotted screws in the mounting rings. Rotate the disposer so that the drain elbow lines up with the drainpipe. Tighten the nuts securely onto the slotted screws to ensure a good seal.

Making the hookups. Fit the coupling and washer onto the drain elbow. Add an elbow fitting on the other end of the trap to adjust to the drainpipe. You may need to shorten the drainpipe to make the connection. Tighten all connections, and run water down through the disposer to check for leaks.

At this point, either plug the disposer into a grounded outlet (see pages 80–81), or shut off the power and wire the unit directly, following the manufacturer's instructions. Then turn the power back on. To be completely safe, it's important to test the unit to make sure it has been properly grounded.

Installing a dishwasher

A built-in dishwasher requires three connections: hot water supply, drainpipe fitting, and a 120-volt, 20-amp, grounded plug-in outlet. (For basic electrical information, see pages 77–82.)

Local codes may require that you also install a venting device, called an air gap, on the sink or countertop. Some municipalities require a permit and an inspection when a built-in dishwasher is installed; check before you begin the work.

Making new connections. For a first-time installation, you'll need to tap into the hot water supply pipe under the sink, and into either the garbage disposer or sink drainpipe for proper drainage.

HOW TO PLUMB A GARBAGE DISPOSER

Attach mounting rings, with gasket and snap ring, to the sink flange; tighten the slotted screws.

Line up the drain elbow on the disposer so it's directly opposite the drainpipe; tighten nuts onto the slotted screws.

Connect the trap to the disposer's drain elbow and to the elbow fitting on the drainpipe.

Begin by shutting off the water supply, either at the shutoff valves under the sink or at the main house shutoff. Drain the supply pipes by turning on the sink faucets. Cut into the hot water supply pipe and install a tee fitting. (If you need any help with pipefitting techniques, consult a professional plumber.) Run flexible copper or plastic tubing (depending on your model) to the location of the water inlet valve on the dishwasher. To simplify future repairs, install a shutoff valve.

Your dishwasher can drain either into the sink drain above the trap or into a garbage disposer. For use with a sink drain, you'll need to buy a threaded waste tee fitting (see drawing below).

To install a waste tee, remove the sink tailpiece (see page 105) and insert a waste tee into the trap. Cut the tailpiece so it fits between the waste tee and the sink strainer assembly. Reattach the tailpiece and clamp the dishwasher drain hose onto the waste tee fitting.

If you already have (or are installing) a garbage disposer, plan to attach the dishwasher drain hose to the disposer drain fitting on the disposer's side. First turn off the electrical circuit that controls the disposer. Then use a screwdriver to punch out the knockout plug inside the fitting. Clamp the dishwasher drain hose to the fitting.

To prevent a backup of waste water into the dishwasher, make a gradual loop with the drain hose to the height of the dishwasher's top before making the connection. If you're required to install an air gap instead of the loop, insert the air gap into the predrilled hole found on some sinks, or into a hole you've drilled at the back of the countertop. Screw the air gap tight from below.

Run one length of hose from the dishwasher to the air gap, and another from the air gap to the waste tee or disposer.

Removing an old dishwasher. If you're simply replacing a dishwasher, the connections should already be made. But you'll have to disconnect and remove the old unit before installing the new one.

First, unfasten any screws or brackets anchoring the unit to the countertop or the floor. Turn off electrical power to the circuit controlling the dishwasher; then shut off the water supply. Disconnect the supply hookup and the drain hose from the dishwasher. With a helper, pull the unit forward to gain access to the electrical connection (unless it's simply under the sink). If the dishwasher is the plug-in type, you're in luck. If it was wired directly, disconnect the wires from the dishwasher.

Completing the installation. Plug in the new dishwasher; then slide it into place. Complete the supply and drain hookups according to the manufacturer's instructions.

Level the dishwasher by adjusting the height of the legs. Anchor the unit to the underside of the countertop with any screws provided. Consider facing the refrigerator to match surrounding cabinetry; panels are available with most modular cabinet lines.

(Continued on next page)

HOW TO CONNECT A DISHWASHER

Install a two-way valve or a tee fitting and shutoff valve in the hot water supply pipe, then add flexible tubing.

To drain into a sink trap, add a threaded waste tee fitting between tailpiece and trap.

To drain into a garbage disposer, connect a dishwasher drain hose to the disposer's drain fitting.

■Fixtures & appliances

Installing a hot water dispenser

Easy-to-install hot water dispensers incorporate a stainless steel faucet connected to an under-counter storage tank. The tank, which in turn is connected to a nearby cold water pipe, has an electric heating coil that keeps water at about 200°F—50° hotter than that produced by the average water heater.

Most units plug into a 120-volt grounded outlet installed under the sink. (For electrical details, see pages 77–82.) Some models, though, are directly wired to a grounded junction box.

Positioning the dispenser. Begin by deciding where you want to place the unit. Commonly, the faucet fits in a hole at the rear of the sink rim, or else mounts directly on the countertop. In the latter case, cut a 1¼-inch-diameter hole in your counter-top near the sink rim with a hole saw or electric drill. Following the manufacturer's instructions, attach the dispenser faucet from beneath the sink. Generally, you'll need only to install a nut and washers to hold the faucet.

From inside the sink cabinet, screw the tank mounting bracket to the wall or cabinet back, making sure it's plumb. The bracket should be located about 14 inches below the underside of the countertop. Next, mount the tank on the bracket.

Making the connections. Before plumbing the unit, shut off the water supply and drain the pipes by opening the sink faucets. Many dispensers come with a self-tapping valve. If yours doesn't, tap into the cold water pipe using a saddle tee fitting (see drawing below). To do this, clamp the fitting to the supply pipe and drill a hole through the fitting into the pipe.

If saddle tees aren't permitted in your area, tap in with a standard tee fitting, then install a shutoff valve and reducer fitting for the dispenser's water supply tube. (If you need help, consult a professional plumber.)

Using the compression nuts provided with the unit, attach one incoming water supply tube between the dispenser and the storage tank, and another between the tank and the cold water supply pipe. Turn on the water supply and check for leaks. Plug in the unit—or shut off the power and connect the wires directly, as required.

Installing a refrigerator

Installing a new refrigerator is easy work—just plug it in to a 120-volt, 20-amp appliance circuit. Your only real challenge will be handling and transporting both the old and the new units.

Disconnecting a refrigerator. When removing the old refrigerator, simply pull it out any way you can to gain access to the plug. If the unit has an automatic icemaker, the fitting attaching the copper supply tubing must be disconnected. Be prepared to remove doors from their hinges, guard rails from stairways, or any other obstructions in the path. Then secure the refrigerator to an appliance dolly and wheel it out.

For safety's sake, plan to store the old unit with its door or doors removed.

Positioning a new refrigerator. Wheel the replacement into a position where you can hook up the icemaker, if necessary, and plug the refrigerator in. Finally push it into place and check level. Adjust the level with shims, as necessary.

A refrigerator can be given a "built-in" look—just wrap modular cabinets around it, or install custom-made cabinets. Be sure to allow ½ inch to 1 inch on all sides for easy removal and air circulation. Add a decorative face panel or manufacturer's trim kit as required.

HOW TO HOOK UP A HOT WATER DISPENSER

First, secure the dispenser faucet to the sink rim or countertop from below, using nut and washers.

Tap into the cold water supply pipe with a saddle tee or standard tee fitting and shutoff valve.

Attach the tank mounting bracket to the wall or cabinet back, then install the storage tank.

Hook up one supply tube from the dispenser to the storage tank, and one from the tank to the supply pipe.

Installing a water line. A water dispenser or icemaker is connected by ¼-inch copper tubing to a cold water supply pipe. To make the connection, use a saddle tee or standard tee fitting and shutoff valve, as detailed under "Installing a hot water dispenser," at left. If the refrigerator can be easily reached from the sink complex, tap in there through the sides of the base cabinets. If the refrigerator is far from the sink, look for another cold water supply pipe to tap (see pages 74–76 for help).

At the refrigerator end, leave a few extra loops of tubing to help you position the unit. Attach the tubing to the refrigerator with a compression union (see drawing below) or other special fitting, following the manufacturer's instructions.

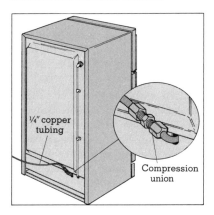
¼" copper tubing

Compression union

Installing a trash compactor

A new trash compactor, like a refrigerator, is simple to hook up—just plug it into a 120-volt, 20-amp grounded outlet.

A typical compactor fits into the same space as a standard 15-inch-wide base cabinet; it can be built in under the countertop, enclosed with an end panel, or used as a free-standing unit.

To install the compactor, move it roughly into position until you can plug in the power cord. Then wrestle it into place (taking care not to scratch the flooring) and level the unit, either by shimming or by adjusting any built-in legs. Fasten the unit to the countertop or cabinets, adding a decorative face panel or trim kit as required.

Installing cooktops, ranges & wall ovens

Cooking equipment offers you a choice of two energy sources—electricity or gas. In addition, it offers three designs—freestanding or "slide-in" range, drop-in range, or a combination of built-in cooktop and separate wall ovens. For a detailed breakdown and evaluation of your options, see pages 57–59.

The only factors limiting your choice are the capacity of your present gas or electrical system, the distance from an existing connection that you plan to move new equipment, and the labor and expense of switching from electricity to gas, or vice versa.

To analyze your present electrical system, see pages 77–78. An electric range, wall oven, or cooktop must be powered by an individual 240-volt circuit. (The exception is a microwave oven, which requires only 120-volt current.) Some appliances are direct-wired; others plug into special 30, 40, or 50-amp outlets mounted nearby. Plugs and outlets are not interchangeable. To determine your needs, consult your appliance dealer or a licensed electrician.

For a discussion of gas system basics, see page 76. If you plan to use the existing line, a gas range can usually be relocated as far as 6 feet from the old gas connection. For new gas lines, you should hire a licensed plumber unless you're very well versed in gas installations. In any case, the work will require inspection by your building department or utility company before hookup.

Once your electrical or gas lines are in order, the actual hookup is straightforward.

Removing a range, oven, or cooktop. Before removing the old unit, first determine the method by which it is fastened (if it is fastened); for help, refer to the appropriate section on page 110. You'll probably need to unfasten some screws or clamps attaching the unit to the underside of the countertop or to adjacent cabinets.

After removing the fasteners, move the appliance just far enough to gain access to the electrical or gas connection. If the appliance is electric, shut off the circuit to the appliance or appliance group before beginning the removal.

Gas appliances should have individual shutoff valves (see drawing below). The valve is open when the handle is parallel to the pipe; to shut off the gas supply, turn the handle until it forms a right angle with the pipe. The appliance is connected to the shutoff valve and main gas line with either solid pipe or flexible tubing and compression fittings.

Solid pipe will need to be cut or unthreaded. A flexible connector can be removed from the shutoff valve with an adjustable wrench.

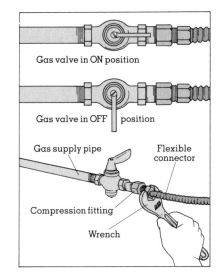
Gas valve in ON position

Gas valve in OFF position

Gas supply pipe

Flexible connector

Compression fitting

Wrench

Some gas appliances also have a 120-volt electrical connection that powers lights, timers, or thermostat. Unplug it or, if the connection is wired directly, shut off power to the circuit before disconnecting the wires.

If at any point you're unsure about how to proceed, call your utility company or seek other knowledgeable help.

Once both the fasteners and power connection are disassembled, the unit can be freely lifted or pulled out of position, loaded onto an appliance dolly, and transported from the room. Be sure you have adequate help for heavy jobs.

(Continued on next page)

■Fixtures & appliances

Installing a freestanding range. Except for the bulkiness of these units, this is a simple job to perform. Be sure the gas shutoff valve or electrical outlet is already in place. Slide the unit in part way until you can make the power hookup; then position it exactly. If the range has adjustable legs, raise or lower them to level the unit; otherwise, use shims as necessary.

Attach flexible cable or plug

If you plan to use an existing gas connection, the new range must be within 6 feet of the shutoff valve. Check local gas or plumbing codes to determine if the connector may be flexible copper, brass, or aluminum, or if it must be solid pipe. A flexible connector is much simpler to install. Use an adjustable wrench to attach the connector's compression nuts to both range and shutoff as required.

Before turning the gas supply back on, it's wise to have utility company personnel check your work. They can inspect for gas leaks or air in the line, and can light and adjust the pilot lights on your new range.

Installing a drop-in range. This type of range is lowered into place between adjacent base cabinets. You'll need to determine the best method for attaching the power connection (either electric plug or gas connector) before, during, or after lifting the unit into place.

Some units have self-supporting flanges that sit on adjacent countertop surfaces. Others are simply lowered into place atop a special cabinet base. Fasten these ranges through side slots into the adjacent cabinets, or into the base itself. Bases and front trim that match

the surrounding cabinetry are available with many cabinet lines, or you can have them custom-made.

Flange supports range

Front trim strip

Support base

Range fastened to adjacent cabinets

Installing a cooktop. Standard electric and gas cooktops or combination cooktop-barbecue units are dropped into a countertop cutout, much as a new sink is installed (see page 105), and then anchored from below with hardware supplied by the manufacturer. The power connection is in the cabinet directly below or to one side of the unit.

Electric cooktops may be plugged in or directly wired to a nearby junction box. A gas cooktop is normally connected by a flexible connector (check local codes), and must be located within 3 feet of its shutoff valve.

DROP-IN COOKTOP

Countertop cutout

Fasten from below

COMMERCIAL GAS COOKTOP

Lowered base cabinet

Gas shutoff valve

Flexible connector

Commercial gas cooktops sit on their own legs on the countertop. Often, a lowered base cabinet is used to align the cooktop with the surrounding countertop. Because of its resistance to heat, tile is frequently used below the cooktop; steel strips help shield adjacent cabinets. The flexible gas connector is commonly run through a hole drilled into the base cabinet below.

Many cooktops, especially those in islands or peninsulas, have special downventing components that direct smoke, grease, and moisture to a fan located in the base cabinet below. From that point, ducting runs out through the wall or down through the cabinet base and below the floor, as shown on page 111.

Installing a wall oven. Separate wall ovens, either singly or in pairs, are housed in specially designed wall cabinets supplied in many sizes. Choose your wall oven first, and take the specifications with you when you shop for cabinets.

Wall ovens typically slide into place and rest atop support shelves. They're fastened to the cabinet through the sides or through overlapping flanges on the front. Trim strips are commonly available to fill any gaps between the ovens and the cabinet front.

The plug-in outlet or gas shutoff valve is usually located below the oven or ovens, inside the cabinet. If you plan both a microwave and a standard electric oven, you'll need both 120-volt and 120/240-volt outlets.

Oven cabinet

Microwave

120-volt outlet for microwave

120/240-volt outlet for wall oven

Wall oven

Installing a ventilation hood

The two basic types of ventilation hood are *ducted* and *ductless*. Though the ductless type is far easier to install (it requires no ductwork), the ducted version is far more efficient.

Before planning any ducting, or purchasing materials, check local mechanical codes for requirements.

Ducting basics. If you're simply replacing a ducted vent hood with a new one, you can probably use the old ducting to vent the new hood.

If you're starting from scratch, keep in mind that the straighter and shorter the path is from the hood to the outside, the more efficient the hood will be. Ducting can run either vertically through the roof or out through the wall.

Ducting is available in both metal and plastic, and is either rectangular or round. The round type is available in both rigid and flexible varieties. The flexible type, though not as strong as the rigid sort, will follow a more twisted course without requiring fittings at each bend. However, if you use round ducting, you'll have to provide a transition fitting where the ducting meets the vent hood.

Join sections of ducting with duct tape. If any elbow fittings are

HOW TO MOUNT A VENT HOOD

To mount a vent hood, trace the duct opening and electrical cable knockout hole on the wall cabinet or wall. Make the cutout with a drill and saber saw. If the cabinet bottom is recessed, add spacers to provide flush mounting surfaces.

required, you'll need access to make the connection. Outside, protect the opening with either a flanged wall cap or a roof cap with integral flashing. Caulk around a wall cap to seal the seams between flange and siding. A roof cap's flashing must first be slipped under the roofing material; then all seams are liberally covered with roofing cement.

Mounting the hood. A vent hood is most commonly mounted on the bottom of a wall cabinet. But first you must cut holes in the cabinet to match knockout holes on the vent's

shell: one for the duct connector and one for the electrical cable.

The hood is screwed to the bottom of the cabinet. If the bottom is recessed, you'll have to add spacers to attach the unit, as shown above.

Hook up the electrical wires according to the manufacturer's instructions, making sure to attach the grounding screw to the grounding bracket on the hood.

Using duct tape or sheet metal screws, connect the vent hood's duct connector to the ducting inside the cabinet. Finally, install light bulbs, lighting panel, and filter panel.

THREE PATHS FOR A VENT DUCT

To rout ducting from a vent hood, run it horizontally in the space between wall cabinets and ceiling, or behind a soffit (A); or take the direct route up through the cabinet and ceiling to the roof (B). A downventing unit vents a cooktop in an island or peninsula (C).

Index

Sunset

Bathrooms
PLANNING & REMODELING

By the Editors of Sunset Books and Sunset Magazine

Built-in vanity houses side-by-side sinks and ample storage; a
wall cabinet adds mirrors and display nooks.

Sunset Publishing Corporation ■ Menlo Park, California

DESIGNER: OSBURN DESIGN

To achieve this dramatic effect, colored joint compound was knife-applied to walls over a lighter tint; a top glaze accents both.

Book Editor
Scott Atkinson

Coordinating Editor
Suzanne Normand Eyre

Design
Joe di Chiarro

Illustrations
Bill Oetinger

Photo Stylist
JoAnn Masaoka Van Atta

Cover: Matching sinks and cabinetry comfortably accommodate two in this colorful master bath. Bathroom design by Osburn Design. Cover design by Naganuma Design & Direction. Photography by Philip Harvey. Photo styling by JoAnn Masaoka Van Atta.

Photography

Jared Chandler: 20 top; **Peter Christiansen:** 28 top, 32 top; **Crandall & Crandall:** 17 top; **Stephen Cridland:** 16 bottom, 27 top; **Jay Graham:** 5, 10, 31 bottom; **Philip Harvey:** 1, 2, 6, 7, 8 top left and bottom left, 9 top, 11, 12, 13, 14, 16 top, 18, 19 top left and top right, 21, 22, 23 top left and top right, 24 top right and bottom, 25, 27 bottom, 28 bottom, 29, 30, 31 top, 32 bottom, 33, 34, 35 bottom left, 37, 46, 48, 51, 64; **David Duncan Livingston:** 15 bottom, 20 bottom, 35 bottom right, 49; **Renee Lynn:** 15 top, 35 top; **Norman A. Plate:** 24 top left, 26 bottom left and bottom right; **Kenneth Rice:** 8 top right; **Brian Vanden Brink:** 19 bottom, 23 bottom, 26 top left; **Tom Wyatt:** 9 bottom, 17 bottom.

Editor, Sunset Books: Elizabeth L. Hogan

First printing April 1994

Time to update your bathroom?

At first glance, a bathroom may seem relatively uncomplicated —a sink, a toilet, and a tub or shower within four walls. But as a look through the pages of this book will prove, there's a lot more to a bathroom than just the basics. Double sinks, whirlpool tubs, stunning tiled surfaces, rich cabinetry—all contribute to turning today's bathrooms into design statements all their own. Now you can achieve the same results.

This new edition offers a wealth of information to guide you, from design ideas for successful floor plans to actual construction techniques. A special section compares the various products on the market today so you can shop wisely for cabinetry, surfacing materials, and fixtures. Whether you're doing the work yourself or hiring professionals for some or all of it, this complete course on bathroom design and construction will provide the help you need.

Special thanks go to Fran Feldman for carefully editing the manuscript. We also wish to thank The Bath & Beyond; Roger Chetrit of Tile Visions; Dillon Tile Supply, Inc.; Menlo Park Hardware Co.; and Plumbing n' Things.

Contents

DESIGN IDEAS

Layouts ▪ Materials ▪ Lighting ▪ Storage

Everyone knows a picture is worth a thousand words. That's why this chapter is packed with full-color photos showing bathroom design ideas that you can apply to your own situation, whether you're remodeling an existing bathroom or starting from scratch.

The first section, "Basic layouts" (pages 6–11), presents a variety of floor plans. Even though you may not have a choice of floor plan, study the photos in this section carefully—you're likely to find details that apply to your bathroom. A related section, "Water works" (pages 12–17), deals with the major plumbing fixtures—sinks, tubs, and showers—around which modern bath design revolves.

"On the surface" (pages 18–23) shows good ways to use surfacing materials ranging from faux painting to stone. "Bright ideas" (pages 24–29) explores natural and artificial lighting, almost always subject to improvement when you're remodeling and an important concern if you're designing a new bath. "Storage solutions" (pages 30–35) concludes the chapter.

View across whirlpool tub includes a master suite's sink area and built-in makeup center. Pink marble lines tub pedestal, floor, and countertops. Elegant wall sconces flank ample mirrors, which stretch space and amplify daylight from an overhead skylight.

Basic layouts

ARCHITECT: LAURENCE ALLEN

Stepped glass-block partition defines large walk-in shower in master bath; glass blocks in exterior walls let in soft, diffused light. Twin sinks sitting atop trim gray European-style cabinets are set off by a green marble countertop and backsplash. Nearby dressing area (out of view) links bedroom to bath and features built-in dressers, marble counters, and warm wool carpeting.

DESIGNER: DEBRA GUTIERREZ

Barrier-free shower design is both beautiful and practical. Incorporated into a stylish marble design is an adjustable hand-held shower head, a grab bar, and a comfortable bench.

Kids' bath begins with a riot of colorful tile. Cork floor is slip-proof. Twin sinks, which overhang a space-saving base cabinet, minimize territorial squabbles. A portable step allows for growing to counter height.

DESIGNER: OSBURN DESIGN

■ Basic layouts

ARCHITECT: DAVID WILLIAMS

DESIGNER: RICK SAMBOL / DESIGN CONSULTANTS

DECORATIVE PAINTING: THE BEARDSLEY COMPANY

Powder rooms occasion bold designs that may not be "practical" for day-to-day bathrooms. In an antique vein, room shown above features a formal parquet floor and a wall-hung sink on shiny chrome legs; painted flowers dominate. Limited understair space shown in photo at left gains weight from textured wallpaper and jet black accents.

DESIGNER: LOU ANN BAUER / BAUER INTERIOR DESIGN

Small washroom combines white wood wainscoting with colorful walls and a hand-painted mirror. Sink fittings atop pedestal sink are actually outdoor faucets.

DESIGNER: ALBERT CAREY, ASID / ACORN KTICHENS & BATHS

With little space to spare, small adult bath has been stretched with mirrors. Hardworking floor plan organizes use areas and incorporates storage by means of vertical dividers.

DESIGNER: RUTH SOFORENKO ASSOCIATES

Tiny white bath has requisite amenities, thanks to careful planning and reliable built-ins. Vanity, sink, tub, and toilet come together in a tight intersection; curves avoid protruding corners that would have blocked foot traffic.

■ Basic layouts

DESIGNER: CATHY NASON ASID INTERIOR DESIGN

DESIGN: LAMPERTI ASSOTICATES

Successful master suite links multiple elements in a single efficient, private retreat. Suite shown above features a stepped glass-block divider that maintains link between bed and bath. Black acrylic soaking tub is on bedroom side of divider; walk-in shower is tucked into a corner. In photo at left, a second suite's exercise area is just a short jog away from soothing tub or seamless shower.

Cedar-lined sauna is a satellite room off a multiroom bath. Twin slat benches, sauna heater, thermostat, and weather-tight door are basic equipment. It's a short walk to shower, visible in background.

Water works

ARCHITECT: J. ALLEN SAYLES

Modern pedestal sink lends its smooth lines to a clean white, symmetrical wall. Mirror anchors design; glass shelf provides trim storage for sink-side accessories. Stylish twin wall sconces shed task light from both directions.

ARCHITECT: J. ALLEN SAYLES

Step-down sinks allow two people to use bathroom at once; each countertop is at a comfortable height for user. Recessed sinks are rimmed with dark blue field tiles; vanities below offer plenty of storage space.

Crystal sink bowl sits atop a transparent shelf in a small powder room. Drain fittings run through transparent glass countertop, providing a design statement of their own.

■ Water works

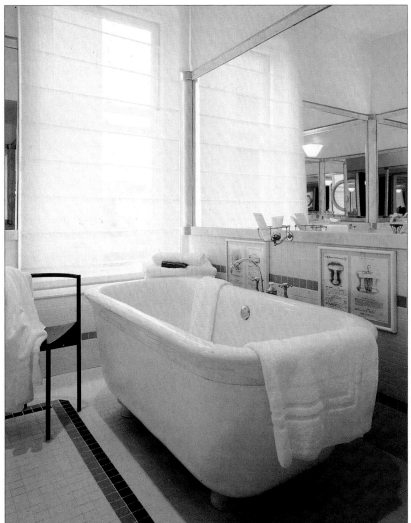

A holdover from the past, stout free-standing tub highlights a brand-new bathroom. Reconditioned with a chrome spout and handles, tub is ready for many more relaxing soaks.

Molded pedestal tub features a water-fall spout and deck-mounted handles. Tub rises above a built-in platform lined with green marble tiles; color is repeated in striped wallpaper.

ARCHITECT: CHARLES DEBBAS

Skylighted soaking area occupies a widened section of a private hallway linking master bedroom and guest room/office. Carefully chosen and shaped materials—slate tiles, maple flooring and cabinetry, and a granite-surfaced tub—create an interior evocative of a Japanese landscape.

DESIGNER: CHADINE FLOOD GONG / CHADINE INTERIOR DESIGN

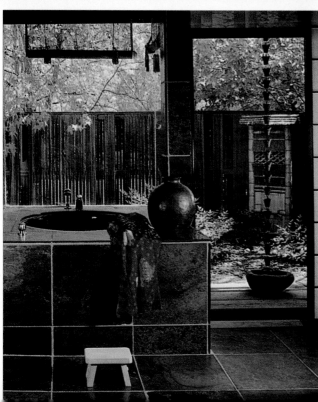

Japanese soaking tub is tranquil centerpiece of a dramatic bath linking indoors with a small Japanese garden outside. Tub platform, floor, and wall surfaces are covered in multicolored African slate, bringing outdoor feeling inside.

■ Water works

ARCHITECT: DAVID WILLIAMS
DESIGNER: RICK SAMBOL / DESIGN CONSULTANTS

Seamless glass steam shower holds down end of a tub platform housing an oval-shaped whirlpool tub. Second-story picture window offers tub-side views; diamond-shaped shower window combines view with privacy.

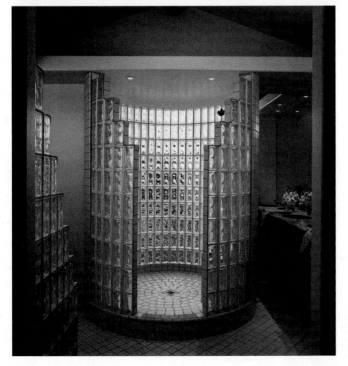

Walk-in shower has a striking curved shape that's echoed in floor tiles. Glass blocks bring in light while maintaining privacy; downlights provide auxiliary light.

ARCHITECT: BO POWELL DESIGN GROUP

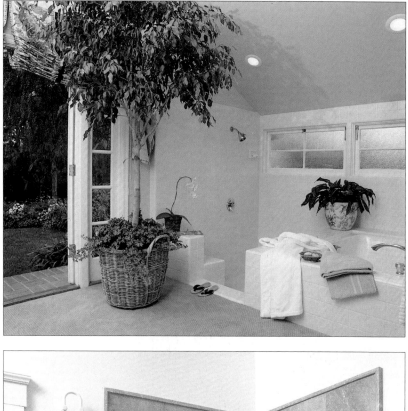

Step-down shower and platform tub are part of an open suite adjacent to a sunny garden. Step-down reduces shower splash; with no surround, open feeling is maintained. Easy-to-clean tile covers all surfaces.

DESIGNER: ELLEN ALVAREZ / DESIGN CABINET SHOWROOMS

Tucked into a corner of a small bath, sleek European shower unit displays an adjustable shower head and massage unit along with a fold-down seat. Curved sliding doors can be removed for cleaning.

On the surface

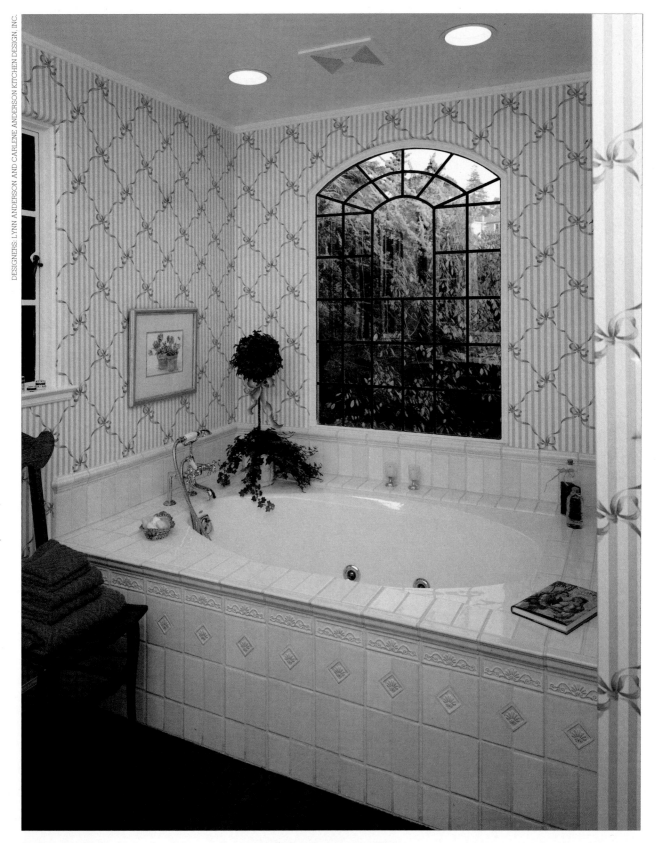

Pink wallpaper lends country cheer to walls surrounding a whirlpool tub. White porcelain tiles facing platform front, tub deck, and backsplash contrast with dark-stained oak floor.

DESIGNER: CHARLOTTE BOYLE INTERIORS
ARCHITECT: J. ALLEN SAYLES

DESIGNER: MONA BRANAGH / PACIFIC BAY INTERIORS

DESIGN: CLASSIC POST & BEAM

Two variations on the pedestal theme: angular adult bath (shown above, at left) gains its fresh effect from a white tile floor and wainscoting punctuated by green trim tiles and chrome accents. Child's bath (shown above, at right) combines a traditional fluted sink with wallpaper and matching cabinet accents; pedestal and floor sport crisp white glazed tile.

Nothing says country comfort like wood—in this case, pine tongue-and-groove paneling, timbers, and window trim. White tile surrounds tub area, heading off moisture damage and allowing for easy cleaning.

■ On the surface

DESIGNER: JOSH CHANDLER

DESIGNER: LAMPERTI ASSOCIATES

DESIGNER: DAVID LIVINGSTON INTERIORS

Bathrooms offer a blank canvas for varied creative expression. In photo above, wall sculpture is joined by an eclectic mix that includes a stainless steel countertop and integral sink, a red tub, textured walls, wood rafters and ceiling, and a dark-stained tile floor.

In a softer style, room at left combines a vanity with amazingly varied slate floor and walls. Sink holes cut in bowl and cabinet accommodate plumbing.

Like a torn masterpiece, a marble countertop gives way to granite, and mirrors yield to wall paint. Polished brass fittings, wall sconces, and angular shapes are repeated endlessly in space-stretching mirrors.

■ On the surface

Textured porcelain tiles marked by subtle variations wrap an oval tub in soft color.
Deck-mounted tub fittings are in a matching muted finish; seamless shower recedes
from view and doesn't interrupt sense of space and quiet.

ARCHITECT: MORIMOTO ARCHITECTS

Bold or subtle, flooring makes a supporting statement in bathrooms. Black and white tile mosaic flooring (above left) lends energy to a quiet bath design; tiles are toasty to the touch, thanks to radiant heating pipes below. In photo above, soft white field tiles and matching grout are punctuated by colorful glazed diagonal inserts.

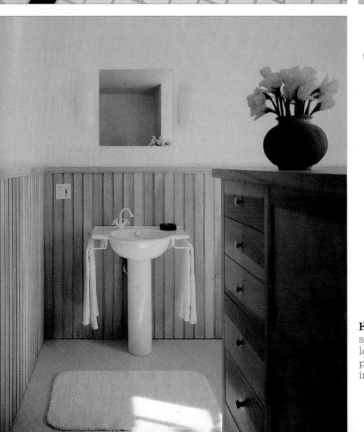

Hardwood wainscoting and chair rail, softened with a white pickling wash, lead the way to a simple European-style pedestal sink. White tile floor and built-in bureau amplify the mood.

Bright ideas

ARCHITECT: REMICK ASSOCIATES

DESIGNER: RICHARD ELMORE

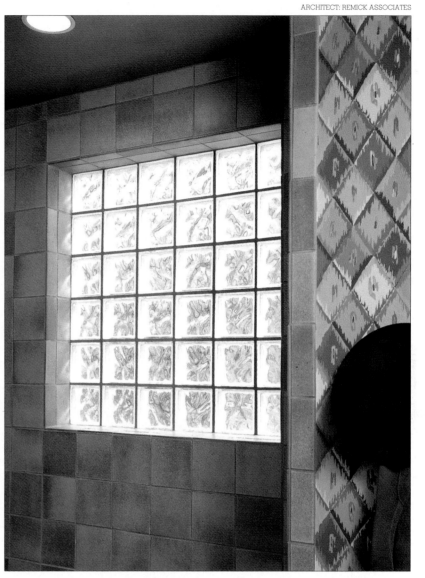

Adding light and design punch while maintaining privacy, glass block is tailor-made for bathroom installation. Curved shower wall shown above left has block below, clear glazing at eye level. Glass-block grouping in photo above delivers soft light to a ground-floor walk-in shower. Single strip of blocks in photo at left brings a flash of light to a child's tub/ shower.

DESIGNER: JIM WALLEN / ACORN KITCHENS & BATHS

Block walls and an opening skylight team up to provide diffuse light and ventilation in a master bath. Block wraps behind both tub and nearby steam shower; mirrors blur boundaries and amplify brightness. Steam shower offers a glimpse of outside through clear blocks up high and in corner.

■ Bright ideas

ARCHITECT: JOHN MORRIS

Enjoy the view without sacrificing privacy. Shown at left, twin roof windows furnish a sunny, private view from an upstairs bath and provide great ventilation, too. Pop-out greenhouse unit shown below and in inset expands a small bathroom and opens it to garden.

DESIGNER: MOLLY RUTH HALE

Second-story privacy offered an opportunity to open master bath to garden: French doors, matching overhead transoms, tub-side double-hung windows, and a skylight do the trick. Indirect soffit fixtures provide quiet light for a nighttime soak.

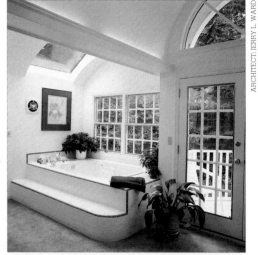

Whirlpool tub in a bathroom bay appears to float into surrounding woodland. Decorative windowpanes focus attention on trees and screen bathers from outside view.

■ Bright ideas

ARCHITECT: JANICE PREGLIASCO

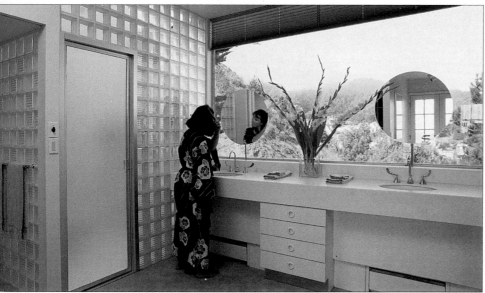

Window, glass blocks, and mirrors brighten this high-ceilinged bathroom. Lollipoplike mirrors above sinks float on exterior view; they're mounted on hardboard backing and strapped to chrome posts set in backsplash.

Light permeates this bright bath. Sources are all visible in mirror: large ridgeline skylights, glass blocks to help spread light, frosted glass doors, and twin wall sconces to provide plenty of task light around stylish pedestal sink.

ARCHITECT: REMICK ASSOCIATES

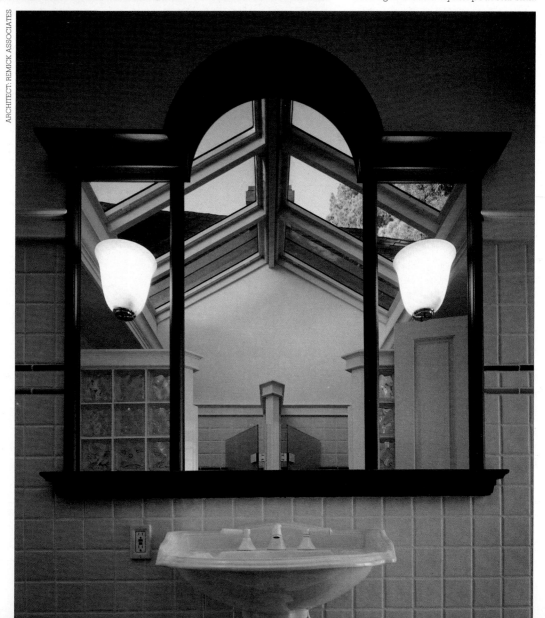

ARCHITECT: CHARLES DEBBAS

DESIGNER: OSBURN DESIGN

In temperate climates, why not open up a wall to summer weather? Bathroom suite utilizes a standard garage door and hardware to open up a sitting area near soaking tub to surrounding hills.

Incandescent/fluorescent strip lights form an integral part of sink-side task area; sealed downlights are visible in mirrors. Frosted windows flank sink, aiding privacy; clear skylights bring in extra daylight.

Storage solutions

Seamless white vanity cabinet is built with frame-and-panel faceframe construction; it forms a perfect base for solid-surface countertop and tile detailing. Wall unit features matching flush doors and glass panels; arched valance, topped with crown molding, houses discreet downlights for sink-side tasks.

DESIGNER: RICK SAMBOL / DESIGN CONSULTANTS AND LYNNE SHILLING

DESIGN: LAMPERTI ASSOCIATES

Stylish European cabinetry built into angle between shower and toilet compartments offers floor-to-ceiling storage and display space on recessed glass shelves. Pinpoint accent lighting comes from low-voltage MR-16 downlights with slot apertures.

Red mahogany cabinets organize every inch of this formal bath done in "club room" style. Base cabinets, lipped shelves, mirror and tub arches, and tub pedestal all match; elegant millwork ties loose ends together.

■ Storage solutions

DESIGNER: CAROLYN VAN LANG

Black-rimmed maple storage unit separates bathroom, with its primary accents, from adjacent bedroom. It's like a kitchen island transported to a bathroom. Jagged marble partition screening bath is reflected in mirror behind sink.

Freestanding deco vanity bridges twin curved pedestals in spacious master suite. Base is veneered with maple; countertop is speckled granite. Twin sinks have waterfall spouts; plumbing is hidden behind pedestal columns.

DESIGNER: GERALD N. JACOBS / JACOBS DESIGN

ARCHITECT: J. ALLEN SAYLES

Dressing area forms a transition zone between bedroom and bath; owners wanted a master suite feel but didn't have space for a separate dressing room. Maple cabinets house plenty of drawers, pegs, cubbyholes, and adjustable shelves; lowered counter section becomes a makeup table.

DESIGNER: MONA BRANAGH / PACIFIC BAY INTERIORS

Antique dresser takes on new life as a bathroom vanity in this traditional setting. Holes were cut in top for a self-rimming sink and deck-mounted fittings; plumbing runs through false drawer.

■ Storage solutions

Glass display shelves bring a touch of elegance and openness to a tiny powder room layout. Triple-thick, laminated shelves are supported discreetly at three points; recess saves space.

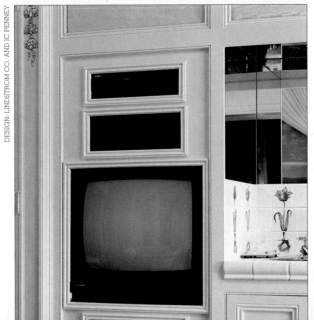

For watching soaps in the suds, television is built into a bathroom wall. Above, cubbyholes hold electronic gear. Ventilation is provided from behind.

Bamboo rods perform as towel bars, bringing nature's forms into bathroom. Double-height unit does double duty.

Sink-side appliance garage built from bird's-eye maple slides out on heavy-duty drawer guides. Power outlet behind lowered drawer back allows bath appliances to remain plugged in.

Up is down, down is up—electric storage unit floats between symmetrical twin sink areas; besides making a dramatic statement, it provides handy storage right where it's needed. Purple dye stain provides color blast, endlessly repeated in mirrors.

PLANNING GUIDELINES

Decision-making ▪ Design ▪ Floor plans ▪ Products

The hallmark of today's bathrooms is style; it can be found in elegant powder rooms, gracious guest baths, efficient family bathrooms, and spacious master suites. Inspired by innovative designs, fashionable fixtures and fittings, and a refreshing palette of colors, the zest for home decorating has progressed to the bathroom from other parts of the house. The introduction of new products and materials—stylish yet durable—has added momentum.

But changes in lifestyle and the economy are at the heart of the bathroom remodeling trend. More and more people are deciding to make the most of the home they already own, rather than move to another one. And in the process they're changing the face of the bathroom. Not long ago, the standard bath was simply a room with utilitarian fixtures. Today's bathroom serves many needs. At its best, it can be a sanctuary from the busy world and a place to pamper yourself.

Planning your new bathroom can be one of the most enjoyable aspects of remodeling; it's the first step toward creating the kind of room you want. In this chapter, you'll learn about bathroom planning, from evaluating your existing bathroom to drawing floor plans for a new one, and determining the best ways to launch your project. The varied choices in fixtures, fittings, and materials are discussed in the "Bathroom showcase" (pages 54–63).

Dramatic master bath features his-and-her sinks and vanities, a flush-mounted whirlpool tub, and a two-person walk-in shower. Sponged and streaked walls, custom tiles, and bird's-eye maple set the color scheme. From the bath, it's just a few steps to an oversize dressing room, abundantly fitted with storage racks, drawers, and cubbyholes.

Getting started

"Where do I begin?" is one of the most-asked questions about remodeling. The answer is to start with an inventory of your existing bathroom. Once you've assessed the room's current condition and developed some remodeling goals, it will be easier to uncover the room's potential for greater comfort, more convenience, and better appearance.

To decide on your primary goals, complete the inventory below. List all the improvements you'd like to make in their order of importance. To make it easier to establish priorities, you can assign a numerical rating to each improvement or designate each as "must do" or "would like to do." The finished list will help you keep your remodeling goals in focus and guide you in setting a budget, working with professionals, and selecting products and materials.

Trends come and go, and the bathroom is not immune to changing fashion. Perhaps it's time to pull the plug on those outdated fixtures, surface treatments, colors, and accessories. Or you may decide to keep your fixtures and tile and redecorate around them with new paint and wallpaper; this approach can be a surprisingly effective and inexpensive way to update a room's appearance.

To help guide your decisions, start collecting ideas. Study the color photographs in this book. Let

---

A BATHROOM INVENTORY

To analyze your present bathroom, take the bathroom inventory that follows—it's one of the most important tools in designing your new bathroom. Think of this exercise as a fact-finding process in which you identify specific conditions you'd like to improve, evaluate strengths and weaknesses, and set goals for remodeling.

First, look at the surfaces. Would the bathroom's style be improved if you changed the walls, floor, ceiling, countertops, or cabinetry? Do your doors and drawers need new hardware? Would new windows, a new bathtub, or a new shower door improve the room?

But don't stop when you've examined those relatively superficial elements. Move on to the fundamentals of the room and everything in it—and the way it all works (or fails to work) for the people who use it.

Layout. Consider the following questions in relation to your bathroom's layout: Does the door open into the room? If so, can it inconvenience someone inside? When open, do cabinet or vanity doors and drawers block the door? Can two people use the sink or vanity area at the same time? Would your family benefit from the added privacy of a compartmentalized bathroom, with tub, shower, or toilet separate from each other and from the vanity? Is there ample room for toweling dry without hitting elbows? Are stored items within easy reach?

Fixtures and fittings. Before you rush out to buy new fixtures and fittings, consider whether the existing ones can be cleaned, refinished, or repaired. If not, decide what features you like and dislike about your current equipment. Are you pleased with the sizes, shapes, and materials? Are the faucets easy to turn on and off? Can you adjust water temperature for the sink and shower as easily as you'd like? Are you content with a bathtub, or would you like a shower also? Would you like to add a whirlpool bath?

Walls, floor, and ceiling. Moisture is the enemy of most room surfaces and subsurfaces and can be a particular problem in bathrooms. Water warps flooring, deteriorates paint, and wilts wallpaper. Examine the surfaces in your present bathroom for chips, cracks, bubbles, mold, mildew, and other maladies. Is your tile uneven? Are the grout and caulking in good condition? Have any subsurfaces been damaged by excess moisture?

If any of your surfaces are in poor condition or you want to make a decorative change, be sure to consider moisture-resistance, maintenance, and durability when you choose new materials. The choices in color, pattern, texture, and style are enormous.

Countertops. Do you have ample counter space in your bathroom? If not, decide where you need more room for storage or display, or simply for a convenient place to put things down. Are existing countertops in good condition? Are joints and corners easy to keep clean? Would you prefer a different type of countertop material, or has the present material been satisfactory?

Storage. Before you think about increasing your storage capacity, clean out and organize your bathroom's existing storage areas. If you're still short of space, determine your most pressing storage needs. Would you like a recessed medicine cabinet, better storage for cleaning supplies, a place for dirty laundry, or a tilt-out bin to hold your bathroom scale? Consider adding a vanity, wall cabinets, or even a floor-to-ceiling unit complete with shelves and bins. Can you enlarge the room to gain space? Is it possible to store some items in a hall closet or other nearby space?

Lighting. Old bathrooms rarely have enough properly placed light fixtures. If your bathroom has only one overhead light or a single fixture above the medicine cabi-them spur your imagination—you're almost certain to find many ideas that you'd like to adapt to your own setting.

Turn, too, to the showcase on pages 54–63, where various types of fixtures and fittings are illustrated and described. Peruse magazines and tour model homes in your neighborhood.

To collect more ideas and get a closer look at new products, visit showrooms and stores displaying bathroom fixtures, cabinetry, light fixtures, wall coverings, tile, and flooring products. As you shop around, try to identify what you like about certain styles. You can obtain catalogues, brochures, and color charts from stores and from manufacturers. Seek out helpful salespersons and ask questions about products that interest you. The answers and advice you receive can be invaluable.

As you accumulate notes, clippings, photographs, and brochures, file your remodeling ideas in a notebook. Choose a binder with several divisions or file your material in separate 9 by 12-inch envelopes. Organize by subjects, such as best overall style, layouts and plans, pleasing color combinations, fixtures and fittings, lighting, and accessory ideas. Then review your remodeling goals and adapt the categories to suit your project.

---

net, you'll certainly want to give some thought to improving the room's artificial lighting. In additional to upgrading general lighting, would you like to add task lighting? Are you pleased with the appearance of existing light fixtures, and is the kind of light (fluorescent or incandescent) what you want? Consider bringing in more natural light. You can do this by adding a skylight, enlarging an existing window, or creating a new window.

Electrical outlets and switches. Note the location and number of electrical outlets and switches. Are there enough outlets? Are switches and outlets conveniently placed? If you need more electrical outlets, you may want to replace a single outlet with a double one. Plan to substitute circuit-breaking GFCI outlets for standard plugs in all wet areas in the bathroom. For greater convenience in a large space, you can install two and three-way switches for lights.

Heating and ventilation. Basic for bathroom comfort are a controlled temperature and good ventilation. No one enjoys the shock of a chilly bathroom on a cold morning. In a poorly ventilated bathroom, you may gasp for air in the middle of a steamy shower or have to stop to wipe off a foggy mirror while shaving. Note any problems caused by poor heating or ventilation, and don't overlook the problem of mold or mildew.

Water and energy conservation. Heating the bathroom and heating water consume a lot of energy. Are the water heater, pipes, and walls well insulated? Is the shower head equipped with a flow restrictor or shut-off valve? If you plan to buy a new toilet, have you considered a water-saving model?

Privacy. Does the door or window of your bathroom open to a public area? If so, you may want to consider relocating the opening or designing special window or exterior treatments to increase privacy. You should also check your bathroom for uninsulated pipes, finishing materials that reflect sound, and insufficient floor, wall, or ceiling insulation.

Accessories. Make a list of your bathroom accessories and note any additions or deletions you'd like to make, as well as any changes you want in quality, quantity, or style. Perhaps you'd like to replace mismatched towel bars and other accessories with a coordinated collection in glass, ceramic, or brightly colored plastic. Do you want the finish on towel bars, mirror frames, and cabinet hardware to match existing or new fittings? Also, look at your towels; aside from being functional, do they complement the room's color scheme? Do you have sufficient towel bars, and are they conveniently placed?

Maintenance. Some bathrooms are easier to maintain than others. Evaluate your bathroom's trouble spots, such as soap buildup, discolored grout, and streaked walls. In planning your project, consider installing smooth, seamless or jointless materials (except flooring) and ones especially designed to withstand moisture. If your fixtures are difficult to clean, you may want to refinish or replace them.

Family needs. A bathroom should be easy for everyone to use. Take time to consider the special needs of family members and regular visitors, including children and elderly or disabled persons. Can an adult bathe a small child safely and comfortably? Is the tub and/or shower equipped with a nonskid base and grab bars? If wheelchair access is a consideration, is the entry wide enough, and is there ample space for easy turning? Can all the fixtures be used without assistance? For more information on barrier-free baths, see page 43.

Your present plan

You've taken a critical look at your bathroom, analyzing its good points and noting where you want to make improvements. If your goals point to simple redecorating or minor remodeling, skip ahead to the design information beginning on page 48 and the "Bathroom showcase" on pages 54–63 for help.

For more ambitious remodeling plans, you'll need to measure the room and draw it to scale. The process of measuring the bathroom elements and perimeter will increase your awareness of the existing space. Scale drawings also serve as a foundation for future design and may satisfy the permit requirements of your local building department. Such plans will also help you communicate your ideas to any professional you hire.

The information here will tell you how to measure your bathroom, record those measurements, and draw a two-dimensional floor plan to scale. You'll also learn how to make elevation drawings of each wall.

Measuring the room

Before you begin taking measurements, draw a rough sketch of the bathroom, its various elements, and any adjacent areas that may be included in the remodeling. Make the sketch as large as the paper allows so you'll have ample room to write in the dimensions. Note any suspected deviations from the standard wall and partition thickness (usually about 5 inches). The sketch should also show all projections, recesses, windows, doors, and door swings.

Tools. Listed below are some tools and supplies that will help you with your measuring and drawing tasks. You can find these tools at hardware, stationery, and art supply stores.

■ Retractable steel measuring tape or folding wooden rule

■ Ruler or T-square

■ Triangle

■ Compass

■ Graph paper (four squares to an inch)

■ Tracing paper

■ Masking tape

■ Pencils

■ Eraser

■ Clipboard or pad with 8½ by 11-inch paper

How to measure. It's important to record the dimensions on the sketch as you measure, using feet and inches as an architect would (you may also want to translate certain dimensions, such as those for tubs and shower enclosures, to inches). Measure to the nearest ⅛ inch, since even a fraction of an inch counts in fitting and spacing bathroom elements. All mea-

surements should be taken to the wall, not to projecting wood trim or baseboards.

First, measure the room's dimensions—the floor, ceiling, and walls; measure each wall at counter height. To find out if the bathroom is square, measure the diagonals (corner to opposite corner). Don't worry if the room isn't square; just be sure your drawing reflects any irregularities.

With the overall dimensions recorded on your sketch, measure the fixtures and other elements in the room and the distances between them, and add this information to your sketch. You can use a wall-by-wall approach, or you can measure by category: fixtures, doors, windows, cabinetry, shelves, and accessories.

Depending on the extent of your remodeling goals, your sketch could include locations of the following: load-bearing walls and partitions, electrical outlets and switches, light fixtures, drains, pipes, and vents. If you want to enlarge your bathroom—or just add more storage space—show relevant adjacent hall space, closets, rooms, and outdoor areas that you may be able to incorporate.

Note any heights that may affect your remodeling plans. These might include the clearance space under a duct or sloping ceiling, the floor-to-ceiling height, and the distance from the floor to the tops and bottoms of the windows.

Drawing to scale

The secrets to drawing a useful floor plan and elevations are a well-prepared sketch with accurate measurements and a reasonable amount of skill at converting those measurements to the scale you choose. Your drawings don't have to be works of art, but they should be precise, complete, and easy to read.

Though architects sometimes use a ¼-inch scale (¼ inch equals 1 foot), using a ½-inch scale for your bathroom remodeling drawings is easier, especially when you want to include all the elements of the room and write their dimensions.

How to draw floor plans. With masking tape, attach the corners of the graph paper to a smooth working surface. Use a ruler, T-square, or triangle to draw all horizontal and vertical lines; make right angles exact. Use a compass to indicate door swings.

To complete the floor plan, refer to your sketch and the sample finished floor plan on the facing page. Indicating walls and partitions by dark, thick lines will make the floor plan easier to read.

How to draw elevations. Elevations, or straight-on views of each bathroom wall, show the visual pattern created by all the elements against that wall. Sketch the elements on each wall, measure carefully, and record the figures as you did for the floor plan; then redraw your elevation sketches on graph paper.

SAMPLE FLOOR PLAN & ELEVATION

The drawings of your existing bathroom should look like the floor plan above and the elevation sketch at right. Be sure to add the appropriate architectural symbols to your floor plan to indicate outlets, switches, windows, and light fixtures.

ARCHITECTURAL SYMBOLS

Architects and designers use a set of standard symbols to indicate certain features on floor plans; some of the most common ones are shown at left. It's a good idea to become familiar with these symbols, since you'll want to use them on your own plans. Also, you'll need to know them to communicate with your building department, contractor, or designer.

Basic layouts

Once you've analyzed your present bathroom's assets and liabilities, it's time to start planning your new one. While brainstorming, try to have some basic layout schemes in mind. The floor plans shown below provide a starting point. Keep in mind that these layouts can be combined, adapted, and expanded to meet your needs. For additional ideas, study the photos on pages 6–35.

The "best" bathroom layout doesn't exist—good layouts vary dramatically. Generally, though, a workable floor plan provides for good access to the room, easy movement within the room, and the convenient use of fixtures and storage units.

Here are some layout guidelines categorized by type of bathroom.

Powder room. This two-fixture room, also known as a guest bath or half-bath, contains a toilet and a sink and perhaps some limited storage space. Fixtures can be placed side by side or on opposite or even adjacent walls, depending on the shape of the room. Very small sinks are available for extra-tight spaces.

Because the guest bathroom is used only occasionally and for short intervals of time, it's a good place to enjoy more decorative but perhaps less durable finishes, such as brass, copper, and upholstery. The door should swing open against a wall, clear of any fixtures. Where space is tight, a pocket door may be the ideal solution.

Consideration should be given to privacy. Preferably, a guest bath should open off a hallway, not directly into the living room, family room, or dining area.

Family bath. The family bath usually contains three fixtures—a toilet, a sink, and a bathtub or shower or combination tub/shower. The fixture arrangement varies, depending on the size and shape of the room. (Several configurations are shown below.) Family baths often have cluster or corridor layouts; they should be at least 5 feet by 7 feet.

To enable several family members to use the bathroom at the same time, consider putting in two sinks. Another possible solution is compartmentalizing, or separating fixture areas. One common arrangement is to isolate the toilet and shower from the sink and grooming area. This configuration can work well to increase privacy when it's not feasible to add a new bathroom.

The family bath is one of the most frequently used rooms in the house. Therefore, be sure to choose durable, moisture-resistant, easy-to-clean fixtures and finishes. Also, be sure to plan adequate storage space for each user's needs.

SAMPLE BATHROOM LAYOUTS

POWDER ROOM
4' by 4'-6"

POWDER ROOM
5' by 5'

POWDER ROOM
3' by 6'

FAMILY BATH   5' by 7'

BACK-TO-BACK   5' by 7' each

FAMILY BATH   7' by 11'

FAMILY BATH
8' by 12'

Children's bath. Ideally, this bathroom is located between two bedrooms used by children, so there's direct access from each room.

If there's space, you may want to consider shared bathing and toilet facilities and an individual sink and dressing area for each child. When several children are sharing one bath, color coding of drawers, towel hooks, and other storage areas can help minimize territorial battles.

Children's baths require special attention to safety and maintenance. Single-lever faucets reduce the chances of a hot-water burn; slip-resistant surfaces prevent accidents. A timer on the light switch keeps your electrical bill down. Plastic laminate countertops and cabinets are a good choice—they're durable and easy to clean. For more information on safety in the bathroom, turn to page 47.

Master bath suite. The master bath has become more than just a place to grab a quick shower and run a comb through your hair. No longer merely a utilitarian space, today's master bath reflects the personality and interests of its owners. Often, it includes dressing and grooming areas, toilet and bathing facilities, and such other amenities as fireplaces, whirlpool baths, oversize tubs, and bidets. Outside this bath is a natural place for a spa, sunbathing deck, or private garden.

Here are some "extras" that you may want to consider for your master bath. Make sure that you provide adequate ventilation to prevent water damage (from splashes and condensation) to delicate objects and equipment.

- Walk-in dressing room
- Exercise room
- Makeup center
- Reading nook
- Home entertainment center
- Art gallery
- Greenhouse or sun room

Barrier-free bath. If you're remodeling to accommodate a disabled or elderly person, be sure you're aware of that person's special needs. Different heights, clearances, and room dimensions may be required. For example, to accommodate a wheelchair, the room must have specific clearances (see page 45). The door should swing out to allow easy movement in and out of the room. The shower needs to be curbless so a wheelchair can roll in unobstructed. You may also want to install grab bars, use levers in place of round door knobs, and choose fixtures and fittings specifically designed for the disabled.

CORRIDOR-TYPE COMPARTMENTALIZED BATH 16' by 5'

CHILDREN'S BATH
6' by 10'

CHILDREN'S BATH
8' by 12'

MASTER BATH WITH GROOMING AREA
20' by 12'

MINIMUM CLEARANCES

SINK

DOUBLE SINK

BATHTUB

TOILET OR BIDET

SHOWER

Locating fixtures

Before you can actually plan your bathroom layout and place your fixtures, it's important to understand some basic facts about plumbing lines, minimum heights and clearances, and fixture location. Only then can you plan a layout that makes sense both structurally and economically.

Once you have all the facts at hand, you'll be ready to experiment with layouts. To do this, trace the scale floor plan of your existing bathroom, including any adjoining space you're planning to "borrow." If you're considering removing or relocating walls, eliminate those existing partitions. As you experiment with different arrangements, set aside any plans you like and start fresh with another tracing of the bathroom's perimeter in its future form.

One of the biggest challenges in designing layouts for your new bathroom is keeping track of your ideas. If they're flowing, you won't want to forget your best inspirations just because you didn't get them down on paper.

One answer is to move paper cutouts around your floor plan and then sketch the best plans you devise with them. To use this method, first draw the perimeter of your existing floor plan and any adjacent areas to be included in the project. Then, using graph paper, make cutouts (to scale) of fixtures, cabinets, countertops, and other elements—both existing features you plan to keep and new ones to be added. Move the cutouts around the floor plan; when you hit on a layout you like, sketch it so you'll have a record of it. When you think you've exhausted the possibilities, compare the plans and evaluate them.

The existing structure

You'll keep costs down and simplify construction if you select a layout that uses the existing water supply, drain lines, and vent stack. If that's not possible, you may want to study the how-to section beginning on page 65 to familiarize yourself with the work that plumbing, wiring, and structural changes entail.

If you're adding on to your house, try to locate the new bathroom near an existing bathroom or near the kitchen. It's also more economical to arrange fixtures against one or two walls, eliminating the need for additional plumbing lines.

Generally, you can move a sink a few inches from its present position with only minor plumbing changes. Your existing supply and drain lines can usually support a second sink. You can extend existing supply and drain lines if the distance from the vent is less than the maximum distance allowed by your local code; if not, you'll have to install a secondary vent—a major undertaking.

If your bathroom has a wood floor with a crawlspace, basement, or first floor underneath, it's relatively simple to move both plumbing and wiring. But in rooms with concrete floors, it's an expensive proposition to move plumbing or wiring that's located under the concrete. To gain access to the lines, you would have to go through the laborious process of breaking up and removing the concrete.

Structural changes, especially those entailing work on load-bearing walls, fall into the category of serious remodeling and may require professional help. Relocating a door or window opening may also involve a lot of work, including framing and finishing. Adding a partition wall, on the other hand, is an easier and less expensive job.

Heights & clearances

Building codes specify minimum required clearances between, beside, and in front of bathroom fixtures to allow adequate room for use, cleaning, and repair. To help in your initial planning, check the minimum clearances shown on the facing page.

Generally, you can locate side-by-side fixtures closer together than fixtures positioned opposite each other. If a sink is opposite a bathtub or toilet, keep a minimum of 30 inches between them. Children, elderly, and disabled persons may require assistance or special fixtures; if you anticipate such needs, allow extra space in your layout.

Shown above, at right, are standard heights for countertops, shower heads, and accessories. If you and others using the bathroom are especially tall or short, you may wish to customize the room to your own requirements. However, when planning such a change, keep one eye on your home's resale value: will potential buyers find these alterations as convenient as you do?

Basic height and clearance guidelines for a barrier-free space are illustrated at right. For additional help, look for an architect or designer who specializes in this expanding field.

Fixture arrangement

It's usually best to position the largest unit—the bathtub or shower—first. Be sure you allow space for convenient access, for cleaning, and, if needed, for bathing a child.

Next, place the sink (or sinks). The most frequently used fixture in the bathroom, the sink should be positioned out of the traffic pattern. Be sure to plan for ample room in front for reaching below the sink and give plenty of elbow room at the sides.

Locate the toilet (and bidet, if you have one) away from the door; often, the toilet is placed beside the tub or shower. A toilet and bidet should be positioned next to each other.

Don't forget about the swing-radius for windows and doors. To resolve a conflict, you could either reverse a standard door's hardware from left to right or substitute a pocket door.

STANDARD HEIGHTS

Soap dishes   Grab bar   Mirror

42" to 48"   66" to 74"   54"   24"   12"   30" to 38"   26"

16" to 24" tub, 30" to 34" tub/shower

12" to 16"

Vanity   Paper holder

BARRIER-FREE GUIDELINES

Shower minimum 4' by 4'

Minimum room dimensions 8' by 8'

Toilet seat 19" to 20" above floor

4'-0"   5'-0" ideal

Sink maximum 34" above floor

Door opening 34", swings out

Finishing touches

Once you've decided on a basic layout and marked the design you've worked out onto a clean tracing of your bathroom's floor plan, you can turn your attention to the walls. Begin by drawing an elevation of each wall and marking on those elevations the fixtures you've already located. Then you'll be ready to add all the other elements that go into your bathroom: storage, mirrors, towel bars, amenities, and heating and ventilation details.

To do this, you can use the same cutout technique you used for the fixtures (see page 44). But now you'll be working on an elevation, not a floor plan, and you'll be preparing a different set of cutouts—straight-on views of fixtures, cabinets, mirrors, and other elements. Arrange these cutouts with an eye for line, shape, and scale (see page 48). The plans you sketch as you move the cutouts around will help you visualize the room as a whole and see relationships between horizontal, vertical, diagonal, and curved lines. Be sure to set aside sketches of the arrangements you like so you can compare them later.

Storage needs

After arranging the fixtures, plan your storage space. Consider what you need to store, how much space you need for it, and how best to organize the space. If you're planning to expand your storage capacity, review your notes from the inventory to pinpoint which items require space.

Consider equipping a vanity or cabinet with racks, shelves, pull-outs, or lazy susans for supplies.

Many bathroom items are candidates for open storage—why not display colorful towels or stacks of soap on open shelving? For a look at a variety of successful storage solutions, see pages 30–35.

Filling in the details

Choosing appropriate fixtures, fittings, and cabinetry will block out your bathroom plan quickly, but don't forget the finishing touches that make or break a handsome, comfortable design. Below, you'll find a checklist of bathroom amenities to consider.

Surfaces. Floor, wall, and countertop surfaces should be durable as well as attractive. For details about the characteristics of the various surface materials, including plastic laminate, solid-surface, wood, stone, and tile, see pages 55 and 62–63 in the section "Bathroom showcase."

Saunas and steam showers. These luxurious features, once found mainly in gyms and health clubs, have recently entered the residential bathroom.

A sauna is a small, wood-lined room (often sold prefabricated) that heats itself to around 200°F. In addition to insulated walls, a solid-core door, and double-paned glass (if any), you'll also need an electric or gas sauna heater. Minimum size for a sauna is about 65 cubic feet per person. But don't make the space overly large—you'll just have more space to heat.

New steam units are small enough to be housed in any number of convenient locations—inside a stor-

ARCHITECT: REMICK ASSOCIATES

Heated towel bars keep bath linens toasty and also serve as radiators. Brass rack harnesses old-fashioned hydronic heat; you can also buy electric versions.

PLAYING IT SAFE IN THE BATHROOM

About 25 percent of all home accidents occur in the bathroom. You can reduce the risk of injury by careful planning and by encouraging safe practices. Here are some guidelines.

■ Install sufficient lighting. Include a night-light, especially if you have small children.

■ Choose tempered glass, plastic, and other shatterproof materials for construction and accessories.

■ Install locks that can be opened from the outside in an emergency.

■ Locate clothes hooks above eye level.

■ Select a tub or shower with a nonslip surface. For existing fixtures, use a rubber bath mat.

■ Install L-shaped or horizontal grab bars, capable of supporting a person weighing 250 pounds, in tub and shower areas. Installation must be done properly—bracing between studs may be required. Plaster-mounted accessories don't provide sufficient support.

■ Anchor any carpeting. Choose area rugs or bath mats with nonskid backing.

■ Avoid scalding by lowering the setting of your water heater or by installing a temperature-limiting mixing valve or a pressure-balancing valve to prevent sudden temperature drops.

■ Test the water temperature before stepping into a shower or tub and when assisting a child or elderly person. Place shower controls where they can be accessed quickly and conveniently.

■ Be sure electrical outlets are grounded and protected with GFCI circuit breakers. Outlets should be out of reach from the shower or bathtub. Install safety covers over unused outlets.

■ Avoid using electrical appliances in wet areas. Keep portable heaters out of the bathroom.

■ If children live in or visit your house, buy medicines (and, when possible, household cleansers) in childproof containers. Store these items in a cabinet equipped with a safety latch. Tape seldom-used non-safety containers closed. Check the contents of your medicine cabinet at least twice a year and discard outdated medicines and those with unreadable or incomplete directions.

■ Keep a first aid kit handy for use in an emergency. Post phone numbers of the nearest emergency rescue unit and poison control center.

---

age cabinet, in an adjacent closet or alcove, or in a tall crawlspace. Besides the steam box, all you need is an airtight shower door, a comfortable bench, and effective ventilation.

Lighting. Don't leave lighting as an afterthought; it should be part of the initial design. A wide range of incandescent, fluorescent, and halogen light sources are on the market today, as well as a huge selection of fixtures to house them.

Design ideas for both natural and artificial light appear on pages 50–51. For a look at how light can be used in bathrooms, see pages 24–29.

Electrical outlets and switches. Tentatively mark the locations of outlets and switches. Every countertop longer than 12 inches should have a two-plug outlet; every wall must have an outlet every 12 feet—or at least one outlet per wall, regardless of size. Be sure that outlets within 6 feet of any wet area are grounded and protected with GFCI circuit breakers.

Switches are usually placed 44 inches above the floor on the open (or latch) side of doorways.

Hardware and accessories. Think now about how you'll coordinate doorknobs, drawer pulls, towel bars, a toilet-paper holder, and other accessories with your fixtures, fittings, and surfaces. Aim for an integrated overall look.

Heating & ventilation

If you want to extend your existing heating system to a new bathroom, check with a professional to be sure your system can handle the added load. You can relocate a hot air register in the floor or in the vanity kickspace by changing the duct work beneath the floor; ducts for wall registers can be rerouted in the stud wall. If you're adding a register, locate it where the duct work can be extended easily from the existing system and where you won't sacrifice wall space.

Hot air duct work is best done by a heating or sheet metal contractor. Extending hot water or steam systems is easier, but it, too, calls for professional help. It may be more practical to equip your bathroom with an electric space heater, which can be recessed in the wall or ceiling, or with an electric heat lamp.

Local building codes may require exhaust fans in certain bathrooms and specify their placement; check the code before you complete your design. Such fans are relatively simple to add or relocate. These units are installed in the ceiling between joists or in the wall between studs, and may require duct work to the outside.

Line, shape & scale

It may never occur to you to consider line, shape, and scale when you draw up your plans. Yet these design elements hold the key to a balanced, visually pleasing design. Take another look at your bathroom elevation sketches to examine these elements. You may want to improve the existing conditions—or perhaps you'll decide to try an entirely new approach.

Line—the dominant theme

Most bathrooms incorporate many different kinds of lines—vertical, horizontal, diagonal, curved, and angular. However, one line usually dominates and characterizes the design. Vertical lines give a sense of height, horizontals add width, diagonals suggest movement, and curved and angular lines impart a sense of grace and dynamism.

Repeating similar lines gives the room a sense of unity. Look at one of your elevation sketches. How do the vertical lines created by the cabinets, vanity, windows, doors, mirrors, and shower or tub unit fit together? Does the horizontal line marking the top of the window align with other horizontal lines in the room, such as the tops of the shower stall, door, and mirror? Clearly, not everything can or should line up perfectly, but the effect is far more pleasing if a number of elements are aligned, particularly when they're the highest features in the room.

Shape—a sense of harmony

Continuity and compatibility in shape also contribute to a unified design. Of course, you needn't repeat the same shape throughout the room—carried too far, that becomes monotonous.

Study the shapes created by doorways, windows, countertops, fixtures, and other elements. Look at patterns in your flooring, wall covering, shower curtain, and towels. Are they different or similar? If they're different, do they clash? If they're similar, are they boring? Consider ways to complement existing shapes or add compatible new ones. For example, if there's an arch over a recessed bathtub, create an arch over a doorway or repeat the arch on the trim of a shelf.

Scale—everything in proportion

When the scale of bathroom elements is in proportion to the overall size of the room, the design feels harmonious. A small bath seems even smaller if equipped with large fixtures and a large vanity. But the same bathroom appears larger, or at least in scale, when equipped with space-saving fixtures, a petite vanity, and open shelves,

Consider the proportions of adjacent features as well. When wall cabinets or linen shelves extend to the ceiling, they often make a room seem top-heavy—and therefore smaller. To counteract this look without losing storage space, place cabinet doors or shelves closer together at the top. Let your floor plan and elevation drawings suggest other ways you can modify the scale of different elements to improve your design.

ARCHITECT: REMICK ASSOCIATES

Squares are everywhere, but size and color contrast set surfaces apart. Easy-to-clean glazed tiles line walls to eye level. Floor mosaics set color accent and lead eye around corner, enlarging sense of space. Tile-high glass-block partition restates square motif and screens shower area while letting light pass through.

Color, texture & pattern

The ways you use color, texture, and pattern play an important part in your design. After you narrow down your selections, make a sample board to see how your choices work together. Color charts for fixtures are readily available, as are paint chips, fabric swatches, and wallpaper and flooring samples.

Choosing your colors

The size and orientation of your bathroom, your personal preferences, and the mood you want to create all affect color selection. Here are some color principles to guide you.

Light colors reflect light, making walls recede; thus, a small bathroom treated with light colors appears more spacious. Dark colors absorb light and can visually lower a ceiling or shorten a narrow room.

When considering colors for a small bathroom, remember that too much contrast has the same effect as a dark color: it reduces the sense of spaciousness. Contrasting colors work well for adding accents or drawing attention to interesting structural elements. But if you need to conceal a problem feature, it's best to use one color throughout the area.

Oranges, yellows, and other colors with a red tone impart a feeling of warmth to a room, but they also contract space. Cool colors—blues, greens, and colors with a blue tone—make an area seem larger. A light, monochromatic color scheme (using different shades of one color) is restful and serene. Contrasting colors add vibrancy and excitement to a design. But a color scheme with contrasting colors can be overpowering unless the tones of the colors are varied. Note, too, that the temperature and intensity of colors will be affected by lighting.

Adding interest with texture & pattern

Texture and pattern work like color in defining a room's style and sense of space. The bathroom's surface materials may include many different textures, from a glossy countertop to smooth wood cabinets to a roughly surfaced quarry-tile floor.

Rough textures absorb light, make colors look duller, and lend a feeling of informality. Smooth textures reflect light and tend to suggest elegance or modernity. Using similar textures helps unify a design and create a mood.

Pattern choices must harmonize with the predominant style of the room. Though pattern is usually associated with wall coverings or a cabinet finish, even natural substances such as wood, brick, and stone create patterns.

While variation in texture and pattern adds interest, too much variety can be overstimulating. It's best to let a strong feature or dominant pattern be the focus of your design and choose other surfaces to complement rather than compete with it.

DESIGNER: FU-TUNG CHENG / CHENG DESIGN

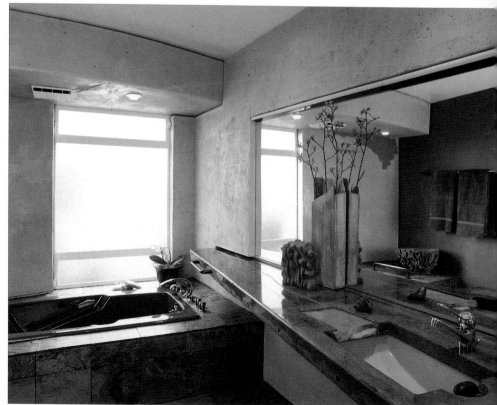

Concrete states an industrial theme, but color and texture add a soft, decorative counterpoint. Clean, cold masonry holds forth on the countertop; masonry is textured and painted on walls and soffits. Variegated slate tiles line floor and tub pedestal.

Lighting guidelines

No matter how beautifully it's decorated, a room with inadequate lighting will be an unpleasant place to be—and difficult to use. In a multiple-use room such as a bathroom, the light levels required range from very soft ambient light to strong directional task lighting. Usually, you can achieve a pleasing level by bringing in natural light through windows and skylights and supplementing it with artificial lighting.

Natural light

To bring natural light into your bathroom, you can use windows and doors (opening to secluded areas) as well as skylights—alone or in combination.

A single window in the middle of a wall often creates a glaring contrast with the surrounding area. To increase the amount of natural light, consider placing windows on adjacent walls or installing a skylight. Either will provide uniform lighting over a larger area. To maximize sunlight, position openings so they face south or west. But to avoid unwanted heat and glare, it's best to locate windows and skylights so they have a northern or eastern exposure.

Windows, available in many styles, may have frames of wood, aluminum, vinyl, or steel. All-vinyl windows and wood windows clad in vinyl or aluminum require the least maintenance.

Though you can have a skylight custom-made, many prefabricated units are available. Some open for ventilation. If there's a space between the ceiling and roof, you'll need a light shaft to direct light to the bathroom below. The shaft may be straight, angled, or splayed.

You can combine glass in different forms (panels and glass blocks, for example) and finishes (clear and translucent) to bring in light and view while still ensuring privacy. Generally, transparent materials are suitable above chin height of the tallest occupant. But be sure to check the heights and locations of neighbors' windows.

Artificial lighting

Artificial lighting can be separated into three categories: task, ambient, and accent. Task lighting illuminates a particular area where a visual activity, such as shaving or applying makeup, takes place. Ambient, or general, lighting fills the undefined areas of a room with a soft level of light—enough, say, for a relaxing soak in a whirlpool tub. Accent lighting, which is primarily decorative, is used to highlight architectural features, set a mood, or provide drama.

Which fixtures are best? Generally speaking, lighting in a bathroom should be small and discreet. Consequently, recessed downlights are very popular. Fitted with the right baffle or shield, those fixtures alone can handle ambient, task, and accent needs.

In a larger bathroom, a separate fixture to light the shower or bath area—or any other distinct part in a compartmentalized design—may be needed. Shower fixtures should be waterproof units fitted with neoprene seals.

Fixtures around a makeup or shaving mirror should spread light over a person's face rather than onto the mirror surface. To avoid heavy shadows, place lights at the sides of the mirror, not just overhead. Wall sconces flanking the mirror not only provide light but also offer an opportunity for a stylish design statement.

And just for fun, why not consider decorative uplights in a soffit or strip lights in a kickspace area? These accents help provide a wash of ambient light and also serve as safe, pleasant night-lights.

Dimmers (also called rheostats) enable you to set a fixture at any level from a soft glow to a radiant brightness. They're also energy savers. It's easy and inexpensive to put incandescent bulbs on dimmers. The initial cost of dimmers for fluorescent lights is greater than for incandescents, and the variety of fixtures with dimmers is limited.

Light bulbs and tubes. Light sources can be grouped in general categories according to the way they produce light.

Incandescent light, the kind used most frequently in homes, is produced by a tungsten thread that burns slowly inside a glass tube. A-bulbs are the old standbys; R and PAR bulbs produce a more controlled beam; silvered-bowl types diffuse light. A number of decorative bulbs are also available.

Low-voltage incandescent lights are especially useful for accent lighting. Operating on 12 or 24 volts, these lights require transformers (which are often built into the fixtures) to step down the voltage from standard 120-volt household circuits.

Fluorescent tubes are unrivaled for energy efficiency; they also last far longer than incandescent bulbs. Older fluorescent tubes have been criticized for noise, flicker, and poor color rendition. Electronic ballasts and better fixture shielding against glare have remedied the first two problems; as for the last one, manufacturers have developed fluorescents in a wide spectrum of colors, from very warm (about 2,700 degrees K) to very cool (about 6,300 degrees K).

Bright, white *quartz halogen* bulbs are excellent for task lighting, pinpoint accenting, and other dramatic accents. Halogen is usually low-voltage but may be standard line current. The popular MR-16 bulb creates the tightest beam; for a longer reach and wider coverage, choose a PAR bulb. There's an abundance of smaller bulb shapes and sizes to fit pendants and undercabinet strip lights.

Halogen has two disadvantages: high initial cost and very high heat. Shop carefully—some fixtures on the market are not UL-approved.

ARCHITECT: MORIMOTO ARCHITECTS

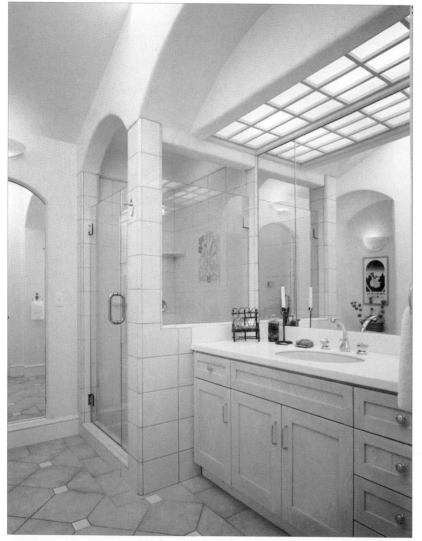

Multiple light sources provide ambient, task, and accent light—day and night. Built-in sink fixture recessed behind "shoji-screen" trim spreads light via diffusing panels. Wall sconces add general light and decorative flair. A skylight brings in welcome sunshine.

DESIGNER: OSBURN DESIGN

Well-chosen accent lighting adds pizzazz to a powder room. Diamond-patterned marble border is highlighted by hidden low-voltage strip lights.

Contemporary pendants follow lines of countertop and repeat in backsplash mirrors. Nonglare bulbs provide plenty of ambient and task light.

ARCHITECT: J. ALLEN SAYLES

Finalizing your plan

The planning process culminates with the drawing of your new floor plan. The floor plan is the basis for the remodeling work, for the preparation of a master list of products and materials, and for the acquisition of any necessary building permits.

Drawing a floor plan

Draw the new floor plan in the same way as you did the existing floor plan (see pages 40–41). On the new plan, include both existing features you want to preserve and all proposed changes, such as new walls, partitions, doors, windows, skylights, light fixtures, electrical switches and outlets, fixtures, cabinets, countertops, and materials. If you prefer, you can hire a designer, drafter, or contractor to draw the final plan for you.

For more complicated projects, your local building department may require additional or more detailed drawings of structural, plumbing, and wiring changes. You may also need to show areas adjacent to the bathroom on the new plan so building officials can determine how the project will affect the rest of your house. Elevation sketches aren't required, but they'll serve as a helpful check in planning the work and ordering materials.

If you're the one ordering the materials for your remodeling project, you'll need to compile a detailed master list. Not only will this launch your work, but it will also help you keep track of purchases and deliveries. For each item that you plan to order, be sure to specify the following information: name and model or serial number, manufacturer, source of material, date of order, delivery date, color, size or dimensions, quantity, price (including tax and delivery charge), and second choice.

Obtaining building permits

To discover which building codes may affect your remodeling project and whether a building permit is required, check with your city or county building department.

You probably won't need a building permit for simple jobs, such as replacing a window with one of the same size, installing a vanity, or changing floor or wall coverings. But for more substantial changes, you may need to apply for one or more of the following permits: structural, plumbing, mechanical heating or cooling, reroofing, or electrical. More complicated projects sometimes require that the design and the working drawings be executed by an architect, designer, or state-licensed contractor.

For your permit, you'll be charged either a flat fee or a percentage of the estimated cost of materials and labor. You may also have to pay a fee to have someone check the plans.

If you're acting as your own contractor, you must ask the building department to inspect the work as it progresses. (A professional contractor handles these inspections without your becoming involved.) The number of inspections depends on the complexity of the job. Failure to obtain a permit or an inspection may result in your having to dismantle completed work.

NEW FLOOR PLAN

In this redesign of the floor plan shown on page 41, there's one big change: the lower, or outside, wall has been pushed out about 3 feet to house a new shower and toilet alcove. A pocket door seals this space, providing privacy while a second person uses the sink or tub areas.

New fixtures include a 5 by 5-foot platform tub and a second deck-mount sink. New light fixtures and electrical outlets complete the plan.

This project would require a professional to prepare detailed drawings of structural, plumbing, and wiring changes. If your project is less complicated, you could probably draw in all the changes yourself. A key to architectural symbols appears on page 41.

WORKING WITH PROFESSIONALS

Major home remodeling projects are not easy work. If you know how to draw plans but dislike physical labor, you'll need someone else to perform the actual work. If you're able to wield a saw and hammer but can't draw a straight line, you may need professional help to prepare the new floor plan or specifications. Some people do the nonspecialized work, such as clearing the site and cleaning up later, but hire experts for everything else. Others let professionals handle the entire project—from drawing plans through applying the finishing touches.

No matter whom you consult, be as precise as possible about what you want and about your budget. Collect pertinent photographs, manufacturer's brochures, and advertisements. Describe the materials, fixtures, and fittings you want to use. Provide your preliminary plans and a rough figure of how much you plan to spend. If you have questions, write them down as you think of them. The more information you can supply and the more informed you are, the better job a professional will be able to do.

Architect or designer?

Either an architect or a designer can draw plans acceptable to building department officials. Each can send out bids, help you select a contractor, and supervise the contractor's work to ensure that your plans and time schedule are being followed. Some architects and designers even double as their own contractors.

Most states do not require designers to be licensed, as architects must be; designers may charge less for their labor. If stress calculations must be made, designers need state-licensed engineers to design the structure and sign the working drawings; architects can do their own calculations.

Many architects are members of the American Institute of Architects (AIA), and many designers belong to the American Institute of Building Designers (AIBD). If you want to work with a bathroom designer, look for members of the National Kitchen & Bath Association (NKBA) or a Certified Bathroom Designer (CBD). Each association has a code of ethics and sponsors continuing programs to inform members about the latest building materials and techniques.

You may also wish to call on the services of an interior designer for finishing touches. These experts specialize in the decorating and furnishing of rooms. They can offer fresh, innovative ideas and advice. Through their contacts, you have access to materials and products not available at the retail level. Many designers belong to the American Society of Interior Designers (ASID), a professional organization.

Architects and designers may charge for time spent in an exploratory interview. For plans, you'll probably be charged on an hourly basis. If you want an architect or designer to select the contractor and keep an eye on construction, plan to pay either an hourly rate or a percentage of the cost of materials and labor—15 to 25 percent is typical. Descriptions of the services to be performed and the amount of the charges should be stated in advance in writing to prevent expensive misunderstandings later on.

Choosing a contractor

Contractors are responsible for construction and all building operations. Often, they're also skilled drafters, able to draw working plans acceptable to building department officials; they can also obtain the necessary building permits.

If you decide to use a contractor, ask architects, designers, and friends for recommendations. To compare bids for the actual construction, contact at least three state-licensed contractors; give each one either an exact description and sketches of the desired remodeling or plans and specifications prepared by an architect or designer. Include a detailed account of who will be responsible for what work.

Don't be tempted to make price your only criterion for selection; reliability, quality of work, and on-time performance are also important. Ask the contractors for the names and phone numbers of recent clients. Call several and ask them how they feel about the contractor; if you can, inspect the contractor's work. Ask for proof of liability insurance; also check bank and credit references to determine the contractor's financial responsibility.

Though some contractors may want a fee based on a percentage of the cost of materials and labor, it's usually wiser to insist on a fixed-price bid. This protects you against both an unexpected rise in the cost of materials (assuming that the contractor does the buying) and the chance that the work will take more time, adding to your labor costs. Many states limit the amount of "good faith" money that contractors can require before work begins.

Hiring subcontractors

When you act as your own general contractor and put various parts of your project out to bid with subcontractors (plumbers, tile setters, and the like), you must use the same care you'd exercise in hiring a general contractor.

Check the references, financial resources, and insurance coverage of a number of subcontractors. Once you've received bids and chosen your subcontractor, work out a detailed contract for each job and carefully supervise all work.

Bathroom showcase

On the following pages is a wonderland of products and materials for the bathroom. Here you can see and compare at a glance a sampling of styles, installation methods, functions, and materials. Though it's by no means exhaustive, this showcase provides the basic information you'll need as you sketch layouts, gather specifications for contracts or ordering, and develop a budget.

Recognizing the need to conserve resources, many manufacturers today offer a variety of water-saving toilets, faucets, shower heads, and hand-held shower attachments, with price and performance comparable to those of their conventional counterparts. These fixtures and fittings can reduce not only the amount of water used but also the amount of energy needed to heat that water.

CABINETS

Today, as changing lifestyles find new expression and bathrooms become grooming centers, exercise gyms, and spas, storage needs and configurations are also changing. One or more base vanities may still form the backbone of the storage scheme, but bath storage areas have become more stylish, their design integrated with mirrors, sink, lighting, and backsplash treatment. Perhaps you'll wish to add a bank of wall cabinets, let built-ins form knee walls between use areas, or plan a floor-to-ceiling unit.

Traditional American cabinets mask the raw front edges of each box with a 1 by 2 faceframe. On European, or frameless, cabinets, a simple narrow trim strip covers raw edges; doors and drawers usually fit to within ¼ inch of each other, revealing a thin sliver of

trim. Door hinges are invisible. Thanks to absolute standardization of every component, frameless cabinets are unsurpassed in versatility.

You can purchase a vanity cabinet with or without countertop and sink. Some manufacturers produce modular cabinet and shelf units for use with their vanities; other units include laundry bins, medicine cabinets, and closets. Standard width is 30 inches, increasing at 3 or 6-inch intervals, but some are as narrow as 12 inches and as wide as 60 inches. Standard heights range from 28 to 36 inches; depths range up to 24 inches.

If you don't find what you're looking for in the bath department, take a look at kitchen units; the differences between cabinet lines are slowly disappearing.

Styles

Wall-hung

Medicine cabinet

Molded top

Wall cabinet

Modular

Shallow-depth with overhanging sink

Double-bowl

COUNTERTOPS

Plastic laminate, ceramic tile, solid-surface acrylic, and stone are the four major countertop materials currently in use. Synthetic marble, popular in the past, is losing ground to solid-surface materials. Wood is sometimes used for countertops, too, but the surface must be carefully sealed to prevent water damage.

Style	Characteristics
Plastic laminate	Laminate comes in a wide range of colors, textures, and patterns. It's durable, easy to clean, water-resistant, and relatively inexpensive. However, it can scratch, scorch, chip, and stain. Also, smooth, reflective surfaces tend to show dirt and water marks. Conventional laminate has a dark backing that shows at its seams; new solid-color laminate, designed to avoid this, is somewhat brittle and more expensive.
	Post-formed tops, premolded and prefabricated, are the least expensive option; a custom top with built-up lip and backsplash looks best but is more costly.
Ceramic tile	Good-looking ceramic tile comes in many colors, textures, and patterns. Installed correctly, it's heatproof, scratch-resistant, and water-resistant. On the other hand, the grout may be hard to keep clean, even when a grout sealer is used. Also, tile's hard, irregular surface can chip delicate glass containers. High-gloss tiles show every smudge.
	Prices range from modest to extravagant, depending on style, accents, and accessory pieces. Nonporous glazed tiles won't soak up spills and stains.
Solid-surface	Durable, water-resistant, nonporous, and easy to clean, this marblelike material allows for a variety of edge details and sink installations, including integral units. Blemishes and scratches can be sanded out.
	Solid-surface countertops are expensive and require firm support from below. Until recently, color selection was limited to white, beige, and almond; now, imitation stone and pastels are readily available. Costs go up for wood inlays and other fancy edge details.
Stone	Granite and marble are beautiful natural materials for countertops. In most areas, you'll find a great selection of colors and figures. Stone is water-resistant, heatproof, easy to clean, and very durable.
	Oil, alcohol, and any acid (even chemicals in some water supplies) can stain marble and damage its high-gloss finish; granite can stand up to all of these. Solid stone slabs are very expensive. Stone tiles, including slate and limestone, are less expensive alternatives.
Synthetic marble	This group of man-made products, collectively known as "cast polymers," includes cultured marble, cultured onyx, and cultured granite. All three are relatively inexpensive and easy to clean. These products are often sold with an integral sink.
	Synthetic marble is not very durable, and scratches and dings are hard to mend (the surface finish is often only a thin veneer). Quality varies widely; look for Cultured Marble Institute or IAPMO certification.
Wood	Wood is handsome, natural, easily installed, and easy on grooming accessories and glass containers. However, wood is harder to keep clean than nonporous materials. If you use it in areas that will get wet (and that includes many bathroom surfaces), thoroughly protect it on all sides with a good sealer, such as polyurethane.
	Maple butcherblock, the most popular ready-made top, is sold in 24, 30, and 36-inch widths; installed price is comparable to ceramic or top-of-the-line laminate. Edge-joined oak, redwood, sugar pine, and teak are also used for counters.

SINKS

Sinks come in many shapes, sizes, colors, materials, and styles. The most commonly available styles are deck-mount, integral sink and countertop, pedestal, and wall-hung. Sinks have either no holes for fittings or holes for 4, 6, or 8-inch faucet assemblies; some also have holes for spray attachments and lotion dispensers (see page 59 for more about sink fittings). You'll find a wide selection of sink materials. Vitreous china, fiberglass-reinforced plastic, enameled cast iron, and enameled steel are the most common. Brass and copper sinks make striking accents, but they require zealous maintenance.

Style	Characteristics
Deck-mount, self-rimming	A self-rimming sink has a molded overlap that's supported by the edge of the countertop cutout. The cutout is undersized, allowing the sink rim to sit on the countertop. This style is easy to install and offers the widest range in shapes, including shell, hexagon, and fluted.
Deck-mount, flush	A surrounding metal frame holds a flush-mount sink to the countertop. The frame comes in several finishes to match fittings. Keeping the joints between the frame, sink, and countertop clean requires some vigilance. This style is usually used with plastic laminate countertops.
Deck-mount, unrimmed	An unrimmed sink is recessed beneath the countertop opening and held in place by metal clips. Fittings are mounted through the countertop or directly on the sink. The sink-countertop joint requires a little extra effort to keep clean. This sink is a good choice for use with tile, plastic laminate, or synthetic marble countertops.
Integral sink and countertop	Made of solid-surface material, synthetic marble, vitreous china, or fiberglass, an integral sink and countertop has no joints, so installation and cleaning are easy. This one-piece molded unit sits on top of a vanity. Sink color can either match the countertop or complement it; edge-banding and other border options abound. Double-bowl units are available.
Pedestal	Pedestal sinks are making a big comeback. Typically made of vitreous china in a wide range of traditional and modern designs, these elegant sinks are easy to install. The pedestal usually hides the plumbing. Some models have old-style vanity legs. Pedestal sinks are generally among the highest-priced basins. There's no storage space beneath.
Wall-hung	Like pedestals, wall-hung sinks are enjoying a revival. Materials and styling are similar; in fact, some designs are available in either version. Generally speaking, these are the least expensive and most compact sink options. Wall-hung units are supported by hangers or angle brackets. If you're installing a wall-hung sink for the first time, plan to add a support ledger.

BATHTUBS

Today's bathtub market overflows with styles. The 30 by 60-inch bathtub, which contributed to the predominance of the 5 by 7-foot bathroom, no longer rules. New and more comfortable tub shapes and sizes are available in an array of colors. Tubs can be purchased in whirlpool models and with grab bars and slip-resistant surfaces for safety. A white tub without special features is still the least expensive.

The boxy, familiar tub is enameled steel, relatively inexpensive, and lightweight. But it's also noisy, cold, and prone to chipping. Enameled cast-iron tubs are more durable and warmer to the touch, but they're very heavy. The most innovative tubs are vacuum-formed acrylic or injection-molded thermoplastic like ABS. These lightweight shells retain heat well, but their shiny surfaces can scratch or dull.

Style	Characteristics
Standard Recessed · Corner	Rectangular tubs come in two styles: recessed and corner. Recessed tubs fit between two side walls and against a back wall; they have one finished side. Corner models have one finished side and end and may be right or left-handed. If space allows, choose a longer model rather than the standard 60 inches; a depth of 16 inches or more is more comfortable than the standard 14 inches.
Platform/sunken	Platform or sunken tubs, most commonly available in enameled cast iron or acrylic, are either set in a raised platform or sunk in the floor. Extra framing is often needed, especially for installation on an upper floor. Interior shapes and features vary. Built-in headrests, seating shelves, and grab bars abound.
Freestanding	An old-fashioned freestanding tub, such as the enduring clawfoot model, makes a nice focal point for a traditional design. You can buy reproductions or a reconditioned original. Such tubs can double as showers with the addition of Victorian-inspired shower head/diverter/curtain rod hardware. Recently, many new sources for renovators' supplies have sprung up; check specialty shops and antique plumbing catalogues.
Whirlpool	Think of these hydromassage units simply as bathtubs with air jets. Jet designs vary; generally, you can opt for high volume and low pressure (a few strong jets) or low pressure and high volume (lots of softer jets). The best whirlpools are adjustable for water volume, air-water mixture, and direction. Because of their extra weight, whirlpools may need special floor framing. They may also require an extra-capacity water heater or separate in-line heater.
Soaking	Soaking tubs have deep interiors. Ideal for use in small spaces, they come in recessed, platform, and corner models, with rectangular or round interiors of fiberglass or acrylic. Hot tubs, with their continuous water supply, can present moisture problems in all but the best-ventilated spaces. They're best used outdoors.

SHOWERS

Many shower options are available, including shower and tub/shower kits that come with or without overlapping wall panels, adhesive, and caulking. You can also purchase shower and tub/shower wall kits to use with existing shower bases and tubs. If shower or tub/shower doors don't come with your kit, you can buy them separately. Because of their size, one-piece molded shower or tub/shower surrounds are used primarily in new homes or additions; if you have oversize doors in your house, you may be able to use one of these units.

Size is important; make sure you carefully measure the installation area and the unit before you buy. Units are available in fiberglass-reinforced plastic, acrylic, plastic laminate, and synthetic marble. Shower stalls made of tin or stainless steel are fading from the plumbing scene.

Style	Characteristics
Shower surrounds	Most shower surrounds require framing for support; you fasten the panel flanges to the framing. The shower base, walls, and door can be purchased individually or in a kit. Some models come with ceilings. For comfort, choose a shower that's at least 3 feet square. Complete assemblies vary in height, but 84 inches is common. Corner and circular shower models are available. Circular showers feature clear or tinted acrylic doors that double as walls.
Tub/shower surrounds	Tub/shower surrounds must also have framing for support. You can purchase the tub, walls, and door in a kit, or buy a separate recessed tub and match it with compatible prefabricated wall panels or a custom wall treatment (such as tile panels). Molded fiberglass wall panels may include molded soap dishes, ledges, and grab bars. You can also add a shower head or install a hand-held shower attachment to convert an existing tub surround to a tub/shower. Shower attachments are mounted to the wall or tub spout.
Shower bases Rectangular　Square　Corner	A shower base can be purchased separately or in a kit that includes a shower surround. Most bases are made of fiberglass, acrylic, or terrazzo, and come in standard sizes in rectangular, square, or corner shapes; all have a predrilled hole for the drain. It's easy to find a base that matches a tub or another fixture, as many manufacturers make both.
Shower doors Swinging　Sliding　Folding	Doors for showers come in a variety of styles: swinging, sliding, and folding, as well as pivot (not shown). Tub/showers typically have sliding or folding doors. Doors and enclosures are commonly made of tempered safety glass with aluminum frames. Frames come in many finishes; you can select one to match your fittings. The glazing can be clear, hammered, pebbled, tinted, or striped. Many sliding doors have towel bars. Swinging, folding, and pivot doors can be installed with right or left openings. Folding doors are constructed of rigid plastic panels or flexible plastic sheeting.

FITTINGS FOR FIXTURES

Fittings are sold separately from fixtures. Select fittings that are durable and easy to use. Cost varies according to material, quality, and design.

Fittings for sinks are available with single, center-set, or spread-fit controls. A single-control fitting has a combined faucet and lever or knob that controls water flow and temperature. A center-set control has separate hot and cold water controls and a faucet, all mounted on a base. A spread-fit control has separate hot and cold water controls and a faucet, each independently mounted. The number of holes in the sink and the distances between them—either 4, 6, or 8 inches—determine which fittings can be used. If fittings are to be attached to the wall or counter, the holes can be placed to suit the fittings.

For tubs and tub/showers, you can use either single or separate controls. Tubs also require a spout and drain. Tub/showers need a spout, shower head, diverter valve, and drain. Water-saver shower heads are readily available. You can purchase single-control fittings with pressure-balancing and temperature-limiting valves.

The best fittings are made of brass and come in several finishes, including chrome, pewter, gold, and bright enamel. Ceramic or nylon-disk designs are generally easier to maintain than older schemes.

Styles

Sink sets

Single-control

Single-control with pull-out sprayer

Center-set

Spread-fit

Spread-fit

Shower sets

Single-control

Temperature-limiting

Separate controls

Spray bars

Adjustable-height head

Tub sets

Single-control

Separate controls

Separate controls

Deck-mount with separate controls

Roman spout with deck-mount controls

Tub/shower sets

Single-control with diverter

Single-control with spout diverter

Separate controls with handle diverter

Separate controls with button diverter

Hand shower

TOILETS & BIDETS

New styling, new colors, and new technologies are updating the tried-and-true water closet. In addition to standard and antique models, toilets now come in sleek European designs, standard or low-profile heights, and rounded or elongated bowl shapes.

A washdown toilet, no longer accepted by many code authorities, is the least expensive, least efficient, and most noisy of the various models. Less noisy is a reverse trap toilet; it has a smaller water area, water seal, and trapway than the washdown.

A siphon jet toilet is quieter and has a larger water surface than the previous two styles, but it's also more costly; because it has a larger trapway, it's less likely to clog.

The new word in toilets is ultra-low-flush. Older toilets use 5 to 7 gallons of water or more per flush. In 1983, codes were changed to require 3½-gallon-per-flush toilets for new construction. But ultra-low-flush (ULF) toilets, which use only 1.6 gallons or less per flush, are already replacing these. Some homeowners complain that ULF toilets require several flushings. One solution to this problem is the pressure-assisted design, which uses a strong air vacuum to power a quick, intensive flush.

A bidet, best installed next to the toilet, is floor mounted and plumbed with hot and cold water. It's used primarily for personal hygiene.

Toilets and bidets are made of vitreous china.

Style	Characteristics
One-piece Low-profile Wall-hung	One-piece toilets are characterized by their low profile, usually 19 to 26 inches high. These units are designed for floor and wall mounting. Available with round or elongated bowls, one-piece toilets have reverse trap, siphon jet, or ultra-low-flush flushing action. Their design, efficiency, and easy installation make them a popular choice.
Two-piece Standard Safety Wall tank Ultra-low-flush	Two-piece toilets come in many models and can be mounted on the floor or on the wall. A wall-hung toilet, available only in siphon jet and siphon action models, offers easy access to the floor for cleaning. If you don't already have a wall-hung toilet, you'll face fairly major alterations to the wall framing and the floor. If you have special needs, consider special toilet designs. The rim of a higher-seat safety toilet is 18 inches above the floor, compared to the 14-inch height of a conventional bowl. A back-outlet toilet has an above-floor drain. It's most frequently used on concrete floors, where it would be difficult and costly to install other toilets or relocate an existing one.
Bidets Center-fit Spread-fit	Available with wall or deck-mount water controls, a bidet comes with a spray spout or a vertical spray located in the center of the bowl. Some have rim jets for rinsing, to maintain bowl cleanliness. Most models also have a pop-up stopper that allows the unit to double as a foot bath or as a basin for washing clothes.

HEATING & VENTILATION

Nothing spoils the soothing effects of a long, hot soak or shower faster than stepping out into a cool bathroom. A small heater in the wall or ceiling may be just what you need to stay warm while toweling off.

Bathroom heaters warm rooms by two methods: convection (usually boosted by a small fan) and radiation. Convection heaters warm the air in a room; the air, in turn, transfers the heat to surfaces and objects that it contacts. Radiant heaters emit infrared or electromagnetic waves that warm the objects and surfaces they hit without warming the intervening air. If you're

installing a new slab or subfloor, you may want to consider radiant heating pipes below.

Most building codes require that bathrooms have either natural or forced ventilation. Forced ventilation, then, is required in windowless bathrooms. In fact, some codes specify that the exhaust fan must be on the same switch as the lights. But even if you have good natural ventilation, an exhaust fan can exchange the air in a bathroom faster than an open window; in bad weather, a fan can keep the elements out and still remove stale air.

Style	Characteristics
Electric heaters Radiant heater with heat lamps Convection heater with light and fan Radiant or convection wall heater	Wall or ceiling-mounted convection heaters usually have an electrically heated resistance coil and a small fan to move the heated air. Radiant heaters using infrared light bulbs may be surface-mounted on the ceiling or recessed between joists. Radiant heating panels are generally flush-mounted on a wall or ceiling.
Gas heaters Convection wall heater Freestanding heater	You'll find heaters available for either propane or natural gas. Though most are convection heaters, there is one radiant type: a catalytic heater. Most gas heaters are flush-mounted on a wall, but in a spacious master suite you might consider an attractive, freestanding "stove" unit. Options include electric ignition and wall-mounted thermostats.
Heated towel bars Hydronic towel bar Electric towel bar	Besides gas and electricity, another heat source has reappeared on the bathroom scene: hot water. The original idea was to warm bath towels, but now these hydronic units—wall or floor-mounted—are being billed as radiators as well. You can find electric versions of the towel bar heater, too.
Exhaust fans Ceiling fan Ceiling fan with light Wall fan	You can buy fans to mount in the wall or ceiling. Some models are combined with a light or a heater, or both. The Home Ventilating Institute recommends that the fan be capable of exchanging the air at least eight times every hour (for details, see page 81). Most fans also have a noise rating measured in sones; the lower the number, the quieter the fan.

FLOORING

Think moisture-resistance when choosing a flooring material for a bathroom. Resilient tiles and sheets, ceramic tile, and properly sealed hardwood and stone are all good candidates. For a touch of comfort, don't rule out carpeting, especially the newer stain-resistant, industrial types.

For safety's sake, a bathroom floor must be slip-resistant, especially in wet areas. Tiles are safest in matte-finish versions. Smaller tiles, with their extra grout spaces, offer more traction than larger tiles. A rubberized mat or throw rug (if it will stay put) can provide firm footing near the tub or shower.

Style	Characteristics
Resilient	Generally made of solid vinyl, rubber, or polyurethane, resilients are flexible, moisture and stain-resistant, easy to install, and simple to maintain. A seemingly endless variety of colors, textures, patterns, and styles is available. Resilient is vulnerable to dents and tears but can be repaired. Tiles can collect moisture between seams if improperly installed. Sheets run up to 12 feet wide, eliminating the need for seaming in many bathrooms; tiles are generally 12 inches square. Vinyl and rubber are comfortable to walk on. Polyurethane finish eliminates waxing. Vinyl is the least expensive option. Some vinyl comes with a photographically applied pattern, but most is inlaid; the latter style is more expensive but wears better. Tiles are often easier to lay than sheet goods.
Ceramic tile	Made of hard-fired slabs of clay, tiles are usually classified as *quarry tile*, commonly unglazed (unfinished) red-clay tiles that are rough and water-resistant; *pavers*, rugged unglazed tiles in earth-tone shades; and *glazed* tile, available in glossy, matte, or textured finishes and in many colors. Tile sizes run the gamut of widths, lengths, and thicknesses. Tile can be cold, noisy, and, if glazed, slippery underfoot. If not properly grouted, tiles can leak moisture. Grout spaces can be tough to keep clean. Cost varies widely; three-dimensional patterns and multicolored glazes can easily double costs. Purer clays fired at higher temperatures generally make costlier but better-wearing tiles.
Wood	Wood contributes warmth to the decor, feels good underfoot, resists wear, and can be refinished. The three basic types are *strip*, narrow tongue-and-groove boards in random lengths; *plank*, tongue-and-groove boards in various widths and random lengths; and *wood tile*, often laid in blocks or squares in parquet fashion. "Floating" floor systems have several veneered strips atop each tongue-and-groove backing board. Wood flooring may be factory-prefinished or unfinished. Moisture will damage wood flooring; also, an adequate floor substructure is crucial. Bleaching and some staining processes may wear unevenly and are difficult to repair. Wood is moderate to expensive in cost, depending on quality, finish, and installation. Floating systems are generally the most expensive.
Stone	Natural stone, such as slate, flagstone, marble, granite, and limestone, has been used for flooring for centuries. Today, its use is even more practical, thanks to the development of sealers and finishes. Easy to maintain, stone flooring is also virtually indestructible. Stone can be used in its natural shape or cut into uniform pieces—rectangular blocks or more formal tiles. Generally, uniform pieces are butted tightly together; irregular flagstone requires grouted joints. The cost of most stone flooring is high. Moreover, the weight of the materials requires a very strong, well-supported subfloor. Some stone—marble in particular—is cold and slippery underfoot. Careful sealing is a must; some stones absorb stains and dirt readily.

WALL COVERINGS

In addition to the shower and tub-surround areas, your bathroom will probably include a good bit of wall space. Bathroom wall treatments must be able to withstand moisture, heat, and high usage. These surfaces also go a long way toward defining the overall impact of your bath. (For details on paint, see page 101.)

Style	Characteristics
Ceramic tiles	Wall tiles are glazed and offer great variety in color and design. Generally lighter and thinner than floor tiles, they're used primarily on interior surfaces—walls, countertops, and ceilings. Their relatively light weight is a plus for vertical installation. The glazed surface is water-resistant, though the bodies are porous.
	Standard sizes for wall tiles range from 3-inch squares to 4¼ by 8½-inch rectangles; thicknesses vary from ¼ to ⅜ inch. Other sizes and shapes are available. Many wall tiles come with matching trim pieces for edges, coves, and corners.
	Wall tiles are also available in pregrouted panels, a handy shortcut that reduces installation time and effort. Designed primarily for tub and shower areas, a panel contains up to 64 tiles, each measuring 4¼ inches square. The panels have flexible, water-repellent grout.
	Ceramic mosaic is one of the most colorful and versatile materials in the tile family. Tiles sold under this name are generally small—2 by 2 inches or less. For this reason, they can be installed on curved surfaces. Mosaics come in sheets, with the tiles mounted on thread mesh or paper backing or joined with silicone rubber. Once they're in place, you grout these sheets like any other wall tiles.
Stone	Marble, slate, limestone, and granite, whether as 8 or 12-inch tiles or wider sheets, can perform a role similar to ceramic tile. Stone tiles are expensive but, used as accents, they can go a long way. Most stone, especially marble, should be thoroughly sealed for wall use; untreated, it can be stained or eaten away by acids in cleaning supplies or even household water.
Glass block	If you're looking for some ambient daylight but don't want to sacrifice privacy, consider glass blocks. You can buy 3 or 4-inch-thick square blocks in many sizes; rectangular blocks are available in a more limited selection. Textures can be smooth, wavy, rippled, bubbly, or crosshatched. Mortarless block systems make an often tricky installation job simpler for do-it-yourselfers.
Wallpaper	Wallpaper for the bathroom should be scrubbable, durable, and stain-resistant. Solid-vinyl wallpapers, which come in a wide variety of colors and textures, fit the bill. New patterns, including some that replicate other surfaces (such as linen), are generally subtle; wallpaper borders add visual punch to ceiling lines and openings. Good ventilation is crucial to keep wallpaper from loosening.
Plaster	The textured, uneven, and slightly rounded edges of plaster give a bathroom a custom, informal look. Plaster is especially popular for Southwest-theme designs. If the surface is too irregular, however, plaster is hard to keep clean.
Wood	Tongue-and-groove wood paneling—natural, stained, bleached, or painted—provides a charming accent to country schemes. Wainscoting is the most popular application; the paneling is separated from wallpaper or paint above by the traditional chair rail.
	Moldings are back in vogue. Specialty shops are likely to have a wide selection and will often custom-match an old favorite to order.

REMODELING BASICS

Installation ▪ Removal ▪ Tools ▪ Techniques

After sifting through a wealth of bathroom remodeling ideas, you've probably selected what's right for your family's special needs. Perhaps you've decided on a quick and easy change—a fresh coat of paint in your favorite color. Or maybe this is the time for the major remodel you've been dreaming about—moving a wall, opening the ceiling with a skylight, installing a gleaming new tub and surrounding tile.

This chapter is designed to help you translate your ideas and dreams into changes in your bathroom. From the basics of structural framing, plumbing, and wiring to the fine points of installing the walls, it's all here for you to read and do. Each project begins with general information on planning and procedures, then takes you through the work with illustrated step-by-step instructions.

Though the directions assume that you have some basic knowledge of building terms, tools, materials, and techniques, you needn't be an expert to do most of the projects in this chapter. If you need more detailed information on procedures, take a look at the *Sunset* books *Basic Carpentry Illustrated*, *Basic Plumbing Illustrated*, and *Basic Home Wiring Illustrated*.

Pedestal sinks are making a comeback, and most models are easy to install. Since plumbing hardware will be visible below the sink, you may wish to invest in decorative supply tubing and shutoff valves. For installation details, see pages 84–85.

Before work begins

Are you ready to remodel? Before plunging into a project, you should have a clear idea of the steps required to complete the job, and the sequence in which they should be done. You'll also need to evaluate your own ability to perform the various tasks. One of your first decisions will be whether to do the work yourself or get professional help.

Can you do the work yourself?

What skills do you need to remodel a bathroom? It depends on the improvements you're planning. Projects such as painting, setting wall tile, and installing floors and cabinets are within easy reach of any homeowner with basic do-it-yourself ability. You'll need a few specialized tools to complete some projects, but you can buy them at a building supply or home improvement center, or perhaps even rent them.

If your plans include complex remodeling projects such as moving bearing walls, running new drain and vent pipes, or wiring new electrical circuits and service panels, you may want to hire professionals to do part or all of the job. But many smaller structural, plumbing, and electrical jobs can be done by a homeowner with some basic experience.

Even if there's little you can build, you may discover a talent for demolition—and save some money. But some contractors may not want to relinquish this task. If you do take it on, be sure to finish by the time the remodeling crew is ready to begin.

Planning your project

Putting careful thought into your preparations can save you extra work and inconvenience later. As the scale of your remodeling project increases, the need for careful planning becomes more critical. If your home has only one bathroom, your goal is to keep it in operating order as much of the time as possible. With careful scheduling, the remodeling time will be easier for the entire family.

Be sure to obtain any necessary permits from your local building department. A contractor, if you hire one, will do this job for you. But if you're doing the work yourself, you'll need to secure permits and arrange for inspections. Finally, before you start work, double-check the priorities listed below.

■ Establish the sequence of jobs to be done, and estimate the time needed for completion.

■ If you're hiring professional help, make sure you have legally binding contracts and schedules with contractors and subcontractors.

■ If electricity, gas, or water must be shut off by the utility company, arrange for the cutoff date.

■ Locate an area for temporarily storing fixtures that have been removed.

■ Measure fixtures for adequate clearance through doorways and hallways, or down staircases.

■ Locate a site for dumping refuse and secure necessary permits.

■ Obtain all other required permits.

■ Arrange for timely delivery of materials and be sure you have all the necessary tools on hand.

Note: If you're contracting the work, you can skip the last three steps; they're normally part of the contractor's service.

How to use this chapter

Reading all the sections of this chapter through quickly will help you to get a general feeling for what's involved in bathroom remodeling.

In the first three sections, you'll find an overview of structural, plumbing, and electrical systems. Even if you don't plan to do the work yourself, you may want to review these sections for background information. Understanding basic systems enables you to plan more effectively and to understand the reasons for code restrictions affecting your plans.

Many of your remodeling hours may be spent tearing out old work. To minimize the effort, we've included removal procedures along with installation instructions in the sections on fixtures, wall coverings, flooring, and cabinets.

If you're planning only one or two small projects, turn directly to the applicable sections for step-by-step instructions.

STEPS IN REMODELING

You can use this chart to plan the general order of removal and installation in remodeling your bathroom, though you may need to alter the suggested order, depending on the scale of your job and the materials you select. For more information, read the appropriate sections on the following pages. Manufacturers' instructions will offer additional guidelines as you go along.

Removal sequence

1. Accessories, decorative elements
2. Furniture, if any
3. Contents of cabinets, closets, shelves
4. Fixtures, plumbing fittings
5. Vanity countertops
6. Vanity cabinets, recessed cabinets, shelves
7. Flooring
8. Light fixtures, as required
9. Wall and ceiling coverings

Installation sequence

1. Structural changes: walls, doors, windows, skylights
2. Rough plumbing changes
3. Electrical wiring
4. Bathtub, shower
5. Wall and ceiling coverings
6. Light fixtures
7. Vanity cabinets, countertops
8. Toilets, bidets, sinks
9. Wall cabinets, shelves
10. Flooring
11. Accessories, decorative elements

Structural basics

Understanding your home's structural shell is a good way to begin any home improvement project, including bathroom remodeling.

Your house's framework probably will conform to the pattern of the "typical house" shown in the illustration below. Starting at the base of the drawing, you'll notice the following framing members: a wooden sill resting on a foundation wall; a series of horizontal, evenly spaced floor joists; and a subfloor (usually plywood sheets) laid atop the joists. This platform supports the first-floor walls, both interior and exterior. The walls are formed by vertical, evenly spaced studs that run between a horizontal sole plate and parallel top plate. The primary wall coverings are fastened directly to the studs.

Depending on the design of the house, one of several types of construction may be used above the first-floor walls. If there's a second story, a layer of ceiling joists rests on the walls; these joists support both the floor above and the ceiling below. A one-story house will have either an "open-beamed" ceiling—flat or pitched—or a "finished" ceiling. With a flat roof, the finished ceiling is attached directly to the rafters. The ceiling below a pitched roof is attached to joists.

Removing a partition wall

Sometimes major bathroom remodeling entails removing all or part of an interior wall to enlarge the space.

Walls that define your bathroom may be bearing or nonbearing. A bearing wall helps support the weight of the house; a nonbearing wall does not. An interior nonbearing wall, often called a partition wall, may be removed without special precautions. The procedure outlined in this section applies to partitions only. If you're considering a remodeling project that involves moving a bearing wall, consult an architect or contractor about problems and procedures.

How can you tell the difference in walls? All exterior walls running perpendicular to ceiling and floor joists are bearing. At least one main interior wall may be a bearing wall.

To determine whether the wall you're planning to move is bearing, climb up into the attic or crawlspace and check the ceiling joists. If they are joined over any wall, that wall is bearing. Even if joists span the entire width of the house, their midsections may be supported by a bearing wall at the point of maximum allowable span. If you have any doubts about the wall, consult an architect, contractor, or building inspector.

Bearing walls (in black)

Nonbearing walls (in white)

Direction of rafters, floor joists, and ceiling joists

Though removing a partition wall is not complicated, it can be quite messy. Cover the floors and fixtures, and wear a dust mask, safety glasses, and gloves. NOTE: Check the wall for signs of wiring, supply and drain pipes, and heating and ventilation ducts; you'll have to reroute them.

Remove the wall covering. First, if there's a door in the wall, remove it from its hinges. Pry off any door trim, ceiling molding, and base molding.

The most common wall covering is gypsum wallboard nailed to wall studs. To remove it, use a prybar (see "Removing gypsum wallboard," page 98).

If the wall covering is plaster and lath, chisel away the plaster and cut the lath backing—wood strips or metal—so that you can pry off the pieces of lath and plaster.

(Continued on next page)

TYPICAL HOUSE STRUCTURE

Rafters

Ceiling joists

Top plate

Header

Wall studs

Rough sill

Subfloor

Floor joists

Sole plate

Joist header

Foundation wall

Sill

■ Structural basics

DISMANTLING THE WALL FRAMING

Saw through the middle of the wall studs; bend the studs sideways to free the nails from the top and sole plates.

Cut gaps through the sole plate with a saw and chisel; insert a prybar in each gap and lift to free the sole plate.

Strip ceiling materials back from the top plate, cut gaps in the plate, and pry out sections of plate.

Dismantle the framing. Remove studs by sawing through the middle of each one; then push and pull them sideways to free the nails (see illustration above).

To remove the sole plate, saw a small section out of the middle down to the finished floor level, chisel through the remaining thickness, and insert a prybar in the gap.

To remove a top plate that lies parallel to the joists, cut ceiling materials back to adjacent joists, and pry off the plate. If the top plate is perpendicular to the joists, you are probably working on a bearing wall and will have to take special precautions (see page 67).

Patch walls, ceiling, and floor. Holes in wallboard and plaster aren't difficult to patch; the real challenge lies in matching a special texture, wallpaper, shade of paint, or well-aged floor. This is not a problem if your remodeling plans call for new wall coverings, ceiling, or flooring. In either case, see the sections "Walls & ceilings" (pages 98–105) and "Flooring" (pages 106–108) for techniques and tips.

Framing a new wall

To subdivide a large bathroom or to enlarge a cramped one, you may need to build a new partition wall or partial wall. Components of wall framing are illustrated below.

Framing a wall is a straightforward task, but you must measure carefully and check the alignment as work progresses. The basic steps are listed below. If you plan to install a doorway, see pages 69–70.

Plot the location. The new wall must be anchored securely to existing ceiling joists, the floor, and, at least on one side, to wall studs. To locate the studs, try knocking with

your fist along the wall until the sound changes from hollow to solid.

If you have wallboard, you can use an inexpensive stud finder; often, though, the nails that hold wallboard to the studs are visible on close inspection.

To locate ceiling joists, use the same methods or, from the attic or crawlspace, drill small holes down through the ceiling on both sides of a joist to serve as reference points below. Adjacent joists and studs should be evenly spaced, usually about 16 or 24 inches apart.

WALL FRAMING COMPONENTS

A wall running perpendicular to the joists will demand the least effort to attach. If wall and joists will run parallel, though, try to center the wall under a single joist; otherwise, you'll need to remove ceiling materials between two parallel joists and install nailing blocks every 2 feet (see illustrations at right). If the side of the new wall falls between existing studs, you'll need to install additional nailing blocks.

On the ceiling, mark both ends of the center line of the new wall. Measure 1¾ inches (half the width of the top plate) on both sides of each mark. Snap parallel lines between corresponding marks with a chalk line; the top plate will occupy the space between the lines.

Position the sole plate. Hang a plumb bob from each end of the lines you just marked and mark these new points on the floor. Snap two more chalk lines to connect these points.

Cut both sole plate and top plate to the desired length. Lay the sole plate between the lines on the floor and nail it in place with 10-penny nails spaced every 2 feet. (If you have a masonry floor, use a masonry bit to drill a bolt hole through the sole plate every 2 or 3 feet. Insert expansion anchors for lag bolts and bolt the sole plate to the floor.)

If you're planning a doorway (see "Framing a doorway," below), don't nail through that section of the plate; it will be cut out later.

Mark stud positions. Lay the top plate against the sole plate, as shown in the illustration. Beginning

ANCHORING A TOP PLATE

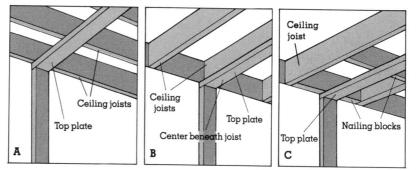

To anchor a top plate, nail to perpendicular joists (A) or to the bottom of the parallel joist (B), or install nailing blocks between parallel joists (C).

at the end that will be attached to an existing stud or to nailing blocks, measure in 1½ inches—the thickness of a 2 by 4 stud—and draw a line across both plates with a combination square. Starting once more from that end, measure and draw lines at 15¼ and 16¾ inches. From these lines, advance 16 inches. Don't worry if the spacing at the far end is less than 16 inches. (If local codes permit, consider a 24-inch spacing—you'll save lumber—and adjust the placement of lines to 23¼ and 24¾ inches.)

Fasten the top plate. While two helpers hold the top plate in position between the lines (marked on the ceiling), nail it to perpendicular joists, to one parallel joist, or to nailing blocks, as shown above.

Attach the studs. Measure and cut the studs to exact length. Attach one end stud (or both) to existing studs or to nailing blocks between studs. Lift

the remaining studs into place one at a time; line them up on the marks, and check plumb with a carpenter's level. Toenail the studs to both top plate and sole plate with 8-penny nails.

Many building codes require horizontal fireblocks between studs. The number of rows depends on the code; if permitted, position blocks to provide an extra nailing surface for wall materials.

Finish. After the studs are installed, it's time to add any electrical outlets and switches (see pages 76–78), as well as any new plumbing (see pages 72–75). It's also time for the building inspector to check your work. Following the inspection, you can finish the walls (see pages 98–105).

Framing a doorway

Your remodeling may call for changing the position of a door and creating a new door opening. Be sure the wall you plan to cut into is a non-bearing wall (see page 67); if it's a bearing wall, consult a professional.

Position the opening. This section assumes that you're installing a standard prehung door and frame. Before starting work, check the manufacturer's "rough opening" dimensions—the exact wall opening required after the new framing is in place.

You'll need to plan an opening large enough to accommodate both

MARKING STUD POSITIONS

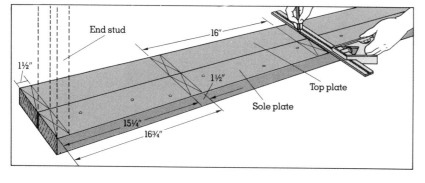

■Structural basics

the rough opening and the rough door framing—an additional 1½ inches on top and sides. If your door didn't come with rough opening dimensions, add an additional ⅜ inch all around for shimming (adjusting level and plumb) the typical door frame.

Often it's simpler to remove the wallboard from floor to ceiling between two bordering studs (the new king studs) that will remain in place. (This is the method illustrated.) In any case, you'll save work later if you can use at least one existing stud as part of the new framing.

Regardless of the method you choose, use a carpenter's level for a straightedge, and mark the outline of the opening on the wall.

Remove wall covering and studs. First remove any base molding. Cut along the outline of the opening with a reciprocating or keyhole saw, being careful to cut only the wallboard, not the studs beneath. Pry the wallboard away from the framing. To remove plaster and lath, chisel through the plaster to expose the lath; then cut the lath, and pry lath and plaster loose.

Cut the studs inside the opening to the height required for the header (see illustration below). Using a combination square, mark these studs on the face and one side, then

cut carefully with a reciprocating or crosscut saw. Remove the cut studs from the sole plate.

Frame the opening. With wall covering and studs removed, you're ready to frame the opening. Measure and cut the header (for a partition wall you can use a 2 by 4 laid flat), and toenail it to the king studs with 8-penny nails. Nail the header to the bottoms of the cripple studs.

Cut the part of the sole plate within the opening, and pry it away from the subfloor (see "Removing a partition wall," page 67).

Cut trimmer studs and nail them to the king studs with 10-penny nails in a staggered pattern. You'll probably need to adjust the width by blocking out a third trimmer from one side, as shown below right. Leave an extra ⅜ inch on each side for shimming, plus space for the door jambs.

Hang the door. A standard prehung door and frame are predrilled for a lockset. The door comes already fitted and attached to the frame with hinges. Pull out the hinge pins to remove the door before you install the frame. Nail the frame in the rough opening, shimming carefully to make the side jambs plumb and the head jamb level. Rehang the

door and install the lockset; then install stop molding and trim (casing).

Closing a doorway

It's easy to eliminate an existing doorway. Simply add new studs within the opening and attach new wall coverings. The only trick is to match the present wall surface.

First, remove the casing around the opening. Then remove the door from its hinges or guide track, and pry any jambs or tracks away from the rough framing.

Next, measure the gap on the floor between the existing trimmer studs; cut a length of 2 by 4 to serve as a new sole plate. Nail it to the floor with 10-penny nails. (If you have a masonry floor, attach the 2 by 4 with lag bolts and expansion anchors).

Measure and cut new studs to fill the space; position one stud beneath each cripple stud. Toenail the studs to the new sole plate and header with 8-penny nails. Add fireblocks between studs if required by the local code.

Strip the wall coverings back far enough to give yourself a firm nailing surface and an even edge. Then add new coverings to match the existing ones, or resurface the entire wall (see pages 98–105). Match or replace the baseboard molding.

FRAMING A DOORWAY

Mark and cut studs within the opening to a height even with the top of the new header, and remove.

Nail the new header to the king studs, then nail through the header into the ends of the new cripple studs.

Nail trimmer studs to the king studs; add a third trimmer, if needed, to make the opening the correct width.

SKYLIGHTING THE BATHROOM

A skylight brings light and an open feeling into windowless interior bathrooms or those where uncovered windows would be a privacy problem.

Installing a skylight in a pitched roof with asphalt or wood shingles is a two-part process: you cut and frame openings in both roof and ceiling, and connect the two openings with a vertical light shaft. (You don't even need a light shaft for a flat roof or open-beamed ceiling.) A description of the installation sequence follows; for more detailed information, consult the manufacturer's instructions or your skylight dealer.

Mark the openings. Begin by measuring and marking the location of the ceiling opening. Then drive nails up through the four corners and center so they'll be visible in the attic. You'll save work if you can use one or two ceiling joists as the edges of your opening.

With a plumb bob, transfer the center mark to the underside of the roof. Mark the roof opening suggested by the manufacturer on the underside of the roof and drive nails through the corners.

Frame the roof opening. Exercise extreme caution when working on the roof; if the pitch is steep or if you have a tile or slate roof, you should leave this part to professionals.

If your skylight must be mounted on a curb frame, build the curb first; 2 by 6 lumber is commonly used.

To determine the actual size of the opening you need to cut, add the dimensions of any framing materials to the rough opening size marked by the nails. You may need to remove some extra shingles or roofing materials down to the sheathing to accommodate the flashing of a curb-mount-

ed skylight or the flange of a self-flashing unit.

Cut the roof opening in successive layers: roofing materials first, sheathing next, and finally the rafters. Before cutting the rafters, support them with 2 by 4s nailed to the ceiling joists below.

To frame the opening, you'll need double headers and possibly trimmers to narrow the width between rafters.

If you're installing a curb-mounted unit, position and flash the curb. Toenail the curb to the rafters or trimmers and to the headers. Flash according to the manufacturer's instructions.

Mount the skylight. For a curb-mounted unit, secure the skylight to the top of the curb with nails and a sealant. Nail a self-flashing unit

through the flange directly to the roof sheathing; then coat the joints and nail holes with roofing cement.

Open the ceiling. Cut through the ceiling materials and then cut the joists. Support joists to be cut by bracing them against adjacent joists. Frame the opening in the manner used for the roof opening.

Build a light shaft. Measure the distance between the ceiling headers and roof headers at each corner and at 16-inch intervals between the corners. Cut studs to fit the measurements and install them as illustrated above. This provides a nailing surface for wall coverings.

To finish, insulate the spaces between studs in the light shaft before fastening wall coverings to the studs. Trim the ceiling opening with molding strips.

Plumbing basics

Whether you're planning to add a single fixture or remodel an entire bathroom, you'll need an introduction to plumbing basics. Replacing an old bathtub, sink, or toilet with a new one at the same location is a straightforward job, but roughing-in (installing) plumbing for fixtures at new locations takes skill and planning.

What follows is an overview of fundamentals—household plumbing systems, plumbing codes, and general procedures for planning, routing, and roughing-in new pipes. This information may help you to decide whether to make your project a do-it-yourself effort or a professional one. If you have doubts, consider a compromise—you might hire a professional to check your plans and install pipes, then make the fixture hookups yourself (see pages 82–97).

If you want to do all the work yourself, read the information that follows before you begin to ensure that you're familiar with the tools and techniques required for the job.

How the system works.

Three complementary sets of pipes work together to fill your home's plumbing needs: the water supply system, and the drain-waste and vent (DWV) systems (see the illustration below).

The supply system. Water for your toilet, tub, shower, and sink enters the house from a public water main or from a source on the property. Water from a water company is usually delivered through a water meter and a main shutoff valve. You'll find the meter either in your basement or crawlspace, or outdoors, near your property line. The main shutoff valve—which turns the water for the whole house on and off—is usually situated near the water meter.

At the water service entrance, the main supply line divides in two—one line branching off to be heated by the water heater, the other remaining as cold water. The two pipes usually run parallel below the first-floor level until they reach the vicinity of a group of fixtures, then

head up through the wall or floor. Sometimes the water supply—hot, cold, or both—passes through a water softener or filter before reaching the fixtures.

Supply pipes are installed with a slight pitch in the runs, sloping back toward the lowest point in the system so that all pipes can be drained. Sometimes at the lowest point there's a valve that can be opened to drain the system—essential for vacation homes in cold climates.

Drain-waste and vent systems. The drain-waste pipes take advantage of gravity to channel waste water and solid wastes to the house sewer line. Vent pipes carry away sewer gas and maintain atmospheric pressure in drainpipes and fixture traps. The traps (curved sections in the fixtures' drainpipes) remain filled with water at all times to keep gases from coming up the drains.

Every house has a 3 or 4-inch-diameter main soil stack that serves a dual function. Below the level of the fixtures, it is your home's primary drainpipe; above the stack it becomes a vent with its upper end protruding through the roof. Drainpipes from individual fixtures, as well as branch drains, connect to the main stack. These pipes lead away from all fixtures at a carefully calculated slope—normally ¼ inch per foot. Since any system may clog now and then, cleanouts usually are placed at the upper end of each horizontal section of drainpipe.

A fixture or fixture group located on a branch drain far from the main stack will have a secondary vent stack of its own rising to the roof.

Planning and layout

This section outlines the planning process and explores some of your options in adding new plumbing. When plotting out any plumbing addition you must balance code restrictions, the limitations of your system's layout, design considerations, and, of course, your own plumbing abilities.

A PLUMBING OVERVIEW

Secondary stack
Vent pipe
Vent pipe
Main stack
Sink trap
Toilet drain
Branch drain
Water heater
Branch drain
Water softener
Main cleanout
Main house drain
Main shutoff valve
Main water supply

Cold water supply
Hot water supply
Vent system
Drain-waste system

Check the codes. Almost any improvement that adds pipe to the system will require approval from local building department officials before you start, and inspection of the work before you close the walls and floor.

Learn what work you may do yourself—some codes require that certain work be done only by licensed plumbers.

Map your system. A detailed map of your present system will give you a clear picture of where it's feasible to tie into supply and drain lines, and whether the present drains and vents are adequate for the use you plan.

Starting in the basement, sketch in the main soil stack, branch drains, house drain, and accessible cleanouts; then trace the networks of hot and cold supply pipes. Also, check the attic or roof for the course of the main stack and any secondary vent stacks. Determine and mark on the sketch the materials and, if possible, the diameters of all pipes (see "Materials," at right).

Layout options. Plan the plumbing for any new fixtures in three parts: supply, drainage, and venting. To minimize cost and keep the work simple, arrange a fixture or group of fixtures so they are as close to the present pipes as possible.

Three economical ways to group your new fixtures (see drawings below) are to:

■ connect an individual fixture to the existing stack (drawing A)

■ add a fixture or group above or below an existing group on the stack

■ tie a fixture (except a toilet) directly into a new or existing branch drain (drawing B)

If your addition is planned for an area across the house from the existing plumbing, you'll probably need to run a new secondary vent stack up through the roof, and a new branch drain to the soil stack (see drawing B below) or to the main house drain via an existing cleanout.

The new vent stack must be installed inside an existing wall (a big job), built into a new oversize or "thickened" wall (see "Build a wet wall," page 74), or concealed in a closet or cabinet. In mild climates, a vent may also run up the exterior of the house, but it must be hidden within a box.

Materials. Decide what kind of pipe you'll need, based on the material of the pipe you'll be tying into.

Your home's supply pipes most likely are either galvanized steel (referred to as "galvanized" or "iron"

pipe) connected by threaded fittings, or rigid copper joined with soldered fittings.

Older DWV pipes probably are made of cast iron, with "hub" or "bell-and-spigot" ends joined by molten lead and oakum. (DWV pipes other than the main stack may be galvanized.)

To extend cast-iron pipes, you may substitute "hubless" fittings (consisting of neoprene gaskets and stainless steel clamps), which are simpler to install than hub fittings.

If you wish to change pipe material in your extension, it's a matter of inserting the appropriate adapter at the fitting end. You might want to change cast-iron or galvanized pipe to copper or plastic pipe. First check your local code, because some areas prohibit use of plastic pipe.

Plumbing codes

Few code restrictions apply to simple extensions of hot and cold water supply pipes, provided your house's water pressure is up to the task. The material and diameter for supply pipes serving each new fixture or appliance are spelled out clearly in the plumbing code. More troublesome are the pipes that make up the DWV system. Codes are quite specific about the following: the size of stacks, drainpipes, and vents serving any new fixture requiring drainage; the critical distance from fixture traps to the stack; and the method of venting fixtures.

Stack, drain, and vent size. The plumbing code will specify minimum diameters for stacks and vents in relation to numbers of *fixture units*. (One fixture unit represents 7.5 gallons or 1 cubic foot of water per minute.) In the code you'll find fixture unit ratings for all plumbing fixtures given in chart form.

To determine drainpipe diameter, look up the fixture or fixtures you're considering on the code's fixture unit chart. Add up the total fixture units; then look up the drain diameter specified for that number of units.

PLUMBING LAYOUT OPTIONS

To drain bathroom plumbing additions, you can either (A) tap into the present main stack, if nearby, or (B) install a new branch drain and secondary vent stack.

(Continued on next page)

■Plumbing basics

Vent pipe sizing criteria also include *length* of vent and *type* of vent, in addition to fixture unit load.

Critical distance. The maximum distance allowed between a fixture's trap and the stack or main drain that it empties into is called the critical distance. No drain outlet may be completely below the level of the trap's crown weir (see illustration below)—if it were, it would act as a siphon, draining the trap. Thus, when the ideal drainpipe slope of ¼ inch per foot is figured in, the length of that drainpipe quickly becomes limited. But if the fixture drain is *vented* properly within the critical distance, the drainpipe may run on indefinitely to the actual stack or main drain.

Stack or vent

Crown weir

¼" per foot slope

Critical distance

Trap

Drainpipe

Venting options. The four basic venting options (see illustration above right)—subject to local code—are wet venting, back venting, individual venting, and indirect venting.

■ *Wet venting* is simplest—the fixture is vented directly through the fixture drain to the soil stack.

■ *Back venting (reventing)* involves running a vent loop up past fixtures to reconnect with the main stack or secondary vent above the fixture level.

■ *Individual (secondary) venting* means running a secondary vent stack up through the roof for a new fixture or group of fixtures distant from the main stack.

VENTING OPTIONS

Wet venting   Back venting (reventing)   Individual (secondary) venting   Indirect venting

■ *Indirect venting* allows you to vent some fixtures (such as a basement shower) into an existing floor drain or laundry tub without further venting.

Roughing-in new plumbing

Once you've planned your plumbing additions, you can begin installation.

Locate and tie into existing pipe. In the mapping stage, you determined the rough locations of the pipes. The next step is to pinpoint them and cut away wall, ceiling, or floor coverings along studs or joists to expose the sections you want to tie into. Be sure to cut out holes large enough to allow you to work comfortably. (For information about wall and floor coverings, see pages 98–108.)

Basically, tying into drainwaste, vent, and supply lines entails cutting a section out of each pipe and inserting a new fitting to join old and new pipe. The method you use to tie into the pipes varies with the pipe material.

Route new pipes. With the connections made, the new DWV and supply pipes are run to the new fixture location. Ideally, new drainpipes should be routed below the bathroom floor. They can be suspended from floor joists by pipe hangers, inserted in the space between parallel joists, or run through

notches or holes drilled in joists that are at right angles to the pipe (if allowed by code). If you have a finished basement or your bathroom is on the second floor, you'll need to cut into the floor or ceiling to install pipes between or through joists, hide the pipes with a dropped ceiling, or box them in. (Remember that drainpipes must slope away from fixtures at a minimum slope of ¼ inch per foot.)

Supply pipes normally follow drainpipes but can be routed directly up through the wall or floor from main horizontal lines. Supply pipes should run parallel, at least 6 inches apart. In cold areas, codes may prohibit supply pipes in exterior walls.

Build a wet wall. The main soil stack, and often a secondary stack, commonly hide inside an oversize house wall called a "wet wall."

Unlike an ordinary 2 by 4 stud wall (shown on page 68), a wet wall has a sole plate and a top plate built from 2 by 6 or 2 by 8 lumber. Additionally, the 2 by 4 studs are set in pairs, with flat sides facing out. This creates maximum space inside the wall for large DWV pipes (which often have an outer diameter greater than 3½ inches) and for fittings, which are wider yet.

You can also "fur out" an existing wall to hide added pipes—attach new 2 by 4s to the old ones, then add new wall coverings. Similarly, a new branch drain that can't run below the floor may be hidden by a raised section of floor.

Roughing-in fixtures

Following are general notes on roughing-in new fixtures that require tying into your present DWV and supply systems, or extending them. Note that fixtures may be required to have air chambers—dead-end pipes that minimize noisy water hammer.

Sink. A sink is comparatively easy to install. Common installations are back-to-back (requires little pipe), within a vanity cabinet (hides pipe runs), and side-by-side. A sink can often be wet vented if it's within the critical distance; otherwise it's back vented. Adding a sink has little impact on the drain's present efficiency (a sink rates low in fixture units).

Supply pipes required: Hot and cold stubouts with shutoff valves; transition fittings, if necessary; flexible tubing above shutoff valves (see "Sink faucets," page 92).

Toilet. The single most troublesome fixture to install, a toilet requires its own vent (2-inch minimum) and at least a 3-inch drain. If it's on a branch drain, a toilet can't be upstream from a sink or shower.

The closet bend and toilet floor flange must be roughed-in first; the floor flange must be positioned at the level of the eventual finished floor.

Supply pipes required: Cold water stubout with shutoff valve; flexible tubing above valve (see "Installing a toilet," page 96).

Shower stall and bathtub. Like sinks, bathtubs and showers rate low in fixture units. They're often positioned on branch drains and are usually wet-vented or back-vented; both enter the stack at floor level or below because of the below-floor trap. A shower's faucet body and shower head assembly are installed while the wall is open; tubs and showers may require support framing.

Supply pipes required: Hot and cold supply lines and a pipe to the shower head (see "Bathtub & shower faucets," page 93).

ROUGHING-IN FIXTURES

Representative roughing-in measurements. Plumbing components illustrated are a sink, toilet, and tub/shower. Use the measurements to help you plan; check local codes and specific fixture dimensions for exact roughing-in requirements.

Electrical basics

What may appear to be a hopelessly tangled maze of wires running through the walls, under the floors, and above the ceiling of your home is actually a well-organized system composed of several electrical circuits. In your bathroom, those circuits supply power to light fixtures, switches, fans, heaters, and electrical outlets.

This section briefly explains your home's electrical system and offers general information about basic electrical improvements so you can better understand the processes involved in making changes to your electrical system. Techniques for installing light fixtures appear on pages 79–80.

Before you do any work yourself, talk with your building department's electrical inspector about local codes, the National Electrical Code (NEC), and your area's requirements for permits and inspections.

Understanding your system

Today most homes have what's called "three-wire" service. The utility company connects three wires to your service entrance panel. Each of two hot wires supplies electricity at approximately 120 volts. A third wire—a neutral one—is maintained at zero volts. (Don't be misled, though; all three wires are live.)

Three-wire service provides both 120-volt and 240-volt capabilities. One hot wire and the neutral wire combine to provide 120 volts—primarily for lights and plug-in outlets. Two hot wires combine to provide 240 volts, often used for electric heaters.

Service entrance panel. This panel is the control center for your electrical system. Inside the panel, you'll usually find the main disconnect (main fuses or circuit breaker), the fuses or circuit breakers protecting each individual circuit, and the grounding connection for the entire system.

Simple circuitry. The word "circuit" means the course electric current travels—in a continuous path from the service entrance panel or a separate subpanel, through one or more devices in your home that use electricity (such as light fixtures or appliances), and back to the panel. The devices are connected to the circuit by parallel wiring. With parallel wiring, a hot, a neutral, and a ground wire (for a 120-volt circuit) run continuously from one fixture box, outlet box, or switch box to another. Wires branch off to individual electrical devices from these continuous wires.

Modern circuit wires are housed together in a cable. Cable contains either one or two hot wires, a neutral wire, and a ground wire—each, except the ground wire, wrapped in its own insulation. (For the best connections, use only cable with all-copper wire.)

Individual wires are color-coded for easy identification. Hot wires are usually black or red, but may be any color other than white, gray, or green. Neutral wires are white or gray. Grounding wires are bare copper or green.

Occasionally, a white wire will be used as a hot wire; it should be taped or painted black near terminals and splices for easy identification.

Grounding. The NEC requires that every circuit have a ground wire. It provides an auxiliary path to ground for any short that might occur in a fixture or appliance. Also, according to the NEC, all bathroom outlets within 6 feet of a water source (sink or tub) must be protected with ground fault circuit interrupters (GFCI). These cut off power within ¹⁄₄₀ of a second if current begins leaking anywhere along the circuit. They may be special circuit breakers or built into an outlet.

Extending a circuit

To extend an existing electrical circuit, you'll need a knack for making wire connections, and the patience to route new cable.

Before you start work, remember: NEVER WORK ON ANY LIVE CIRCUIT, FIXTURE, PLUG-IN OUTLET, OR SWITCH. Your life may depend on it. Turn off the circuit breaker or remove the fuse and make sure no one but you can turn the electricity back on.

The steps in extending a circuit are outlined below. Generally, you route new cable from box to box; you install new boxes where you want to add outlets, fixtures, or switches; and then you tap into a power source —an existing outlet, switch, or fixture box.

To install a new circuit, the work is much the same, except that you connect into a service panel or subpanel instead of into an existing outlet, switch, or fixture box.

Select a power source. A circuit can be tapped for power at almost any accessible outlet, switch, or fixture box of the appropriate voltage. (The exceptions are a switch box without a neutral wire and a fixture box at the end of a circuit.) The box you tap into must be large enough to hold new wires in addition to exist-

ROUTING CABLE TO OUTLETS

Original box · Cut wall covering · Wall studs · Drill ¾" holes, or notch studs · Box hole · Box hole · Cable ing wires, and must have knockout holes through which you can run the new cable.

Select and locate new boxes. If wall or ceiling coverings have not yet been installed, choose an outlet or switch box you nail to studs or joists. If wall or ceiling coverings are already in place, choose cut-in boxes that don't have to be secured to studs or joists. Requirements regarding boxes for mounting ceiling fixtures are outlined on pages 79–80.

Unless codes prohibit the use of plastic, you can use either plastic or metal boxes. Metal boxes, though sturdier, must be grounded; plastic boxes cost less and need not be grounded, though the circuit must have a ground wire.

To find a suitable box location, first turn off power to all circuits that may be behind the wall or ceiling. Drill a small test hole and probe through it with a length of stiff insulated wire until you find an empty space.

Unless old boxes are at different levels, place new outlet boxes 12 to 18 inches above the floor, switch boxes or outlet boxes above a counter 44 inches above the floor. Never place boxes near a tub or shower.

If you're adding a new wall, you may be required by code to add an outlet every 12 feet, or one per wall regardless of the wall's length.

When you've determined the correct locations, trace the outline of each box on the wall or ceiling (omit protruding brackets). Then cut along the outlines.

Route and connect new cable. After the box holes are cut, run cable from the power source to each new box location. (Wait until you have the new boxes wired and the outlets, switches, and fixtures connected before you make the actual hookup to the source.)

Where you have access from an unfinished basement, an unfloored attic, or a garage adjacent to the bathroom, it's easy to run cable either attached to the joists or studs

or through holes drilled in them.

Where walls and ceilings are covered on both sides, you'll have to fish cable through them, using electrician's fish tape (illustrated below) or a length of stiff wire with one end bent into a blunt, tight hook.

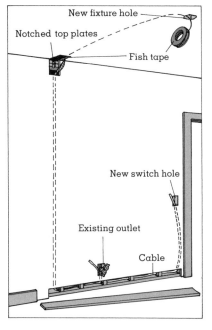

New fixture hole
Notched top plates
Fish tape
New switch hole
Existing outlet
Cable

After routing new cable, secure the cable to each new box. Slip a cable connector onto the end of the cable and insert the cable and connector into a knockout in the box. Fasten the connector to the box, leaving 6 to 8 inches of cable sticking out for wiring connections. Then mount the box to the ceiling or wall and wire as described below.

Wire plug-in outlets. An outlet must have the same amperage and voltage rating as the circuit. If you have aluminum wiring, be sure to use the correct outlet; it will be identified by the letters CO-ALR. An outlet marked CU-AL should be used only with copper wire. If installing a GFCI outlet, follow the manufacturer's directions.

If you're adding a grounded outlet to a circuit that does not contain a grounding wire, you'll have to run a separate grounding wire from the new outlet to a nearby cold water pipe. (One method is shown on page 79; for help, consult an electrician.)

The drawing below shows how to wire a plug-in bathroom outlet with both halves live. The box is assumed to be metal; if you use a plastic box, there's no need to ground the box, but you'll have to attach a grounding wire to each outlet. Simply loop the end of the wire under the grounding screw. Connect the hot wire to the brass screw of the outlet, the neutral wire to the silver screw, and the ground wire to the green screw.

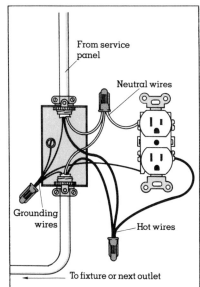

From service panel
Neutral wires
Grounding wires
Hot wires
To fixture or next outlet

Wire single-pole switches. One single-pole switch may control one or more light fixtures, a heater, a ventilating fan, or several outlets.

Like outlets, the switch must have the same amperage and voltage rating as the circuit. If you have aluminum wiring, be sure to use a switch marked with the letters CO-ALR.

When wiring switches, remember that they are installed only on hot wires. The switches illustrated on page 78 have no grounding wires because the toggles on most home switches are made of shockproof plastic. If switches are housed in plastic boxes, the boxes do not need to be grounded. When installing a plastic switch box at the end of a circuit, secure the end of the grounding wire between the switch bracket and the mounting screw. If the switch is in the middle of a circuit,

■ Electrical basics

WIRING SINGLE-POLE SWITCHES

IF POWER ENTERS SWITCH BOX

IF POWER ENTERS FIXTURE BOX

Grounding wires

Neutral wires

Hot wires

From service panel

3-conductor cable

Hot wires

Grounding wires

Neutral wires

From service panel

To next fixture

WIRING A GFCI

Incoming wires

TEST RESET

Outgoing wires

Grounding wires

---

just twist the ends of the ground wires together and cover them with a wirenut.

Single-pole switches have two screw terminals of the same color (usually brass) for wire connections, and a definite right-side up. You should be able to read the words ON and OFF embossed on the toggle. It makes no difference which hot wire goes to which terminal. The cable can be run first either to the fixture or to the switch—whichever is the more convenient route.

Wire a GFCI. The protection value of an outlet-style GFCI has made it standard in new construction. Depending on the model, the GFCI may also protect all other devices downstream (away from the source) from it, but it will not protect any outlets upstream (toward the source).

A GFCI receptacle is wired like an ordinary outlet, except that you must connect incoming hot and neutral wires to the "line," or input, terminals, and any outgoing wires to the "load" side. If your model in-

cludes a built-in grounding jumper, attach it to the other ground wires in the box with a wirenut, as shown above.

Wire into the power source. After you've wired new outlets and switches, you're ready to make the final connections. Connections to three types of boxes used as power sources are illustrated below. Wirenuts join and protect the stripped ends of spliced wires within the boxes.

WIRING INTO A POWER SOURCE

FIXTURE BOX AS POWER SOURCE

From service panel

Grounding wires

To existing switch

Neutral wires

Hot wires (white wire should be painted black near splice)

To new boxes

OUTLET BOX AS POWER SOURCE

From service panel

Hot wires

Grounding wires

Neutral wires

To new boxes

SWITCH BOX AS POWER SOURCE

From service panel

Hot wires

Grounding wires

To new boxes

Neutral wires

To existing light

Installing light fixtures

Most bathrooms need both task lighting for specific areas and general lighting. For a discussion of lighting choices, see page 50.

Basically, to replace an existing light fixture with one of the same type, you disconnect the wires of the old fixture and hook up new wires. Adding a new fixture where there was none before is more complicated. You must first run new cable from a power source and install a fixture box and a switch.

Below are instructions for installing two types of light fixtures—surface-mounted and recessed.

Surface-mounted fixtures. Attach these fixtures directly to a wall or ceiling fixture box, or suspend ceiling fixtures from a fixture box by chains or cord. New fixtures usually come with their own mounting hardware, adaptable to any fixture box.

Sometimes, though, the weight of the new fixture or the wiring necessary for proper grounding requires that you replace the box before installing the fixture.

Electrical code requirements sometimes allow ceiling fixtures weighing less than 24 ounces to be mounted on cut-in boxes held in position by the ceiling material. For a more secure installation and for heavier fixtures, you must fasten the box to a framing member or a special bracket secured to the joists. Do not attach fixtures heavier than 6 pounds to the box with screws through the fixture's metal canopy; use the hardware supplied by the manufacturer or check with your electrical inspector.

The NEC requires that all incandescent and fluorescent fixtures with exposed metal parts be grounded. If the fixture box is not grounded (as is the case when your present house wiring includes no grounding wire), you'll have to extend a grounding wire from the box to the nearest cold water pipe, as shown above right. The pipe must be metal, unbroken by plastic fittings or runs along its length. Bypass a problem spot or your water meter with a "jumper" wire. It's a good idea to ask a licensed electrician or building inspector to check your work.

Grounding strap
#12 copper wire
Cold water pipe

A cord or chain-hung fixture must also have a grounding wire run from the socket to the box. Most new fixtures are prewired with a grounding wire.

Then install your new surface-mounted fixture as described below.

■ **To replace an existing fixture with a new one,** first turn off the circuit. Remove the shade, if any, from the

SURFACE-MOUNTED FIXTURES

Hot wires
Junction box
FLUORESCENT PANEL
Neutral wires
CEILING-MOUNTED FIXTURE
Grounding jumper
Neutral wires
Hanger bar
Hot wires
Mounting screw
Diffusing panel
Canopy
Fluorescent tube holders
Cap nuts
WALL-MOUNTED FIXTURE
Grounding wire
Pivot bar
Hot wires
Neutral wires
Decorative ball globe

■ Electrical basics

old fixture. Unscrew the canopy from the fixture box, and detach the mounting bar if there is one. Now make a sketch of how the wires are connected. If the wires are spliced with wirenuts, unscrew them and untwist the wires. If the wires are spliced and wrapped with electrician's tape, simply unwind the tape and untwist the wires.

Match the wires of the new fixture to the old wires shown in your sketch, and splice with wirenuts. Secure the new fixtures as recommended by the manufacturer, using any new hardware included.

■ **To install a fixture in a new location,** you must route a new cable from a power source and install new fixture and switch boxes. New cable routed to the fixture box should include a grounding wire to be attached to the box's grounding screw. If more than one cable enters the box (for example, a separate cable from the switch box), you'll need to attach the end of a short length of bare 12-gauge wire (a "jumper") to the grounding screw, and use a wirenut to splice the other end to the ends of the grounding wires in the cables.

RECESSED DOWNLIGHTS

Once you've routed the new cable and grounded the fixture box, wire in the new fixture—black wire to black, white to white; cap all splices with wirenuts. Then mount the fixture with hardware supplied by the manufacturer.

Recessed ceiling fixtures. Common recessed fixtures include incandescent circular or square downlights and larger fluorescent ceiling, or "troffer," panels. You'll need to cut a hole in the ceiling between the joists, or remove tiles or panels from a suspended ceiling, to install either type. Larger troffer panels may also require 2 by 4 blocking between joists for support.

Recessed fixtures need several inches of clearance above the finished ceiling. They're most easily installed below an unfinished attic or crawlspace. Because of the heat generated by many downlights, you must either buy a special zero-clearance model (type ICT), or plan to remove insulation within 3 inches of the fixture and make sure that no other combustible materials come within ½ inch.

Most low-voltage downlights come with an integral transformer

attached to the frame; if yours doesn't, you'll first need to mount an external transformer nearby and then route wire to the fixture.

If there's no crawlspace above the ceiling, find the joists (see page 68); don't forget to shut off power to any circuits that might be wired behind the ceiling before drilling exploratory holes.

Once you've determined the proper location for the fixture housing, trace its outline on the ceiling with a pencil; use a keyhole saw or saber saw to cut the hole. Brace a plaster ceiling as you cut.

If you don't have access from above, look for a remodeling fixture. The version shown above, at left, slips through the ceiling hole and clips onto the edge of the ceiling. The fixture trim then snaps onto the housing from below. (Hook up the wires to the circuit before securing the fixture and trim.)

So-called new work or rough-in downlights with adjustable hanger bars, such as the model shown above, at right, are easy to install from above. Simply nail the ends of the bars to joists on either side; then clip the trim or baffle into place from below.

CLIMATE CONTROL: HEATING & VENTILATION

Certain elements of your bathroom's climate—steam, excess heat, early morning chill—can be annoying and unpleasant. When you remodel, consider adding an exhaust fan to freshen the air and draw out destructive moisture, and a heater to warm you on cool days. Installing these climate controllers is within the grasp of most do-it-yourselfers. For more details on both fans and heaters, see page 61.

Heating the bathroom

Because electric heaters are easy to install and clean to operate, they're the most popular choice for heating bathrooms. In addition to the standard wall and ceiling-mounted units, you'll find heaters combined with exhaust fans, lights, or both. Many units require a dedicated 120 or 240-volt circuit, so shop carefully.

Gas heaters that can be recessed into a wall between two studs are available in a variety of styles and sizes. Regardless of how they heat, all gas models require a gas supply line and must be vented to the outside.

Choose the location of your heater carefully. Of course, you'll want to place it where someone getting out of the tub or shower will benefit from it (this is particularly true of radiant heaters, which heat objects directly). But don't locate the heater where someone will bump against its hot surfaces, or where it might char or ignite curtains or towels.

Since gas heaters require a vent to the outside, you'll probably want to place the heater on an outside wall. Otherwise, you'll have to run the vent through the attic or crawlspace and out through the roof. It's best to have a professional run gas lines; in any case, you must have the work tested and inspected before the gas is turned on.

Ventilating the bathroom

You can buy fans to mount in the wall or in the ceiling. Some models are combined with a light or a heater; some have both.

It's important that your exhaust fan have adequate capacity. The Home Ventilating Institute (HVI) rec-
ommends that the fan be capable of exchanging the air at least eight times every hour. To determine the required fan capacity in cubic feet per minute (CFM) for a bathroom with an 8-foot ceiling, multiply the room's length and width in feet by 1.1.

For example, if your bathroom is 6 by 9 feet, you would calculate the required fan capacity as follows:

$$6 \times 9 \times 1.1 = 59.4 \text{ CFM}$$

Rounding off, you would need fan capacity of at least 60 CFM. If your fan must exhaust through a long duct or several elbows, you'll need greater capacity to overcome the increased resistance. Follow the dealer's or manufacturer's recommendations.

Ideally, your fan should be mounted as close to the shower or tub as possible. It should also be as far away as possible from the source of replacement air (the door, for instance). In addition, you'll want the exhaust duct to be as short and straight as possible. If you have trouble finding a location that meets all three requirements, you may want to consult a professional.

THREE WAYS TO DUCT EXHAUST FANS

Ceiling fan ventilates through duct either to roof cap on roof or to grill in soffit under the eave.

Wall fan on inside wall also ventilates through duct to cap on roof or to grill in soffit under the eave.

Wall fan on outside wall, installed between wall studs, ventilates through wall directly to outside.

Sinks

Replacing the bathroom sink (also known as a lavatory or basin) is one of the quickest ways to give your bathroom a new look without getting involved in a complex and expensive remodeling project.

This section will show you how to remove and install the four basic types of sinks: integral sink and countertop, pedestal, wall-hung, and deck-mount. For more information on the many sink models and materials, see page 56.

If you're planning to add a sink or to move one, you may want to consult a professional about extending supply, drain, and vent lines (see pages 72–75). But to replace a sink, extensive experience with plumbing isn't a requirement.

REMOVING A SINK

Unless you're installing a new floor covering, be sure to protect the bathroom floor with a piece of cardboard or plywood before you begin work. You'll also want a bucket and a supply of rags or sponges nearby to soak up excess water.

To loosen corroded plumbing connections, douse them with penetrating oil an hour before you start.

Disconnecting the plumbing

If the sink faucet is mounted on the countertop and you don't plan to replace the faucet, it isn't necessary to disconnect the water supply lines. If the faucet is connected to the sink, you do need to disconnect the supply lines.

Be sure to turn off the water at the sink shutoff valves or at the main valve before doing any work. Disconnect the supply lines at the shutoff valves, placing a bucket underneath them to catch any water, and open the faucets so the lines can drain.

If your sink isn't equipped with shutoff valves, disconnect the supply lines at the faucet inlet shanks, as explained on page 92—and plan to add shutoff valves before you connect the plumbing to the new sink (or

have a professional plumber do the work for you).

Next, move the bucket underneath the trap. If the trap has a cleanout plug, remove it to drain the water, then loosen the slip nuts and remove the trap. If there is no cleanout plug, remove the trap and dump the water into the bucket.

Disconnect the pop-up drain assembly by loosening the clevis screw and then removing the spring clip that connects the stopper and pivot rod to the pop-up rod on the faucet (see "Removing a sink faucet," page 92).

The tailpiece, drain body, and sink flange, as well as the faucet, will now come out with the sink. If you plan to reuse the old faucet, remove it carefully from the sink and set aside.

Removing an integral sink & countertop

An integral sink is molded as part of the countertop, and the unit is secured to the top of a vanity cabinet. Look underneath for any metal clips or wooden braces securing the unit, and remove them. Then lift off the whole unit.

If you can't remove the unit easily, insert the end of a small prybar in the joint between the countertop and vanity cabinet at a back corner. Carefully lift up the prybar to break the sealing material between the countertop and the vanity. If the joint is too narrow to accept the end of a prybar, cut through the sealing ma-

terial with a hot putty knife, then pry or lift up the countertop.

Removing a pedestal sink

Most pedestal sinks are made of two pieces—the sink and the pedestal or base. Look in the opening at the rear of the pedestal to locate a nut or bolt holding the sink down. If you find one, remove it. Lift off the sink and set it aside.

The pedestal is usually bolted to the floor. You may find the bolts on the base, or on the inside of the pedestal (see illustration above right). Undo the bolts and remove the pedestal. If you can't move it after removing the bolts, rock it back and forth, and then lift it out. If the pedestal is recessed into a ceramic tile floor, you may have to remove the surrounding floor tiles with a cold chisel and soft-headed steel hammer. Rock the pedestal back and forth to break any remaining seal with the floor. Lift the pedestal up and set it aside.

Hold-down bolt

Base sealed to tile floor

Removing a wall-hung sink

To remove a wall-hung sink, first unscrew the legs, if any, that support the front of the sink. Check underneath for any bolts securing the sink to the mounting bracket on the wall (see illustration below), and remove them. Then lift the sink straight up and off the mounting bracket.

Mounting slots

Mounting bracket

Water supply lines

Drain stubout

Shutoff valves

Removing a deck-mount sink

There are three basic types of deck-mount sinks used in vanity countertops: self-rimming or rimless sinks, flush-mount sinks, and unrimmed or recessed sinks. All may be secured to the countertop with lugs or clamps that must be unscrewed before you remove the sink.

Self-rimming or rimless sinks. These have a molded flange that sits on the countertop. Once you have removed any lugs or clamps from underneath, just use a hot putty knife or other knife to cut through the

sealing material between sink and countertop; then pry up the sink to break the seal and lift it out.

Countertop

Molded flange

Putty or caulking

Putty knife

Flush-mount sinks. Have a helper support the sink while you undo the lugs or clamps that secure the sink's metal rim to the countertop. (If you're working alone, you can support the sink with a 2 by 4 and a wood block tied together through the drain; see illustration below.) After you remove the lugs or clamps, cut through the sealing material between the rim and the countertop with a hot putty knife or other knife. Pry up the rim to free the sink; then lift straight up.

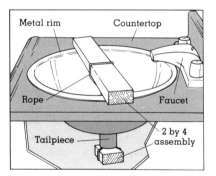

Metal rim

Countertop

Rope

Faucet

Tailpiece

2 by 4 assembly

Unrimmed or recessed sinks. An unrimmed or recessed sink is secured to the underside of the countertop. The easiest way to remove the sink is to first take off the countertop. Check underneath for any brackets and remove them. Then insert a prybar into the joint between the countertop and the vanity cabinet near a rear corner, and pry up. Turn the countertop bottom side up and rest it on a padded surface. Undo the lugs or clamps securing the sink, and lift it off the countertop.

Sink

Putty or caulking

Clamps

Underside of countertop

When the countertop is tiled, the flange usually rests on top of the plywood base for the tile. Look underneath; if you don't see any clips or brackets, you'll have to remove the tile surrounding the edge of the sink. With a soft-headed steel hammer and cold chisel, remove enough tile so that you can lift the sink from the countertop. (Be sure to protect your eyes with goggles.) If you can't find matching replacement tile and need to reuse the old tiles, remove them carefully to avoid breaking them.

Plywood backing

Flange

Cold chisel

Quarter-round tiles

INSTALLING A SINK

If you're installing a sink at a new location instead of replacing an existing one, you'll need to extend the supply, drain, and vent pipes (see pages 72–75).

If you'd like your sink to be higher than standard, you can raise the vanity of an integral or deck-mount sink by building a base under it. If you're installing a wall-hung sink, simply mount the bracket higher. You can't adjust the height of a pedestal sink, but you may be able to buy a taller model.

(Continued on next page)

■Sinks

MOUNTING A DUAL-HANDLE FAUCET

Apply putty to bottom edge of the faucet if there is no rubber gasket to seal it to sink's surface.

Set the faucet in place, insert the inlet shanks through the sink holes, and press down. Add washers and locknuts.

Attach flexible supply lines to the faucet's inlet shanks, using pipe joint compound and coupling nuts.

Before installing the sink, you'll need to install the faucet and the sink flange.

Installing the faucet & sink flange

Whether the faucet is to be mounted on the countertop or on the sink itself, you'll find it easier to install the faucet before you set the sink in place. The main steps are illustrated above. First make sure that the mounting surface is clean. If your faucet came with a rubber gasket, place it on the bottom of the faucet. For a faucet without a gasket, put a bead of plumber's putty around the bottom edge of the faucet.

Set the faucet in position, and press it down onto the sink or countertop surface. Assemble the washers and locknuts on the inlet shanks, and then tighten the nuts. Remove excess putty from around the faucet. Connect the supply lines to the inlet shanks and tighten the coupling nuts. For more information on installing faucets, see pages 92–93.

Now install the sink flange and drain. To attach the flange, run a bead of plumber's putty around the drain hole of the sink. Press the flange into the puttied hole. Put the locknut, metal washer, and flat rubber washer on the drain body in that order. Insert the threaded end of the drain body into the bottom of the sink and screw it onto the flange. Then tighten the locknut until it is snug (do not overtighten).

Installing an integral sink & countertop

Cover the top edges of the vanity cabinet with a sealant recommended by the manufacturer. Place the countertop unit on the cabinet flush with the back edge. Make sure the overhang—if any—is equal on the left and right. Press along the countertop edges to complete the seal, and check around the perimeter, removing any excess sealant.

If your unit came with mounting brackets, use them to secure the countertop to the vanity. Seal the joint between the countertop and the wall with caulking compound.

Installing a pedestal sink

Position a *dual-handle faucet* as shown above. Assemble the washers and locknuts on the inlet shanks; then tighten the nuts. Remove excess putty from around the faucet. Connect the supply lines to the inlet shanks.

Most *single-lever faucets* include short supply tubes; simply tighten the locknuts on the threaded stubs from below. For details, see pages 92–93.

Position the sink on top of the pedestal and, if required by the manufacturer, bolt the two together as directed.

Installing a wall-hung sink

For new installations, you'll need to remove the wall coverings and wallboard. Notch two studs directly behind the sink's proposed location, and nail or screw a 1 by 6 or 1 by 8 mounting board flush to the stud fronts; then re-cover the wall.

Before you attach the mounting bracket to the wall mounting board, check to see that it fits the sink. Refer to the manufacturer's instructions to properly position the bracket. Generally, you center the bracket over the drainpipe, then level it at the desired height from the floor. Fasten the bracket to the mounting board with woodscrews, making sure that it's level. Then carefully lower the sink onto the mounting bracket.

Because the mounting bracket can bend or break under the weight of a large wall-hung sink, the manufacturer may recommend that adjustable legs be inserted into the holes under the front corners of the sink. Screw the legs down until the sink is level; be sure to keep the legs plumb.

Seal the joint between the back of the sink and the wall with caulking compound.

Installing a deck-mount sink

If your countertop doesn't have a hole for the sink, you'll need to cut one. For a self-rimming or an unrimmed sink, mark the hole, using the templates supplied with the sink. If you didn't receive a template, cut one from paper; it should fit loosely around the outside of the sink bowl where the bowl meets the flange.

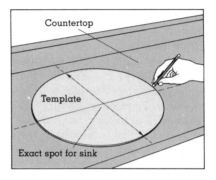

For a flush-mount sink, trace the bottom edge of the sink's metal framing rim directly onto the spot where the sink will sit in the countertop.

After you mark the location of the cutout, drill a starting hole, then use a saber saw to cut the opening.

Install your deck-mount sink as described below.

Self-rimming or rimless sinks.

First, run a bead of caulking compound or plumber's putty around the underside of the flange. Set the sink on the countertop and press it down until the putty oozes out. Install any lugs or clamps according to the manufacturer's instructions. Remove excess putty.

Flush-mount sinks.

Apply a bead of caulking compound or plumber's putty around the sink lip. Fasten the metal framing rim around the lip, following the manufacturer's directions. Next, apply a bead of caulking compound or plumber's putty around the top edge of the countertop sink opening, and set the sink and rim in place. Secure the sink and rim to the underside of the countertop with the lugs or clamps provided. Wipe off excess putty.

Unrimmed or recessed sinks.

Turn the countertop upside down and apply plumber's putty or caulking compound on the underside, around the edge of the sink opening. Set the sink in place, checking from the other side to be sure it is centered in the opening. Anchor the sink as recommended by the manufacturer. If you're finishing the countertop with ceramic tile, you can mount the sink atop the plywood base and then edge it with tile trim.

Connecting the plumbing

Once the sink is installed, connect the water supply lines to the shutoff valves and tighten the coupling nuts. Then connect the trap to the drainpipe and tailpiece, and tighten the slip nuts (see drawing, page 82). Connect the pop-up stopper to the faucet pop-up rod (see page 93). Turn on the water at the shutoff valves or main shutoff; check for leaks.

Bathtubs

Installing or replacing a bathtub can be a complicated job—one that takes careful planning. But a gleaming new tub in your bathroom is well worth the effort.

Your tub choices range from porcelain-enameled cast iron or steel to lightweight fiberglass-reinforced plastic. The waterproof wall covering around a tub (called a surround) can be tile or panels of fiberglass-reinforced plastic or coated hardboard.

If you're building a new bathroom, you can create an entire bath area with a tub and surround manufactured as a one-piece unit. These units are not recommended for remodeling projects, though, since they are usually too large to fit through a door and must be moved in before the bathroom walls are framed. For remodeling, your best choice is a tub with separate wall panels or tiles.

Before you install a tub in a new location, check local building codes for support requirements; a bathtub filled with water is extremely heavy and needs plenty of support. You should also check the plumbing code requirements for extending the water supply and drain-waste and vent systems (see page 73). Consider getting professional help to build the framing and to rough-in plumbing for a new installation.

In this section, you'll find general directions for removing and installing bathtubs and wall coverings. For detailed product information, see page 57.

REMOVING A BATHTUB

There are three main steps to this job: disconnecting the appropriate plumbing, removing part or all of the wall covering, and removing the tub itself.

Disconnecting the plumbing

Generally it's not necessary to turn off the water unless you're replacing the faucet body. If you do need to turn off the water, do so at the fixture shutoff valves (if you can reach them through an access door in an adjoining room or hallway) or at the main shutoff valve. Open the faucets to drain the pipes.

Next, remove any fittings—spout, faucet parts, shower head, and diverter handle—that will be in the way. To remove the tub, you'll also have to unscrew and remove the overflow cover and drain lever. By pulling out this fitting, you'll also remove the bathtub drain assembly if it's a trip-lever type.

If you have a pop-up stopper, pull it out with the rocker linkage after removing the overflow cover (see illustration below).

If there's an access door or access from the basement or crawlspace, use a pipe wrench to loosen the coupling nuts from behind the tub; disconnect the trap and waste tee, as shown below, at right. If you can't get access to the drain plumbing, you can work from inside the tub; disconnect the tub from the overflow pipe and drainpipe by unscrewing the overflow retainer flange and drain flange.

Removing the wall covering

Most bathtubs are recessed; that is, they are surrounded by walls on three sides. Depending on whether you want to replace the tub only, or the tub and the wall covering, you'll need to remove all or part of the surrounding tiles or panels. Before doing this, remove any fittings, such as the shower head, that are in the way (if you haven't yet done so).

Tile. If there are wall or floor tiles along the edge of the tub, free the tub by chipping out approximately 4 inches to the nearest grout joint (see illustration above right). On the walls, remove the plaster or gypsum wallboard backing at the same time, so that several inches of the wall studs are exposed. Use a cold chisel and soft-headed steel hammer to remove the tile, and be sure to protect your eyes from fragments by wearing goggles.

If you're removing a recessed tub, you must also remove enough tile (and other obstructions) from the floor and walls to be able to slide the tub out of its recess.

Fiberglass panels. Take out the wall panels by first removing the

DISCONNECTING THE PLUMBING

Remove faucet and diverter parts and spout, leaving stubout for spout and faucet and diverter stems.

Unscrew overflow cover, then pull out drain assembly—first the overflow cover and lift linkage, then the pop-up stopper.

Loosen slip nuts and remove trap from underneath tub; then disconnect and remove overflow pipe.

REMOVING WALL COVERINGS

For tile walls, chip away a 4-inch strip of tile and backing from walls; remove an equivalent strip from a tile floor.

For fiberglass panels, pry panel flange and pull panel and any backing off the wall studs.

gypsum wallboard or molding from the panel flanges. With a prybar, pry the panels, along with any backing, off the studs. Once the end panels are removed, you can take out the back panel, leaving the exposed wall studs (see illustration above).

Removing the tub

The tub's bulk will make this one of your biggest jobs. To get the tub out, you may first have to remove the bathroom door or even cut a hole in the wall opposite the tub plumbing. Plan exactly how you'll route the tub through and out of the house. You'll need helpers to move it, especially if it's a heavy steel or cast-iron fixture.

Steel or cast-iron tubs. Locate and remove from the wall studs any nails or screws at the top of the tub's flange (lip) that may be holding the tub in place. With at least one helper (probably three for a cast-iron tub), lift up the tub with a prybar and slide two or three soaped wooden runners under it (see illustration at right). Then slide the tub out of the recess.

Fiberglass tubs. To remove a fiberglass or plastic tub, pull out all nails or screws driven into the wall studs through the flange. Reach between the studs and grasp the tub under the flange (see illustration far right); with the aid of a helper, if necessary, pull the tub up off its supports and out of the recess.

INSTALLING A BATHTUB

If you're replacing an old tub with a new one, carefully inspect the subfloor where the tub will be installed for level and for moisture damage, and make any necessary repairs or adjustments.

If you're installing a tub in a new location, you'll do the framing and rough-in the plumbing first (see "Structural basics," pages 67–70, and "Plumbing basics," pages 72–75).

Setting, leveling & securing the tub

This is the most crucial part of the installation process. A tub must be correctly supported and carefully secured in a level position so that it will drain properly and all plumbing connections can be made easily.

MOVING THE TUB

To move a steel or cast-iron tub, slide it across floor on soaped wooden runners. You'll need several helpers .

To move a fiberglass tub, grasp it under back of the flange and lift it up and out. A helper will make the job easier.

Steel or cast-iron tubs. These heavy tubs require either vertical or horizontal wood supports (see "Four ways to support a tub" on the following page). Horizontal supports are 1 by 4s or 2 by 4s, nailed across the wall studs so that the tub's flange rests on them. Vertical supports are 2 by 4s nailed to each stud. Position the supports so that the tub will be level both from end to end and from back to front.

If your tub is steel, you can attach prefabricated metal hangers to the studs with woodscrews to support the tub.

When you've attached the appropriate supports, slide your new tub along soaped wooden runners into position (see illustration below). With the aid of several helpers, lift it so that the flanges rest on the supports. Check the tub at both ends to see that it's level. If not, insert shims between the tub and wall supports or floor to level it. To prevent the tub from slipping, anchor it by driving nails or screws into the studs tight against the top of the flange.

Fiberglass tubs. If necessary, temporarily remove any protruding stubouts. Then, with a helper, set the tub on wood supports, tight against the rear studs.

Once the tub is in position, check on top for level at both ends, shimming where needed, as for steel and cast-iron models. Drill holes in the tub flange and carefully nail or screw through the holes into the studs.

(Continued on next page)

■Bathtubs

Connecting the plumbing

Once the tub is secured in position, reconnect the overflow pipe, trap, and drain assembly. (Be careful not to overtighten the nuts and crack the tub's surface.) Make sure you connect the overflow pipe with the tub drainpipe on the side of the trap nearest the bathtub, not on the far side.

If you're reusing existing wall coverings, install the faucet and spout, plus a diverter and shower head as required. If you plan on a new wall covering (see below), connect the fittings afterwards.

Installing the wall covering

Before patching or re-covering the walls with either tile or panels, turn on the water and check the drain and supply pipes for leaks.

If you plan to install a tiled wall, see pages 103–105. If you're starting from scratch, it's best to use cement backer board as a base.

To install new fiberglass panels, cover any exposed studs with gypsum wallboard (cut to accommodate the plumbing) or cement backer board. Then follow the procedure below.

Drill pipe holes. To install a panel over pipe stubouts and faucet and

FOUR WAYS TO SUPPORT A TUB

Support a new tub in one of these ways: nail or screw fiberglass tub flange to studs (A); support steel tub with metal hangers (B); nail vertical 2 by 4s to studs to support metal tubs (C); nail horizontal 2 by 4s to support metal tubs (D).

diverter stems, you'll need to mark and drill it accurately (see illustration below). Measure and mark the panel by holding it up against the stubouts and stems. Drill slightly oversized holes in the panel with a spade bit, backing the panel with a wood plank to prevent splintering.

Set panels. Apply mastic in S-patterns to the backs of the panels (see illustration below), and press

the panels in place around the top of the tub, according to manufacturer's directions. If panels are to be nailed or screwed to the studs, predrill all nail holes.

Finish and seal panels. Seal all gaps between the wall covering and the stubouts and stems with silicone caulk. Finally, attach the faucet and diverter parts, spout, and shower head.

INSTALLING PANELS AROUND A TUB

After carefully marking one panel to fit over the stubouts and faucet and diverter stems, drill holes in it with a spade bit.

Apply mastic to panel in S-patterns while panel rests on planks laid across a pair of sawhorses.

Press panel into place on the wall, fitting it over stubouts and faucet and diverter stems.

Showers

From elegant ceramic tile to easy-to-install fiberglass or plastic panels, your choices are many when it comes to replacing or adding a shower in your home. And if you're installing a completely new bathroom, you can also choose a molded one-piece shower enclosure. (These are not recommended for remodeling projects because they won't fit through most bathroom doors.)

In this section you'll find instructions for removing all types of showers (including the older metal units) and for installing tile and fiberglass-reinforced or plastic-paneled showers. For more details on the various models, see page 58.

REMOVING A SHOWER

Most showers consist of three walls with waterproof wall covering, such as tile or panels, and a separate base, mounted in a wood frame. Removing a shower is a three-step procedure: disconnecting the plumbing, removing the wall covering, and removing the base. If the shower is a one-piece unit, you'll also have to cut a hole in a wall to get it out, unless you cut the unit into pieces.

If you're changing the location of a shower or permanently removing it, you'll probably want to dismantle the wood frame and remove the plumbing.

Disconnecting the plumbing

First remove the shower door or the rod and curtain. Then turn off the water supply at the fixture shutoff valves (sometimes accessible through an access door in an adjoining hallway or closet) or at the main shutoff valve. Open the faucets to drain the pipes. Then sponge the shower base dry.

Remove the faucet handles and other trim parts, leaving the faucet stems. Then remove the shower head with a pipe wrench tape-wrapped to avoid scarring the fixture (see illustration above).

DISCONNECTING SHOWER PLUMBING

Use pipe wrench wrapped with tape to remove shower head. (Faucet parts have already been removed.)

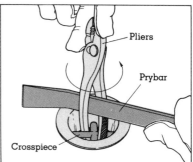

After removing drain cover, use pliers and prybar to unscrew crosspiece from drain.

Unscrew and pry up the drain cover, and with a pair of pliers and a small prybar, unscrew the crosspiece (see illustration). If you're removing a one-piece shower enclosure, you'll also have to disconnect the drainpipe and remove protruding faucet stems and fittings that might get in the way when you tip the unit to pull it out. Finally, plug the drain opening with a rag to prevent debris from falling into it.

Removing the wall covering

The removal procedure you'll follow depends on whether you have a tiled shower, walls covered with fiberglass panels, or an older metal shower.

After you've removed the wall covering, check for moisture damage to the frame and to any soundproofing insulation secured across the inside of the frame. Repair or replace if necessary.

Tile. Ceramic tile is the most difficult wall covering to remove. If the existing tile is clean, smooth, and securely attached, you can avoid removing it by using it as a backing for a new tile surface. If you must remove it, proceed with caution and wear goggles while you work.

(Continued on next page)

REMOVING SHOWER WALLS

For tile walls, chip and pry off tile and wallboard backing to expose entire frame of shower.

For panel walls, remove any wallboard or molding covering panel flanges; then pry panels off frame.

■Showers

To remove tile set in mortar, you must break up the tile, mortar, and any backing with a sledge hammer. Remove it down to the wood frame, being careful not to hit and damage the wall studs. You may want to hire a tile professional for this part of the project.

If the tile is set on wallboard with adhesive, use a cold chisel and soft-headed steel hammer to chip away small sections of tile and backing. Then insert a prybar and pry off large sections of tile and backing until the entire frame is exposed (see illustration, page 89).

Fiberglass panels. First remove any molding or wallboard covering the panel flanges. Then pry panels, along with any backing and nails, off the wood frame (see illustration, page 89). If you're removing a one-piece enclosure, you may have to cut it apart to get it out (a saber saw with a plastic-cutting blade will do the job quickly).

Metal showers. Remove metal shower walls by unscrewing them at the edges and then at the front and back corners. These screws hold the shower walls to each other and sometimes to a wood frame. If the screws are rusted, cut the screw heads off with a hacksaw or cold chisel; then separate the walls with a hard pull.

Removing the base

The base may be tile on a mortar bed, or it may be a fiberglass unit. Tile is difficult to remove because it's laid in mortar; fiberglass bases are simply pried out.

After you've removed the base, inspect the subfloor and framing for moisture damage, and repair where necessary.

Tile on mortar. As with tile walls, check first to see if you can lay the new tile over the old. If not, use a sledge hammer to break up and remove all tile and mortar down to the subfloor. You may be able to pry up one side of the base and slip a

wedge under it to make it easier to break up. Wear goggles to protect your eyes from tile or mortar fragments.

Fiberglass. Remove all nails or screws from the flange around the top of the base. Pry the base off the floor with a prybar; lift it out.

Nails removed from flange

Prybar

INSTALLING A SHOWER

When you replace an old shower, the plumbing—and probably the wood frame—will already be in place.

If you're putting a shower in a new location, you must first frame the shower walls using 2 by 4s (see "Structural basics," pages 67–70). Make accurate measurements (follow the manufacturer's directions to frame a fiberglass shower); keep framing square and plumb.

Once the frame is complete, you'll also need to rough-in supply and drain lines, and install the faucet and pipe for the shower head (see pages 72–75 and 94).

Now you're ready to install the shower—first the base, then the walls.

Installing the base

Installing a watertight tiled base on a mortar bed is a highly complicated project not recommended for beginners. If you want this type of base in either a tile or panel shower, consider having a professional build it.

To install a fiberglass or plastic base, position it over the drain outlet. Connect the base to the drain by screwing in the crosspiece (see il-

lustration, page 89), and cover the opening with rags to keep debris from falling in. Follow the manufacturer's directions to secure the base to the frame (nailing is shown below). Later, remove the rags and attach the drain cover.

Studs

Nails

Fiberglass base

Installing the wall covering

Once the base is secured, you're ready to cover the shower's side and back walls with tile or panels.

Tile. Like a tile base, tile walls can be tricky to install. If you want tile on a mortar bed, you may want to hire a tile contractor to install it. If you're planning to back the tile with either water-resistant wallboard or cement backer board, you may decide to do the job yourself.

First, prepare the backing. Cut holes for the shower head stubout and faucet stems; then nail the backing to the frame (see illustration above right).

Plan the layout of your tile by marking horizontal and vertical working lines on the shower wall (see illustrations above right). Using thin-set adhesive, tile the back wall. Then move on to the sides, cutting tiles to fit around the shower stubout and faucet stems.

Set ceramic tile accessories. Allow the tile to set (for the required time, consult the adhesive manufacturer's instructions) before grouting all the joints between the tiles. When the grout has set, you can seal it. For more information on establishing working lines, setting tile, and grouting joints, turn to pages 103–105; or ask your tile dealer.

INSTALLING TILE ON SHOWER WALLS

To attach wallboard or backer board to a wood shower frame, nail along the length of the 2 by 4 studs.

Mark working lines, both horizontal and vertical, then set tile on shower walls in a pyramid pattern.

Backing is positioned to leave ½-inch gap above base; leave ¼-inch gap for caulking tile.

Fiberglass panels. Shower panels of fiberglass usually come with manufacturer's directions for installation. Some require no backing (except perhaps soundproofing insulation); others require separate water-resistant wallboard backing.

For both types of panels, measure and mark on one panel the locations of the shower head stubout and faucet stems. Lay the marked panel across two sawhorses, and with a spade bit, drill slightly oversized holes for your fittings. Support the panels with wood planks so you don't splinter them as you drill (see illustration below).

If the base of your shower has channels on the outside edges for sealant, clean out any debris from them. Then fill the groove at the back with the sealant recommended by the manufacturer (see illustration below). Also apply adhesive to the reverse side of the back panel according to manufacturer's directions.

Install the back panel by fitting it into the groove on the base, then pressing it against the frame to make a complete seal. Next, fill the other grooves on the base with seal-

ant and install the side panels; they may snap or clip to the back panel. Screw or nail the flanges of the panels to the framing. Install cover moldings over the nails or screws, if required.

Connecting the plumbing

Once you've installed the wall coverings, caulk around all openings; then re-attach the shower head, escutcheons, and faucet handles.

Finally, hang the shower door, or mount a curtain rod and hang a shower curtain.

INSTALLING FIBERGLASS SHOWER PANELS

Mark a panel for stubout hole and faucet stem, set panel on supporting planks and sawhorses, and drill holes.

Channel in shower base holds panel tightly in place; sealant prevents moisture from getting behind panels.

Press panel to the frame, guiding head stubout and faucet stems through holes; nail or screw panel flange to frame.

Faucets

Whether you're replacing an old faucet or selecting fittings for a new sink or bathtub, you'll find a wide variety of faucet types and styles from which to choose. The product information on page 59 can help you make your selection.

In this section, you'll find information on removing and installing two different types of widely used bathroom faucets: deck-mount models for sinks, and wall-mount models for bathtubs and showers.

SINK FAUCETS

In choosing a deck-mount faucet, be sure that the faucet's inlet shanks are spaced to fit the holes in your sink. If you're replacing a faucet, it's wise to take the old one with you when you shop. You'll also need new water supply lines, so take them with you, too.

Choose a unit that comes with clear installation instructions, and make sure that repair kits or replacement parts are readily available.

Removing a sink faucet

Before removing the faucet, turn off the water at the sink shutoff valves or main shutoff valve. Place a bucket under the valves and use a wrench to remove the coupling nuts connecting the water supply lines to the valves. Open the faucet and allow the water to drain from the lines.

If your sink has a pop-up drain, you'll need to disconnect it before removing the faucet. Unfasten the clevis screw and spring clip that secure the pivot rod to the pop-up rod, and remove the pop-up rod from the faucet body (see drawing on facing page).

With an adjustable or basin wrench, reach up behind the sink and remove the coupling nuts holding the supply lines to the inlet shanks on the faucet (see illustration above). Use the wrench to remove the locknuts from the shanks. Take off the washers; then lift up the faucet and remove it from the sink or countertop.

Installing a sink faucet

Before you start, have an adjustable wrench on hand. If your new faucet doesn't come with a rubber gasket, you'll also need a supply of plumber's putty.

If you're installing a new faucet on an old sink, make sure the area around the faucet is free of dirt and mineral buildup.

The basic steps in installing a sink faucet are outlined below, but since procedures vary with the type of faucet, you should also look carefully at the manufacturer's instructions.

Mounting the faucet. If your new faucet doesn't have a rubber gasket on the bottom, apply a bead of plumber's putty around the underside of the outside edge.

The faucet may have either inlet shanks or inlet tubes and threaded mounting studs. Insert the inlet shanks or tubes down through the holes in the mounting surface; press the faucet onto the surface. For a faucet with inlet shanks, screw the washers and locknuts onto the shanks by hand (see illustration at left); tighten with a wrench. If your faucet has tubes, assemble and tighten the washers and nuts on the mounting studs (see drawing below).

Connecting the plumbing. Two types of flexible supply lines are available: chrome-plated corrugated metal tubing and plastic tubing. Because it's a little better looking, metal tubing is usually used when the supply lines are visible. Gaskets and coupling nuts are sold separately, so be sure they fit the faucet and the shutoff valves. Plastic tubing is sold with gaskets and coupling nuts already assembled.

Before connecting the supply lines, apply pipe joint compound to the threads on the inlet shanks and shutoff valves, or to the threads on the fittings at the ends of the tubing.

INSTALLING A SINGLE-LEVER FAUCET

Position the faucet, threading inlet tubes through the sink hole; then tighten the locknuts on mounting studs.

Extend flexible tubing from inlet tubes as required; attach it to shutoff valves with an adjustable wrench.

Then connect the supply lines to the inlet shanks or tubes (see illustration on facing page). Tighten the coupling nuts with a wrench. Gently bend the supply lines to meet the shutoff valves, and secure them to the valves with coupling nuts. Tighten the nuts with an adjustable wrench, then turn on the water and check for leaks.

If you're installing a new pop-up drain assembly, follow the manufacturer's instructions. Connect the pop-up rod to the new pivot rod, using the fastenings supplied with the new drain assembly.

BATHTUB & SHOWER FAUCETS

Faucets for bathtubs and showers are either compression models (usually with separate hot and cold water controls) or washerless models (with a single lever or knob to control the flow and mix of hot and cold water). In both types (see illustration above right), the faucet body is mounted directly on the water supply pipes inside the wall.

You can either renovate a bathtub or shower faucet, or completely replace it. If the faucet body is in good condition, you may simply want to replace some of the faucet parts. If the faucet body is in poor condition, or if you want to change the type of

TWO TYPES OF BATHTUB AND SHOWER FAUCETS

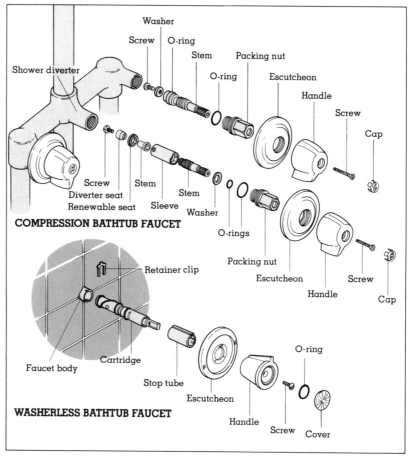

COMPRESSION BATHTUB FAUCET

WASHERLESS BATHTUB FAUCET

faucet you have, you may have to replace the entire assembly. You'll also need to replace the complete faucet if you want to add a shower head above an existing bathtub (see "Adding a shower faucet," page 94). The following sections tell you how to renovate or replace a faucet.

Renovating a bathtub or shower faucet

To renovate a faucet, you can replace faucet parts—stems, handles, and trim (such as escutcheons)— and the tub spout or shower head. In a tub, you might also replace the diverter—the mechanism that redirects water to the shower pipe. To find the correct replacement parts, it's a good idea to disassemble the old faucet first, then take the parts with you to the store when you shop for new ones.

Before you start work, turn off the water at the bathtub or shower shutoff valves or at the main shutoff valve. (Bathtub or shower shutoff valves may be accessible through a panel in an adjoining room, hall, or closet.)

The drawings on this page show you how typical compression and washerless faucets are put together, but the assembly may vary with individual models. As you disassemble your faucet, take notes and make a sketch of the parts and the sequence of assembly so you'll be able to put the faucet back together. First remove faucet handles, trim, and stem parts; then remove the diverter (if necessary). Finally, remove the tub spout or shower head with a tape-wrapped pipe wrench.

When you're ready to assemble the new fittings, simply reverse the procedure.

(Continued on next page)

■Faucets

REMOVING A BATHTUB FAUCET

Diverter handle
Spout
Tape-wrapped pipe wrench

Remove spout from wall stubout by turning counterclockwise with a tape-wrapped pipe wrench.

Cut-away wall covering
Faucet body
Spout stubout
Hot-water supply pipe
Cold-water supply pipe

Remove faucet body from supply pipes by unscrewing or unsoldering the connections.

Replacing a bathtub or shower faucet

Replacing a complete bathtub or shower faucet involves cutting away the wall covering and removing the faucet body from the supply pipes with wrenches or a small propane torch. You'll need to take the old faucet body with you when you buy a new one, to be sure of getting the correct size. If you've never done any pipefitting, you may want to get professional help to install the new faucet body.

Getting to the faucet body. First remove the faucet handles and trim, and the shower head or tub spout and diverter. To work on the faucet body and the pipes behind the wall, open the access door or panel if one is available. If not, cut a hole in the bathroom wall large enough to allow you to work on the faucet body and pipes comfortably (see illustration at right). Then turn off the water at the bathtub shutoff valves or main shutoff valve.

Removing the faucet body. The illustration above shows how a bathtub or shower faucet body is mounted onto the water supply pipes. It may be attached with either threaded or soldered connections. If you find threaded connections, un-

screw them. Use one wrench on the supply pipe to hold it steady, and one wrench on the coupling, turning it counterclockwise. If you find soldered copper connections, unsolder them, using a small propane torch.

Installing the faucet body. If your tub or shower is not equipped with individual shutoff valves, you may want to add them now (or consult a professional plumber for help). To install a faucet body on threaded pipe fittings, apply pipe joint compound to the male threads of the pipes and screw the connecting coupling nuts down tight.

For copper pipe, solder couplings to the pipes and screw them onto the faucet body. If the faucet body must be soldered directly to the pipe, first remove the valve and diverter stems.

After the pipes are connected to the faucet body, turn the water on and check for leaks. To make certain the pipes can't vibrate when the water is turned on and off, anchor them and the faucet body firmly to the wall studs or support with pipe straps before patching and re-covering the wall.

Carefully measure and mark the positions of the new faucet, spout, and shower head stubouts on the replacement wall covering. Then

prepare and replace the wall covering, and attach the new fittings.

Adding a shower faucet

To add a shower head above your old bathtub, you'll have to replace the old faucet assembly with one equipped with a shower outlet and diverter valve. In addition, you'll have to install a shower pipe in the wall, as shown below.

If your tub surround is tiled, the tile will have to be removed so you can add the shower pipe. Cut your access hole large enough to install the shower pipe. From the shower outlet on the faucet body, run a ½-inch pipe up the wall to the desired height (see illustration, page 75) and top it with an elbow. Nail a 2 by 4 wood support behind the elbow and anchor the pipe to it with a pipe strap.

To avoid scratching the shower arm while you're repairing the wall covering, thread a 6-inch galvanized nipple into the elbow in place of the shower arm.

Wall studs
Elbow
Pipe strap
Support
Shower pipe
Pipe strap
Faucet body

Finally, clean the pipe threads and install the shower arm and shower head, using pipe joint compound on the male threads of the fittings. Repair or replace wall coverings as required (see pages 98–105).

Toilets & bidets

Removing or installing a toilet or bidet is not very complicated, especially when the plumbing is already in place. During major remodeling involving the floor or walls, remember that toilets and bidets are the first fixtures to remove and the last to install.

For product information on various models, see page 60.

TOILETS

Conventional two-piece toilets have a floor-mounted bowl with a tank mounted on the bowl. Older types with floor-mounted bowls may have the tank mounted on the wall. One-piece toilets, with the bowl and tank mounted on the floor as a single unit, are becoming increasingly popular with homeowners. (One-piece wall-hung models that connect directly to the stack in the wall are also available.) This section deals primarily with conventional floor-mounted toilets.

Before you begin work, be sure to check any code requirements for a new or replacement toilet.

Removing a toilet

The procedure for removing a toilet varies with the type of fixture. For a two-piece toilet, you remove the tank first, then the bowl. (For a one-piece toilet, you remove the tank and bowl at the same time.)

Disconnect the water supply. Before you begin work, turn off the water at the fixture shutoff valve or main shutoff valve. Flush the toilet twice to empty the bowl and tank; then sponge out any remaining water. To remove the toilet seat and lid, unfasten the nuts on the two bolts projecting down through the bowl's back edge. Unfasten the coupling nut on the water supply line (see illustration below) underneath the tank. If the line is kinked or corroded, replace it when you install the new toilet.

Remove the tank. If you're removing a bowl-mounted toilet tank, detach the empty tank from the bowl as follows: Locate the mounting bolts inside the tank at the bottom. Hold them stationary with a screwdriver while you use a wrench to unfasten the nuts underneath the tank (see illustration below). You'll find it easier to remove the nuts if a helper holds the screwdriver. Then lift up the tank and remove it.

In a wall-mounted tank, a pipe usually connects the tank and bowl. Loosen the couplings on the pipe and remove it. Then reach inside the tank with a wrench and unscrew the nuts on the hanger bolts—these attach the tank to the hanger bracket on the wall. Now you can remove the tank.

Remove the bowl. The following instructions apply to most floor-mounted toilet bowls. At the base of the bowl near the floor, pry off the caps covering the hold-down floor bolts. Unscrew the nuts from the bolts. If the nuts have rusted on, soak them with penetrating oil or cut the bolts off with a hacksaw.

Gently rock the bowl from side to side, breaking the seal between the bowl and the floor. Lift the bowl straight up, keeping it level so any remaining water doesn't spill from its trap (see illustration below).

Stuff a rag into the open drain-pipe to prevent sewer gas from escaping and to keep debris from falling into the opening.

(Continued on next page)

REMOVING A FLOOR-MOUNTED TOILET

Loosen the coupling nut on the water supply line at the bottom of the tank, using a wrench.

Detach the tank from the bowl by loosening mounting bolts with a screwdriver and a wrench.

Lift the bowl straight up off the floor flange, keeping it level to avoid spilling any remaining water.

■ Toilets & bidets

Installing a toilet

The amount of work needed to install a new toilet depends on whether it will be in a new location. Hooking up a toilet in a new location is a challenging project because you must extend supply, drain, and vent pipes (see pages 72–75). You may want to have a professional run the piping to the desired spot and then complete the installation yourself.

Replacing an old fixture with a new one at the same location is a one-afternoon project that you can do yourself. The only crucial dimension you need to check on a new toilet is its roughing-in size—the distance from the wall to the center of the drainpipe (most are 12 inches).

You can usually determine roughing-in size before removing the old bowl—just measure from the wall to one of the two hold-down bolts that secure the bowl to the floor. (If the bowl has four hold-down bolts, measure to one of the rear bolts.) Your new toilet's roughing-in size can be shorter than that of the fixture you're replacing, but if it's longer, the new toilet won't fit.

Once you've determined that the fixture will fit, you're ready to install it. The following general instructions apply to two-piece floor-mounted toilets. The key steps are illustrated at right. (For a one-piece, floor-mounted toilet, install the bowl as described below, then connect the water supply.)

Prepare the floor flange. This fitting connects the bowl to the floor and drainpipe.

Remove the rags and, with a putty knife, scrape off the wax bowl ring that formed the seal between the bowl and the flange. Thoroughly scrape the flange so that the new ring will form a leakproof seal.

If the old flange is cracked or broken, or if its surface is rough, replace it with a new flange, matched to the existing drainpipe material. (Use a plastic flange with plastic pipe, cast iron with a cast iron pipe.) Remove the old hold-down bolts from the floor flange, then insert the new bolts through the flange. If necessary, hold them upright with plumber's putty. Align the bolts with the center of the drainpipe.

Install the bowl ring. Turn the new bowl upside down on a cushioned surface. Place the new bowl ring over the toilet horn (outlet) on the bottom of the bowl, and apply plumber's putty around the bowl's bottom edge.

Place the bowl. Check that all packing material has been removed from the new bowl, and all rags from the drainpipe. Then gently lower the bowl into place over the flange, using the bolts as guides. To form the seal, press down firmly while twisting slightly.

Check the bowl with a level—from side to side and from front to back; use copper or brass washers to shim underneath the bowl where necessary. Be careful not to break the seal. Hand tighten the washers and nuts onto the hold-down bolts; you'll tighten them permanently after the tank is in place.

Attach the tank. For a bowl-mounted tank, fit the rubber gasket

INSTALLING A FLOOR-MOUNTED TOILET

Thoroughly scrape the old bowl ring from the floor flange, using a putty knife or similar tool.

Position the new bowl ring over the toilet horn on the bottom of the bowl as it rests on a cushioned surface.

Level the bowl once it's in place, using small copper or brass washers to shim underneath, if necessary.

Attach the tank to the bowl using mounting bolts, with rubber gasket and tank cushion in place.

over the end of the flush valve that projects through the bottom of the tank. Place the rubber tank cushion on the rear of the bowl. After positioning the tank on the bowl, insert the mounting bolts through their holes in the bottom of the tank so they pass through the tank cushion and the back of the bowl. Then tighten the nuts and washers onto the bolts. (Secure wall-mounted tanks to hanger brackets with bolts through the back of the tank. Assemble the large pipe between bowl and tank and tighten the couplings.)

Now you can attach the bowl to the floor permanently. Use a wrench to tighten the hold-down nuts at the base of the bowl, but don't overtighten them or you'll crack the bowl. Check to see that the bowl is still level and doesn't rock. Fill the caps with plumber's putty and place them over the nuts. Seal the joint between the base of the bowl and the floor with a bead of caulking compound.

Attach the toilet seat by inserting mounting bolts through the holes in the back of the bowl; then assemble the washers and nuts onto the bolts and tighten.

Connect the plumbing. Connect the water supply line to the underside of the tank. If your old plumbing had no fixture shutoff valve, install one now (consult a professional plumber for help). Finally, turn on the water and check for leaks.

BIDETS

A bidet—a one-piece fixture—is usually installed next to the toilet. Unlike a toilet, a bidet has a sink-type drain and trap and is plumbed for hot and cold water. (For product information, see page 60.)

Removing a bidet

A bidet is usually not difficult to remove. You just disconnect two water supply lines, a drainpipe, and the hold-down bolts.

Disconnect the plumbing. Before doing any work, turn off the

water at the fixture shutoff valves or main shutoff valve. Open all faucets; then unfasten the coupling nuts on the hot and cold water supply lines, so that all remaining water will be completely drained. These lines are either freestanding or attached to the wall behind the bidet. (Some bidets may be plumbed with mixing valves in the wall and a single water supply line running to the fixture.)

Behind and under the back of the bidet, you'll find the drainpipe connection and usually a pop-up drain assembly. First, loosen the clevis screw (see illustration on page 93) and disconnect this assembly. Then loosen the slip nuts on the trap and remove it.

Remove the bidet. Pry the caps off the flange at the base of the bidet and remove the nuts underneath them. If the nuts are rusted, soak them with penetrating oil or cut the bolts with a hacksaw.

Lift the bidet straight up off the hold-down bolts that secure it to the floor. You may need to rock the fixture gently first to break the caulk seal (if there is one) around the base.

Stuff a rag into the drainpipe to prevent debris from falling into the opening.

Installing a bidet

A bidet must be mounted to the floor with hold-down bolts. If you're hooking up a new bidet in an existing location and want to use the existing floor bolts, the distance between bolt holes must be the same as for the original fixture. Also make sure the fittings on the new model are compatible with the existing water supply and drain lines.

If you're installing a bidet in a new location, you'll need to extend supply pipes and drainpipes (see pages 72–75). Unless you're experienced in home plumbing, you'll probably want to hire a professional for this part of the job.

Position the bidet. Remove all packing material from the bidet and

TYPICAL BIDET

Clearance to finished wall as required

Hot and cold water controls

Pop-up drain

Supply line and shutoff

Hold-down bolt

Drainpipe

Trap

place the fixture so that its drain opening is directly over the drainpipe. If it's a new installation rather than a replacement, mark the locations for the hold-down bolts on the floor, using the holes in the bidet's flange as guides; then remove the bidet, drill holes sized for the bolts, and screw the bolts through the floor. Turn the bidet upside down onto a cushioned surface and apply plumber's putty around the bottom edge.

Remove the rag from the drainpipe and set the bidet back in position, using the bolts as guides.

Level the bidet, from side to side and from front to back, using copper or brass washers to shim beneath the bottom edge, if necessary. If you do shim, you may need to reseal the fixture to the floor. Hand tighten washers and nuts onto the hold-down bolts; you'll tighten them further after the plumbing connections are made. Connect the pop-up drain assembly, if there is one.

Connect the plumbing. Connect the drain and the two water supply lines. Once all connections are made, use a wrench to tighten the nuts on these lines, as well as the nuts on the hold-down bolts. (Don't overtighten the hold-down bolts or you'll crack the fixture.) Fill the caps with plumber's putty and place them over the nuts on the bidet flange. Turn on the water and check for leaks.

Walls & ceilings

A new moisture-resistant wall or ceiling can improve the bathroom's appearance and make the room easier to maintain at the same time.

This section will show you how to remove and apply the most popular wall treatments in today's bathrooms—gypsum wallboard, wallpaper, and ceramic tile. (For information on painting, see the special feature on page 101.)

GYPSUM WALLBOARD

This versatile wall covering has a gypsum core faced with thick paper. You can use it as finish material, putting paint or wallpaper over it, or you can use it as a backing for other materials, such as tile, wood, or panels of plastic-coated hardboard.

A special water-resistant grade is available for use around tubs, showers, and other damp areas. This wallboard is usually identified by a blue or green paper cover. It's best not to use it where you plan to paint or wallpaper, though—the compound you must use to finish joints between panels of water-resistant wallboard is nearly impossible to sand, so every imperfection will show through.

Panels are generally 4 feet wide and 8 feet long. (Lengths over 8 feet can be specially ordered.) Common thicknesses are ⅜ inch for wallboard used as a backing, ½ inch for wallboard used as finish wall covering.

INSTALLING WALLBOARD ON A WALL

Lift each wallboard panel into position and center the edges over wall studs. Then nail the panel to the studs, dimpling the wallboard surface slightly with the hammer. Stagger panels in adjacent rows so that ends don't line up.

Removing gypsum wallboard

If your bathroom's existing wallboard has only minor cracks or holes, you can probably repair it by filling in the cracks with ready-mixed spackling compound, then sanding smooth. But if it's wet, mildewed, or badly damaged, you'll have to remove it before installing other wall covering.

Use a broad-bladed prybar and a claw hammer to remove wallboard. Wear a dust mask to avoid inhaling gypsum dust, and cover all fixtures and the floor with drop cloths. Finally, be sure to turn off electrical power to the bathroom by flipping a circuit breaker or removing a fuse, so you won't risk hitting a live wire with the prybar.

Your wallboard may be nailed at intervals along the wall studs, or nailed only around the outside edges and sealed to the studs with adhesive. In either case, the removal procedure is the same.

Break through a taped seam between panels with the prybar. Then pry up the panel, using the stud for leverage, until you loosen a large piece. With both hands, pull the piece of wallboard off the studs. (Some of the nails will probably come off with it.) If the wallboard is attached with adhesive, you can leave the backing paper on the studs.

Once you've completely stripped the wallboard away from the studs, work through the area a second time and pull out any remaining nails.

CUTTING GYPSUM WALLBOARD

Cut wallboard along pencil or chalk line marked on front face, using utility knife guided by straightedge.

Break gypsum core by placing edges of stacked 2 by 4s under cut and pressing down on panel.

Complete cut by turning panel over, bending wallboard back, and cutting through back paper with utility knife.

INSTALLING WALLBOARD ON A CEILING

Ceiling joists

Wallboard

Drywall screws

It takes two to install a wallboard ceiling. Prop each panel in place with your heads; screw or nail first in the center and then where it will take the weight off your heads.

Installing gypsum wallboard

Installing gypsum wallboard is a three-step procedure. You measure and cut panels to size, hang them, and finish the seams and corners with wallboard compound and tape. Handle bulky panels carefully as you work; take care not to bend or break the corners or tear the paper covers.

Cut the wallboard. Though you'll use some full-size panels, you'll also need to cut pieces to fit around obstacles such as doors, windows, fixtures, and cabinets.

To make a straight, simple cut, first mark a line on the front of the panel with a pencil and straightedge, or snap a chalkline. Cut through the front paper with a utility knife; use a straightedge to guide the knife. Break the gypsum core by bending the board toward the back, as shown in the drawing on page 98. Finally, cut the paper on the back along the bend. Smooth the cut edge with a perforated rasp.

To fit wallboard around doors, windows, and other openings, measure and mark carefully. Measure from vertical edges of the opening to the edge of the nearest panel or a corner; measure from horizontal edges to the floor. Transfer the measurements to the wallboard and

make the cutout with a keyhole saw. For mid-panel cutouts, drill a pilot hole, then use a keyhole saw to make the cutout.

Basic wall application. Wall panels may be positioned either vertically or horizontally—that is, with the long edges either parallel or perpendicular to wall studs. Most professionals prefer the latter method because it helps bridge irregularities between studs and results in a stronger wall. But if your wall is higher than 8 feet, you may not want to use this method, since the extra height requires more cutting and creates too many joints.

Before installing wall panels, mark the stud locations on the floor and ceiling.

Starting at a corner, place the first panel tight against the ceiling and secure it with nails, drywall screws, or construction adhesive supplemented by nails. Drive in nails with a hammer, dimpling the wallboard surface without puncturing the paper. Fastener spacings are subject to local codes, but typical nail spacing is every 8 inches along panel ends and edges and along intermediate supports (called "in the field").

Apply additional panels in the same manner. If you're applying wallboard horizontally, stagger the end

joints in the bottom row so they don't line up with the joints in the top row.

Basic ceiling application. Methods for installing a wallboard ceiling are basically the same as those for walls. If you're covering both walls and ceiling, do the ceiling first.

Fasten panels perpendicular to joists with annular ring nails, drywall screws, or a combination of nails and construction adhesive. Screws are quick and strong, but you'll need a power screw gun or drill with adjustable clutch to drive them. Typical fastener spacing is every 7 inches along panel ends and at intermediate joists.

Because you'll need to support the heavy panels while fastening them, installing a wallboard ceiling is a two-person job. First, secure each panel at the center with nails or screws; then place the next few fasteners where they'll take the weight off your heads (see drawing above left).

Tape the joints and corners. If your wallboard will be a backing for paneling, you won't need to tape and conceal joints or corners. But if you're painting, wallpapering, or installing tile, you must finish the wallboard carefully. You'll need these basic tools and materials: 6 and 10-inch taping knives, a corner tool, sandpaper, wallboard tape, and taping compound (water-resistant wallboard requires water-resistant compound). See NOTE, page 100, for special instructions on taping water-resistant wallboard.

Finishing is done in stages over a period of days. To tape a joint between panels, first apply a smooth layer of taping compound over the joint with a 6-inch taping knife (see drawing on page 100). Before the compound dries, use the knife to embed wallboard tape into it, and apply another thin coat of compound over the tape, smoothing it gently with the knife.

Tape and finish all joints between panels in the same manner. Then, with smooth, even strokes of

■ Walls & ceilings

TAPING WALLBOARD JOINTS

Apply a smooth layer of taping compound over wallboard joint, using a 6-inch taping knife.

Embed wallboard tape into the compound before it dries, and apply another thin layer of compound.

Apply a second coat a few inches on each side of joint, feathering compound out to edges.

the 6-inch knife, cover the nail dimples in the field with compound.

Allow the taping compound to dry for at least 24 hours; then sand lightly until the surface is smooth. Wear a face mask and goggles while sanding, and make sure the room is well ventilated.

Now use a 10-inch knife to apply a second coat of compound, extending it a few inches on each side of the taped joint. Feather the compound out toward the edges.

Let the second coat dry, sand it, then apply a final coat. Use the 10-inch knife to smooth out and feather the edges, covering all dimples and joints. Once the compound dries, sand it again to remove even minor imperfections.

NOTE: To finish water-resistant wallboard that will be backing for ceramic tile, first embed the tape in water-resistant taping compound along panel joints; then remove all excess compound with a taping knife. Apply a second thin coat over the wet taping coat and fill any nail dimples. Do not leave excess compound—it can't be sanded dry.

To tape an inside corner, it's easiest to use precreased tape. Apply a smooth layer of compound to the wallboard on either side of the corner. Measure and tear the tape, fold it in half vertically along the prepared crease, and press it into the corner with a taping knife or corner tool. Apply a thin layer of compound over the tape and smooth it out; then finish as you did the other joints.

Nail metal cornerbeads to all exterior corners to protect them. Apply compound to each side of the corner with a 6-inch knife. When it's dry, sand it smooth. With a 10-inch knife, apply a second coat of compound, feathering it. Allow to dry, then sand away imperfections.

Textured versus smooth finish. Though many people prefer the smooth look, texture can hide a less-than-perfect taping job—and add some visual interest to an uninterrupted wall. Some joint compounds double as texturing compounds; other effects may require special texturing materials. Ask your dealer for recommendations.

Professionals often apply texturing with a spray gun, but others produce good results by daubing, swirling, or splattering the compound with a sponge, paint roller, or stiff brush—whatever tool produces the desired appearance.

Let the compound set up until slightly stiff; then even it out as required with a wide float or trowel. Allow the finished surface to dry for at least 24 hours before painting.

Hanging new wallpaper

Next to paint, wallpaper is the most popular covering for bathroom walls. Easier than ever to install, wallpaper is available in a kaleidoscope of colors and patterns.

Choices for the bathroom. A wallpaper for the bathroom should

be scrubbable, durable, and stain-resistant. Solid vinyl wallpapers, available in a wide variety of colors and textures, fit the bill. Vinyl coatings also give wallpaper a washable surface but aren't notably durable or grease-resistant.

If you're a beginner, you may want to consider prepasted and pre-trimmed paper.

To find an adhesive suitable for your material, check the manufacturer's instructions or ask your dealer.

Preparing the surface. To prepare for papering, you'll need to remove all light fixtures and faceplates. Thoroughly clean and rinse the surface. Most manufacturers recommend that you completely remove any old wallpaper before hanging a nonporous covering like solid vinyl.

If the existing paper is strippable, it will come off easily when you pull it up at a corner or seam. To remove nonstrippable wallpaper, use either a steamer (available for rent from your dealer) or a spray bottle filled with very hot water. Before steaming, break the surface of the old paper by sanding it with very coarse sandpaper or by pulling a sawblade sideways across the wall.

Within a few minutes of steaming (wait longer if it's a nonporous material), you can begin to remove the old paper. Using a broad knife, work down from the top of the wall, scraping off the old wallpaper.

If yours is a new gypsum wallboard surface, tape all joints between panels before papering. When

PAINTING: TIPS FOR A PROFESSIONAL FINISH

A fresh coat of paint is the fastest way to brighten up your bathroom. Here are some guidelines to help you do a professional-looking job.

Selecting tools & materials

One key to a good paint job is to choose the right materials.

Paint. Your basic choices in paint are water-base, or latex, paint and oil-base, or alkyd, paint. Latex is easy to work with, and best of all, you can clean up wet paint with soap and water. Alkyd paint provides high gloss and will hang on a little harder than latex; however, alkyds are harder to apply and require cleanup with mineral spirits.

In general, high resin content is the mark of durable, abrasion-resistant, flexible paint—the kind you need in a bathroom. Usually, the higher the resin content, the higher the gloss; so look for products labeled gloss or semigloss if you want a tough, washable finish.

An excellent choice for bathroom cabinets and woodwork is quick-drying alkyd enamel. It has a brilliant, tilelike finish that's extremely durable.

Tools. Natural bristle brushes are traditionally used to apply oil-base alkyd enamel paints; synthetic bristles are best for latex products. For window sashes and trim, choose a 1½ or 2-inch angled sash brush. A 2 or 3-inch brush or a paint pad is best for woodwork, doors, and cabinets.

Preparing the surface

To prevent cracking and peeling after the new paint dries, you must begin with surfaces that are smooth and clean.

It's possible to paint over wallpaper that's smooth and attached firmly to the wall. Apply a sealing primer such as pigmented shellac or a flat oil-base enamel undercoat. Let the sealer dry completely before you paint. It's often safer, though, to remove the wallpaper, especially if it's tearing and flaking.

Repairing the finish. For an old painted finish, sanding is sufficient if the surface is flaking lightly. Wash dirty areas on wood surfaces before sanding.

Roughen glossy paint surfaces with sandpaper so the new paint will adhere. (Rough, bare wood also needs sanding, as do patched areas.)

When a wood finish is in such bad condition that painting over it is impossible, you'll have to strip it. You can use an electric paint softener or heat gun, or a commercial liquid paint remover. With either method, you take off the softened paint with a broad knife or scraper, then sand the surface lightly until it's clean and smooth.

Once you've prepared the surface, carefully inspect it for small holes and cracks.

To repair small holes in wallboard, use spackling compound. For details on repairing other surfaces, consult a wall covering specialist.

Finally, dust everything in the bathroom, then vacuum the floor. With an abrasive cleaner, sponge the areas you plan to paint, then rinse. Allow about 24 hours for all washed areas to dry completely.

Prime the surface. Before doing any finish painting, be sure to prime the surface. Use the primer recommended by the paint manufacturer for the type of surface you'll be painting.

Applying the paint

To avoid painting yourself into a corner, you'll want to follow the working sequence outlined below.

Ceiling. If you're painting both ceiling and walls, begin with the ceiling. Paint the entire surface in one session. It's best to paint in 2 by 3-foot rectangles, starting in a corner and working across the shortest dimension of the ceiling.

On the first section, use a brush or special corner pad to paint a narrow strip next to the wall line and around any fixtures. Then finish the section with a roller, overlapping any brush marks. Work your way back and forth across the ceiling, painting one section at a time. Then go on to the walls.

Walls. Mentally divide a wall into 3-foot-square sections, starting from a corner at the ceiling line and working down the wall. As with ceilings, paint the edges of each section first with a brush or corner roller. Paint along the ceiling line and corners, and around fixtures and edges of doors or windows. Finish each section with a roller or brush, overlapping any brush marks.

At the bottom of the walls above the floor or baseboard, and along the edges of vanities and medicine cabinets, use a brush and painting guide to get a neat, even edge. Be sure to overlap any remaining brush marks with your roller.

As a final step, return to the ceiling line and again work down in 3-foot sections.

■ Walls & ceilings

dry, sand the wall smooth and apply a coat of flat, oil-base primer-sealer.

To apply wallpaper over previously painted surfaces that are in good condition, clean off all the dirt, grease, and oil, and let it dry. If latex paint was used, or if you can't determine the type, apply an oil-base undercoat over the old paint.

Ready to start? Plan the best place to hang your first strip. If you're papering all four walls with a patterned paper, the last strip you hang probably won't match the first, so plan to start and finish in the least conspicuous place—usually a corner, door casing, or window casing.

Most house walls are not straight and plumb, so you'll need to establish a plumb line. Figure the width of your first strip of wallpaper minus ½ inch (which will overlap the corner or casing); measure that distance from your starting point, and mark the wall. Using a carpenter's level as a straightedge, draw a line through your mark that's perfectly plumb. Extend the line until it reaches from floor to ceiling.

It's a good idea to measure the wall height before cutting each strip of wallpaper. Allow 2 inches extra at the top and bottom. Be sure also to allow for pattern match.

Using a razor knife, cut the strips. Number them on the back at the top edge so you can apply them in the proper sequence.

With some wallpapers, you'll need to spread adhesive on the backing with a wide, soft paint roller or pasting brush; other papers are prepasted—all you have to do is soak them in water before hanging.

After pasting or soaking, strips should be "booked" (see below).

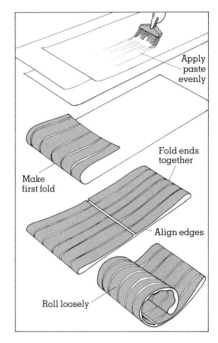

Apply paste evenly

Make first fold

Fold ends together

Align edges

Roll loosely

Trim the edges of the wallpaper at this stage, if necessary.

Hanging the wallpaper. First, position a stepladder next to the plumb line you've marked. Open the top fold of the first booked strip, raising it so that it overlaps the ceiling line by 2 inches. Carefully align the strip's edge with the plumb line.

Using a smoothing brush, press the strip against the wall. Smooth out all wrinkles and air bubbles. Then release the lower portion of the strip and smooth it into place.

Carefully roll the edges flat, if necessary, with a seam roller. To trim along the ceiling and baseboard, use a broad knife and a very sharp razor knife. With a sponge dipped in lukewarm water, remove any excess adhesive before it dries.

Unfold your second strip on the wall in the same way you did the first. Gently butt the second strip against the first, aligning the pattern as you move down the wall. Continue around the room.

Dealing with corners. Because few rooms have perfectly straight corners, you'll have to measure from the edge of the preceding strip to the corner; do this at three heights. Cut a strip ½ inch wider than the widest measurement. Butting the strip to the

HANGING THE FIRST STRIP

2" overlap — Plumb line (A)

½" overlap (B)

Seam roller (C)

Broad knife — Razor knife (D)

Sponge (E)

To hang wallpaper, first open the top fold of the strip, overlap the ceiling line, and align the strip's edge with the plumb line (A); press the strip against the wall with a smoothing brush (B). Release the lower fold and smooth into place; roll the edges flat with a seam roller (C). Trim the strip along the ceiling and baseboard with a broad knife and a razor knife (D). Remove excess adhesive with a sponge dipped in lukewarm water (E).

preceding strip, brush it firmly into and around the corner. At the top and bottom corners, cut the overlap so the strip will lie flat.

Next, measure the width of the leftover piece of wallpaper. On the adjacent wall, measure the same distance from the corner and make a plumb line at that point.

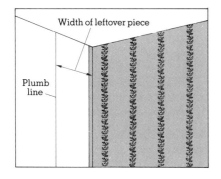

Position one edge of the strip along the plumb line; the other edge will cover the ½-inch overlap. (If you're hanging vinyl wallpaper, you should apply a vinyl-to-vinyl adhesive on top of the overlap.)

Cutouts. It's easy to cut around switches and outlets. Remove all faceplates before hanging the wallpaper; then, before making the cutout, shut off the electricity.

Hang the paper as described above. Then use a razor knife to make an X-shaped cut over the opening, extending the cuts to each corner. Trim the excess along the edges of the opening with the razor knife and a broad knife.

CERAMIC TILE

Few wall coverings have the decorative impact and durability of ceramic tile. It's a natural choice for any wall that might be sprayed or splashed—water, dirt, and soap film clean away in seconds.

On these pages you'll learn how to remove and install ceramic tile. For information on various types of wall tile, see page 63. If your plans call for a ceramic tile floor, install the floor tiles before setting tiles on the wall (see page 108).

Removing ceramic tile

Removing wall tile set in mortar is a tough job. If possible, replace only those tiles that are damaged. If tiles are clean and smooth and the wall surface is flat, consider installing the new tiles directly over them.

If you must remove old tile, proceed with caution (see "Removing the wall covering" on page 89). You may prefer to have a professional remove tile that is set in mortar.

If your wall tile is set on gypsum wallboard, you can more easily remove it yourself. Wearing goggles and a dust mask, use a cold chisel and soft-headed steel hammer to chip through the tile and backing. Once you've removed small sections, insert a prybar and pry off large sections until the wall studs are exposed.

Next, inspect the exposed wall framing for any water damage, and replace framing members if necessary. Then you can install backing for your new tile or for another wall covering of your choice.

Installing ceramic tile

Plan and prepare carefully before you install tile. First measure your bathroom and sketch your walls on graph paper. Choose and plan the placement of special trim pieces, such as bullnose, cove, and quarter-round edging tiles, as well as ceramic accessories—soap dishes, paper holders, and toothbrush holders. Your dealer can help you to select trim pieces.

Once you've designed your walls and selected tile, you're ready to begin. Described below are the steps you'll follow to install your tile, from backing to finished wall. (If you're installing pregrouted tile panels, follow the manufacturer's instructions.)

Before you start, remove baseboards and window and door trim, wall-mounted accessories and lights, and, if necessary, the toilet, bidet, and sink.

Prepare the backing surface. This is probably the most important step in installing wall tile successfully. Backing must be solid, flat, clean, and dry.

You can use existing gypsum wallboard or even existing wood or tile as backing if it's in good condition. You may need to clean, smooth out, or prime these surfaces before you're ready for new tile; ask your tile dealer for recommendations.

You may also opt for new wallboard backing. But for wet areas, it's safest to install cement backer board, available in 3-foot widths and various lengths. Standard panel thickness for new installations is ½ inch; fasten panels to wall studs with 1½-inch galvanized roofing nails. Fill joints between panels and at edges with thin-set adhesive or mortar. Though it's not strictly necessary, a waterproof membrane behind the backer board helps ensure a watertight wall.

For setting tiles on bathroom walls, choose either thin-set (cement-base) or epoxy adhesive. Thin-set adhesive, when mixed with a latex additive, is adequate for most jobs; epoxy is slightly more difficult to work with and more expensive. The same distinctions apply to cement-base and epoxy grouts. Read the labels and consult your tile dealer to determine which adhesive and grout are best for your situation.

Once your backing is prepared, you're ready to mark working lines.

Mark working lines. Accurate horizontal and vertical working lines help you keep tiles properly aligned so that your finished wall will look level and even. The horizontal working line should be near the bottom of the wall, because tiling up a wall is easier than tiling down.

If you're tiling around a tub, establish working lines there first. This way, you can plan for a row of full (uncut) tiles just above the tub, at bathers' eye level. This works out best if the tub is level to within ⅛ inch. Locate the high point of the tub lip with your level, and measure up one tile width plus ⅛ inch. Mark a level line on the wall through this point; then extend it carefully across

■ Walls & ceilings

all adjoining walls. This will give you a bottom row of full tiles around the tub. (You can fill in any small gaps below them with caulking later.)

If your tub is not level to within ⅛ inch, locate the horizontal working line from the low point of the tub lip, and follow the above method. You'll have to cut the bottom row of tiles to fit.

Then, on walls adjoining the tub, establish a line close to the floor. Start at the working line you extended from the tub wall and measure down a full number of tiles, including grout joints. Leave a space at least one full tile high above the floor. Mark the horizontal working line for this wall through this point with a straightedge and level (see illustration below).

To establish a line on a wall not adjoining a tub, find the lowest point by setting a level on the floor at various locations against the walls to be tiled. At the lowest point, place a tile against the wall and mark its top edge on the wall. If you're installing a cove base, set a cove tile on the floor and a wall tile above it (allow for grout joint); then mark the top of the wall tile. Using a level and straightedge, draw a horizontal line through the mark across the wall. Extend this line onto other walls to be tiled.

After marking your horizontal working lines, nail battens (1 by 2-

PATTERNS FOR SETTING TILE

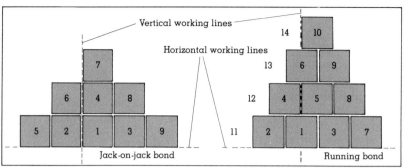

Jack-on-jack bond | Running bond

inch wood strips) all along the walls with their top edges on the lines. These will be your horizontal guides.

To establish a vertical working line, locate the midpoint of a wall and mark it on the horizontal working line. Starting at this point, set up a row of loose tiles on the batten to see how they'll fit at the ends of the wall.

If you'll end up with less than half a tile on both ends, move your mark one-half a tile to the right or left to avoid ending the rows with narrow pieces. Then extend the vertical working line through your mark and up the wall with a straightedge and level (see illustration below).

If you don't plan to tile to the ceiling line, mark the point where the highest tile will be set. Using a level, draw a horizontal line through this point across the wall.

Finally, be sure to mark locations of ceramic towel bars, soap dishes, and other accessories.

Set the tile. First, prepare the tile adhesive according to the manufacturer's directions. (Be sure to keep your working area well ventilated.)

To determine how large an area to cover at one time, consult the adhesive container label for the open time—the length of time you have to work with the adhesive after spreading. Comb the adhesive with a notched trowel to form ridges.

When you set the tiles, place each one with a slight twist—don't slide it. Keep spacing for grout joints uniform. Some tiles have small ceramic spacing lugs molded onto their edges; if your tiles don't have them, drive 6-penny finishing nails into the wallboard to act as temporary spacing guides (see illustration on facing page).

The way you'll begin setting tiles depends on which bond you use—jack-on-jack (with joints lined up) or running bond (with staggered joints).

For jack-on-jack, set the first tile on the batten so that one side is aligned exactly with the vertical working line. Set additional tiles as shown in the illustration above, forming a pyramid pattern. For running bond, *center* the first tile on the vertical working line, then follow the pyramid pattern (illustrated above), as you set the tile.

With either bond, continue setting tiles upward and toward the ends of the wall in the pattern illustrated. After laying several tiles, set

WORKING LINES FOR TILE

Extend horizontal working line around tub to adjoining walls, then measure to floor. Extend lines along adjoining walls.

To establish vertical working line, locate midpoint of wall (A), then adjust (B) according to size of end tiles.

them into the adhesive by sliding a carpet-wrapped piece of plywood across the tiles as you tap it gently with a hammer.

Cut tiles to fit at the end of each horizontal row and at the top near the ceiling. (Use a rented tile cutter to cut straight pieces; use tile nippers to cut out irregular shapes.) For the top row of a wainscoting or other installation that doesn't reach the ceiling, set bullnose or cap tiles.

When you come to a wall where there are electrical outlets or switches, turn off the power to them. Remove the cover plates, if installed, and pull the outlets and switches from their boxes, but don't disconnect them. Cut and fit tiles around the boxes, then remount the outlets and switches.

On inside corners, butt tiles together. On outside corners, set one column of bullnose tiles to cover the unfinished edges of the tiles on each adjoining wall.

INSTALLING WALL TILE

To **space wall tiles** not molded with spacing lugs, place 6-penny finishing nails between tiles.

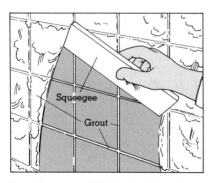

Spread grout on tile, forcing it into joints with a float or squeegee until they're full. Remove excess.

Around windows, finish off the sides and sill with bullnose tiles cut to fit.

Install ceramic accessories such as soap dishes in spaces you left open when tiling. Tape the accessories in place while the adhesive sets.

Now check your work. If anything is out of alignment, wiggle it into position before the adhesive sets. Clean adhesive from the face of

To set bottom row of tiles, remove batten on working line, mark tile and cut. Set in adhesive as for other tiles.

Use bathtub caulk to seal all openings between fixtures or pipes and tile.

tiles and accessories, and from joint spaces.

When the adhesive has set, carefully remove the battens. Twist nail spacers as you pull them out from the wall.

Spread adhesive at the bottom of the wall where the battens were, and set the remaining tiles, cutting them as needed.

Grout the tile. Before grouting, allow the adhesive to set properly—usually, you must allow 16 hours for epoxy-base adhesive and 48 hours for the cement-base type.

Remove any excess adhesive from the tile joints. Then mix the grout recommended for your tile, and spread it on the surface of the tile with a rubber-faced float or a squeegee, forcing it into the tile joints until they're completely filled. Scrape off excess grout from the tile, working diagonally across the surface.

Wipe the tiles with a wet sponge to remove any remaining grout. Rinse and wring out the sponge frequently, wiping until the grout joints are smooth and level with the tile surface. When the tiles are as clean as you can get them, let the grout dry until a haze appears over the surface. Then polish the haze off the tiles with a soft cloth. Finish (tool) the joints with the end of a toothbrush handle.

Seal tile and grout. Installations with unglazed tile or with cement-based grouts need to be protected by a grout and tile sealer. Most sealers for bathroom tile have a silicone base.

Follow manufacturer's instructions for applying these sealers. Both tiles and grout should be dry. On new tile, wait at least 2 weeks—this will give the grout a chance to cure completely. Apply a moderate amount of sealer, and wipe off any excess to prevent the tile from discoloring.

Finally, use caulking to seal all openings or gaps between pipes or fixtures and tile. Replace all trim, accessories, and fixtures.

Flooring

Two requirements for bathroom floors are moisture resistance and durability. Resilient flooring and ceramic tile are ideal choices on both counts. If you're completely remodeling your bathroom, it's a good time to put in ceramic tile, since it's ideally installed with cabinets, doors, and fixtures removed from the room. If you're replacing only the floor, resilient flooring is a good choice; it can be installed around most fixtures and cabinets.

The information in this section assumes that your floor is supported by a standard subfloor, with joists or beams below (see drawing on page 67). If your home is built on a concrete slab and your flooring will be installed over it, you need to make sure that the slab is dry, level, and clean before you begin any work.

RESILIENT SHEET FLOORING

Resilient sheet flooring is available with smooth or textured surfaces, in plain colors or in patterns. Though a few types are available in widths up to 12 feet, most sheet flooring is only 6 feet wide; seams may be necessary.

Plan the new floor. Take exact measurements of the floor and make a scale drawing on graph paper. If your room is very irregular, you may want to make a full-size paper pattern of the floor instead of the scale drawing.

Prepare the subfloor. Both old resilient and wood flooring make acceptable bases for new resilient sheets, provided their surfaces are completely smooth and level. Old resilient flooring must be solid, not cushioned, and firmly bonded to the subfloor. Uneven wood floors may need a rough sanding. Both types must be thoroughly cleaned, and any loose pieces must be secured.

If the old floor is cushioned or in poor condition, it should be removed down to the subfloor, if possible. If the old flooring is impossible to remove without damaging the sub-

floor, or if the subfloor is in poor condition, cover the old flooring with ¼-inch underlayment-grade plywood or untempered hardboard. (If there are signs of water damage or insect infestation, consult a professional.)

Cut the flooring. The most critical step in laying sheet flooring is making the first rough cuts accurately. You may want your flooring dealer to make these first cuts for you; if so, you'll need to supply a floor plan.

To cut the flooring to size yourself, unroll the material in a large room. Transfer the floor plan directly onto the new flooring, using chalk or a water-soluble felt-tip pen, a carpenter's square, and a straightedge.

If your flooring will have a seam, be sure to allow for overlap or for matching the pattern (if any) on adjoining sheets. If your flooring has simulated grout or mortar joints, plan to cut the seam along the midpoint of the joint.

Using a linoleum or utility knife, cut the flooring so it's roughly 3 inches oversize on all sides (the excess will be trimmed away after the flooring has been put in place).

Cut 3" extra

Actual room size

If a seam is necessary, cut and install the piece of flooring that requires the most intricate fitting first; then cut and install the second sheet.

Install the flooring. Following are instructions for laying resilient sheet flooring using adhesive. Some types of sheet flooring can be laid *without* adhesive. In this case, you simply roll out the flooring and shift

it until it's in the proper position, then apply adhesive around the edges or staple the edges in place. If you're considering this easy installation method, check with your flooring dealer to be sure the material you've selected doesn't require adhesive.

If you're installing a single piece of flooring, you can spread adhesive over the entire subfloor at once, or spread adhesive in steps as the flooring is unrolled. Check the adhesive's open time (the time you have to work with the adhesive while it's still tacky); follow the directions of the adhesive manufacturer.

If the entire floor has been covered with adhesive, slowly roll the flooring out across the floor, taking care to set the flooring firmly into the adhesive as you go. If you're working a section at a time, spread adhesive and unroll the flooring as you go.

If you're installing flooring with seams, spread the adhesive on the subfloor as directed by the adhesive manufacturer, but stop 8 or 9 inches from the seam. Then position the first sheet on the floor.

Next, position the second sheet of flooring carefully so that it overlaps the first sheet by at least 2 inches; make sure the design is perfectly aligned. Then roll up the flooring and spread adhesive over the remainder of the floor, stopping 8 or 9 inches from the edge of the first sheet of flooring. Reposition the second sheet of flooring, starting at the seam; again, take care to align the design perfectly. Then roll the flooring out, setting it into the adhesive.

When the flooring is in position, trim away excess flooring at each end of the seam in a half-moon shape so ends butt against the wall.

Using a steel straightedge and a sharp utility knife, make a straight cut (about ½ or ⅝ inch from the edge of the top sheet) down through both sheets. Lift up the flooring on either side of the seam, remove the two overlap strips, and spread adhesive on the subfloor under the seam.

Use the recommended solvent to clean adhesive from around the seam. When the seam is dry and

TRIMMING RESILIENT SHEETS

To trim inside corners, cut excess flooring away a little at a time until flooring lies flat in corner.

To trim outside corners, use utility knife to cut straight down to where wall and floor meet.

To trim along walls, cut flooring with a utility knife and straightedge, leaving a ⅛-inch gap for expansion.

clean, use the recommended seam sealer to fuse the two pieces.

Trim to fit. When the flooring has been positioned, you'll need to make a series of relief cuts at all corners so the flooring will lie flat (see above).

At outside corners, start at the top of the excess flooring and cut straight down to the point where the wall and floor meet. At inside corners, cut the excess flooring away a little at a time until it lies flat.

To remove the excess flooring along a wall, press the flooring into a right angle where the floor and wall join, using an 18 to 24-inch-long piece of 2 by 4. Then lay a heavy metal straightedge along the wall and trim the flooring with a utility knife, leaving a gap of about ⅛ inch between the edge of the flooring and the wall to allow the material to expand without buckling.

RESILIENT TILE FLOORING

Resilient tiles come in two standard sizes, 9-inch and 12-inch square. Other sizes and shapes are available by special order.

To find the amount of tile you need, find the area of the floor, subtracting for any large protrusions. Add 5 percent so you'll have extra tiles for cutting and later repairs. If your design uses more than one color, estimate how many tiles of

each kind you'll need by drawing your design with colored pencils.

Place the tiles. Laying resilient tiles involves three steps: marking the working lines, spreading the adhesive (unless you're using self-stick tiles), and placing the tiles. These steps are similar to those for ceramic tile (for details, see page 108). But unlike ceramic units, resilient tiles are laid tightly against each other, and, because they're made with machine precision, they must be laid out in perfectly straight lines.

Once a tile is in position, press it firmly in place. Lay half a dozen or so, setting them by going over them with a rolling pin. If you're using self-stick tiles, take extra care

to position them exactly before you press them into place (they're hard to remove once they're fixed to the floor). Also note the arrows on the back of self-stick tiles—lay the tiles with the arrows going the same way.

Cut the tile. To cut tiles, score them along the mark with a utility knife; then snap the tile along the line. For intricate cuts, use heavy scissors. (The tiles will cut more easily if warmed in sunlight or over a furnace vent.)

To mark border and corner tiles for cutting, position a loose tile exactly over one of the tiles in the last row closest to the wall (see below). Place another loose tile on top of the first, butting it against the wall. Using this tile as a guide, mark the tile beneath for cutting.

TRIMMING RESILIENT TILES

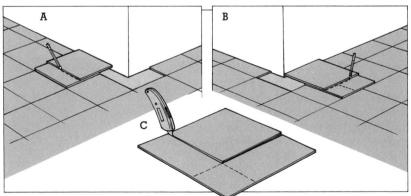

To lay out a border tile, first place a loose tile on top of the last full tile nearest the wall; then place a second tile over the first, butting it against the wall, and mark it for cutting (A). This same technique can be used to mark L-shaped tiles for outside corners (B). Score tiles with a utility knife (C).

∎Flooring

CERAMIC TILE FLOORING

Installing a new floor of ceramic tile can be a very satisfying do-it-yourself project. New, easy-to-install tiles and improved adhesives and grouts make it possible for a careful, patient do-it-yourselfer to create a floor of professional quality.

Because it's usually possible to use existing ceramic tile as a subfloor (see "Prepare the subfloor," below), this section covers installation only—not removal. It's not easy to remove an old tile floor, particularly if the tiles were laid in mortar. So if removal is necessary, it's best to consult a professional.

Installing a ceramic tile floor is essentially a three-step operation: you lay evenly spaced tiles in a bed of adhesive atop a properly prepared subfloor, fill the joint spaces between tiles with grout, and seal the floor for durability and easy cleaning. In this section you'll find basic instructions for laying tile flooring; if you need more detailed information, turn to a contractor or your tile supplier.

Prepare the subfloor. Ceramic tile, masonry, wood, and resilient (except the cushion type) floors can be successfully covered with ceramic tile—provided the old floor is well-bonded, level, clean, and dry.

If the existing flooring is in poor condition, you'll need to repair, cover, or remove it before you can proceed. Fasten loose ceramic, masonry, or resilient flooring with adhesive; nail down loose wood flooring; fill gouges in resilient flooring; and sand wood floors smooth.

If the existing flooring is so badly damaged that it's beyond repair—or if a cushioned resilient flooring has been used—it will need to be removed down to the subfloor, if possible. If the old flooring is impossible to remove without damaging the subfloor underneath, or if the subfloor is in poor condition, you can cover the old flooring with ¼-inch underlayment-grade plywood or untempered hardboard.

Your tile dealer can recommend the best adhesive for your new tile floor (the type of adhesive depends on the type of flooring you'll be covering). Follow your dealer's instructions for preparing the subfloor, and be sure to check the directions on the adhesive container, as well.

Establish working lines. The key to laying straight rows of tile is to first establish accurate working lines. Following are instructions for laying out working lines starting from the center of the room. This method makes it easy to keep rows even and is the best method to use if the room is out of square or if you've chosen a tile with a definite pattern or design.

Locate the center point on each of two opposite walls, and snap a chalk line on the floor between the two points. Then find the centers of the other two walls and stretch your chalk line at right angles to the first line; snap this line only after you've used a carpenter's square to determine that the two lines cross at a precise right angle. If they don't, adjust the lines until they do.

Make a dry run before you actually set the tiles in adhesive. Lay one row of tiles along each working line, from the center of the room to each of two adjoining walls. Be sure to allow proper spacing for grout joints. Adjust your working lines as necessary to avoid very narrow border tiles.

If you're working over a wood subfloor, temporarily nail batten boards along the two working lines that outline the quarter of the room farthest from the door; the battens

will provide a rigid guide for the first row of tiles. (If you're working over a masonry subfloor, you'll have to use the chalk lines as your guides.) You'll set tiles using the sequence shown below, completing the floor quarter by quarter. Work on the quarter by the doorway last.

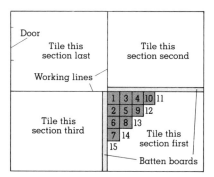

Set the tiles. Using a notched trowel, start spreading adhesive. Cover about a square yard at first, or the area you can comfortably tile before the adhesive begins to set.

Using a gentle twisting motion, place the first tile in the corner formed by the two battens (or chalk lines). With the same motion, place a second tile alongside the first. Continue laying tiles, following the sequence illustrated. Use molded plastic spacers to establish the proper width for the grout joints.

As the tiles are laid, set a piece of carpet-wrapped wood over them, and gently tap the wood with a mallet or hammer to "beat in" the tiles. Keep checking with a carpenter's square or straightedge to make sure each row is straight. Wiggle any stray tiles back into position.

To fit border tiles, measure each space carefully, subtract the width of two grout joints, and mark each tile for any necessary cuts.

When you complete the first quarter of the floor, remove the batten boards, then proceed with the next quarter. After all the tiles are placed, remove the spacers and clean the tile surface so it's completely free of adhesive.

Grout and seal the tile according to the instructions for wall tile on page 105.

Cabinets & countertops

In many homes, the need for bathroom storage has increased as people have collected more and more paraphernalia—bulky electric grooming appliances, children's bath toys, and cleaning supplies. For many families, a medicine cabinet just doesn't provide enough space.

This section will show you how to gain space by installing floor-mounted vanity cabinets, then topping them with countertops of plastic laminate or ceramic tile.

VANITY CABINETS

You can select a vanity cabinet to complement almost any style of bathroom. The vanity may be fitted with various types of countertops and sinks (see pages 54–56).

No matter what countertop and sink you prefer, the methods for removing and installing a prefabricated vanity cabinet in your bathroom are the same.

If a vanity cabinet higher than standard height is more comfortable, add a frame of suitable height underneath the bottom before installing the cabinet.

Removing a vanity cabinet

To remove a plumbed vanity, you'll need to disconnect the plumbing and remove the sink and countertop (see pages 82–83).

Pry away any vinyl wall base, floor covering, or molding from the base cabinet's kickspace or sides.

Old vanity cabinets are usually attached to wall studs with screws or nails through nailing strips at the back of each unit. Sometimes they're also fastened to the floor. Screws are easy to remove unless they're old and stripped. To remove nails, you may need to pry the cabinet away from the wall or floor with a prybar. To prevent damage, use a wood scrap between the prybar and the wall or floor. For a vanity with a solid back, you may have to first shut off the water at the main valve and remove the sink shutoff valves to pull the vanity away from the wall.

Installing a vanity cabinet

Before you begin, remove any baseboard, moldings, or wall base that might interfere. From the floor, measure up 34½ inches—the height of a standard vanity cabinet. Take several measurements and use the highest mark for your reference point. Draw a level line through the mark and across the wall.

If the vanity has a solid back, measure, mark, and cut the holes for the drain and water supply pipes, using a keyhole or saber saw.

For both solid and open-back vanities, locate and mark all wall studs (see page 68) in the wall above where the vanity will be installed. Move the vanity into place.

Level the top of the vanity side-to-side and front-to-back, shimming between the vanity and floor as needed. Both shims and irregularities in the floor can be hidden by baseboard trim.

Some cabinets are designed with "scribing strips" along the sides. Other manufacturers offer decorative panels to "finish" the end of a cabinet run. Both designs include extra material you can shave down to achieve a perfect fit between the cabinet and an irregular wall.

To scribe a cabinet, first position it; then run a length of masking tape down the side to be scribed. Setting the points of a compass with pencil to the widest gap between the scribing strip and the wall, run the compass pivot down the wall next to the strip, as illustrated below. The wall's irregularities will be marked on the tape. Remove the vanity from the wall and use a block plane, file, or power belt sander to trim the scribing strip to the line. Then reinstall the cabinet.

If your cabinet doesn't have scribing strips, you can cover any large irregularities between the wall and cabinet with decorative molding. Scribe the molding as required.

When the cabinet is aligned with your reference marks on the wall, extend the stud location marks down to the hanger strip on the back of the vanity, drill pilot holes through the strip into the wall studs, and secure the vanity to the studs with woodscrews or drywall screws. If the studs aren't accessible, fasten the vanity with wall anchors.

Once the vanity cabinet is secure, install the countertop and sink, then connect the water supply lines, the trap, and the pop-up drain (see pages 83–85).

INSTALLING A VANITY CABINET

Compass and pencil

Masking tape

Vanity cabinet

Scribe and trim sides of vanity to make a snug fit when wall is out of plumb or is uneven.

Hanger strip

Wall studs

Screws

Plumbing connections

Secure vanity cabinet to studs by screwing through hanger strip across the back. Drill pilot holes first.

■ Cabinets & countertops

POST-FORMED LAMINATE COUNTERTOP

Endsplash

Backsplash

Scribing strip

1 by 1 batten

1 by 1 batten

1⅛″ woodscrew

Endcap

COUNTERTOPS

Plastic laminate and tile are two popular materials for countertops. Both are durable, water-resistant, and straightforward to install.

Installing a plastic laminate countertop

Laminate countertops are divided into two types: post-formed and self-rimmed. Post-formed countertops are premolded one-piece tops, from curved backsplash to bullnosed front. The term "self-rimmed" means that you apply the laminate of your choice over a core material.

Post-formed countertop. Since post-formed countertops come only

in standard sizes, you'll normally need to buy one slightly larger than you need and cut it to length. To cut the countertop with a handsaw, mark the cut line on the face. Mark the back if you're using a power saw. Use masking tape to protect the cutting line against chipping (you'll probably have to redraw the line, this time on the tape). Smooth the edge of the cut with a file or sandpaper. Plan to cover that end with an endsplash or endcap (a preshaped strip of matching laminate).

Endsplashes are screwed into the edge of the countertop or into "built-down" wood battens attached to the edge, as shown above. Endcaps are glued to an open end with contact cement or, in some cases, pressed into place with a hot iron.

Countertops, like cabinets, rarely fit uniformly against walls. Usually, the back edge of a post-formed countertop comes with a scribing strip that can be trimmed to follow the exact contours of the wall. Follow the instructions for scribing cabinets on page 109.

Fasten the countertop to the cabinets by running screws from below through the cabinet corner gussets or top frame and through any shims or wood blocks. Use woodscrews just long enough to penetrate ½ inch into the countertop core. Run a bead of silicone sealant along all exposed seams between the countertop and walls.

Self-rimmed countertop. To build your own laminate countertop, you'll need to choose the laminate (¹⁄₁₆-inch thickness is the standard) and cut the core material to size from ¾-inch plywood or high-density particle board.

Build down the edges of the core with 1 by 3 battens (see drawing below). Then you can laminate the countertop (do sides and front strips first and then the top surface).

Measure each surface to be laminated, adding at least ¼ inch to all dimensions as a margin for error. Mark the cutting line. Score the line with a sharp utility knife; then cut with a fine-toothed saw (face up with a handsaw or table saw, face down with a circular saw or saber saw).

Apply contact cement to both the laminate back and the core surface to be joined, and allow the cement to dry for 20 to 30 minutes. Carefully check alignment before joining the two; once joined, the laminate can't be moved. Press the laminate into place, using a roller or a rolling pin to ensure even contact.

Use a block plane to trim the laminate flush with the core's edges; then dress it with a file. Or trim with an electric router equipped with a laminate-trimming bit.

Backsplashes or endsplashes should be cut from the same core material as the main countertop, then butt-joined to the countertop with sealant and woodscrews.

SELF-RIMMED LAMINATE COUNTERTOP

Laminate top

Backsplash

2½″ woodscrew

Scribing strip

4″

¾″ plywood or particle board core

Edge strip

1 by 3 battens

1⅛″ woodscrew

Installing a ceramic tile countertop

Wall tiles, lighter and thinner than floor tiles, are the normal choice for countertops and backsplashes. Standard sizes range from 3 inches by 3 inches to 4½ inches by 8½ inches, with thicknesses varying from ¼ inch to ⅜ inch. Another choice, mosaic tiles (see page 63), makes your job easier, especially in backsplash areas.

Prepare the base. Before laying tile, remove any old countertops; then install ¾-inch exterior plywood cut flush with the cabinet top, screwing it to the cabinet frame from below. For moisture-tight results, add a waterproof membrane, followed by a layer of cement backer board on top.

Surfaces may need to be primed or sealed before tile is applied. To determine the best base and preparation for your job, read the information on the adhesive container or ask your tile supplier.

Plan the layout. Before you start laying tile, you must decide how you want to trim the countertop edge and the sink. For ideas, see the drawing below.

If you decide to use wood trim, seal the wood and attach it to the cabinet face with finishing nails. When in place, the wood strip's top edge should be positioned at the

HOW TO SET COUNTERTOP TILES

First, set edge tiles in place, starting from the center line, after buttering the backs with adhesive.

Next, install field tiles. Use a square to keep the tiles perpendicular to the edge trim.

same height as the finished tile. A recessed sink, commonly used with tile countertops, is also installed at this time (see page 85).

On the front edge of your plywood base, locate and mark the point where the center of the sink or midpoint of a blank countertop will be. Lay the edge tiles out on the countertop, starting from your mark. Some tiles have small ceramic lugs molded onto their edges to keep spacing equal; if your tiles don't, use plastic spacers, available from your tile supplier.

Carefully position the rest of the "field" tiles on the countertop. Observing the layout, make any necessary adjustments to eliminate narrow cuts or difficult fits.

If the countertop will have a backsplash or will turn a corner, be sure to figure the cove or corner tiles into your layout.

Mark reference points of your layout on the plywood base to help you re-create it later; then remove the tile.

Set the tiles. Set all trim tiles before spreading adhesive for the field tiles. Thin-set adhesive, mixed with latex additive, is water-resistant and easy to use.

Butter the back of each front-edge tile and press it into place, aligning it with the reference marks. If your edge trim consists of two tile rows, set the vertical piece first.

Next, butter any back cove tiles and set them against the wall. If you've installed a recessed sink, lay the sink trim next. Be sure to caulk between the sink and the base before setting the trim. If you're using quarter-round trim, you can either miter the corners or use special corner pieces available with some patterns.

Spread adhesive over a section of the countertop. Begin laying the field tiles, working from front to back (see illustration, above). Cut tiles to fit as necessary. As you lay the tiles, check the alignment frequently with a carpenter's square.

To set the tiles and level their faces, slide a 1-foot-square scrap of cloth-covered plywood over them and tap the scrap with a hammer.

Unless you're tiling up to an overhead cabinet or window sill, use bullnose tiles for the last row. If a wall contains electrical switches or plug-in outlets, you can cut tiles in two and use tile nippers to nip out a hole.

Apply the grout. Remove any spacers and clean the tile surface and grout joints until they're free of adhesive. Allow thin-set adhesive to set for 24 hours before grouting the joints. For details on grouting tools and techniques, see page 105.

After grouting, wait at least 2 weeks for the grout to cure; then apply a recommended sealer.

Index

Boldface numbers refer to color photographs.

Combined Index

A comprehensive index to both
volumes appears on the following
pages. This is in addition to the
individual book indexes that
appear on page 128 of each title.

Kitchens

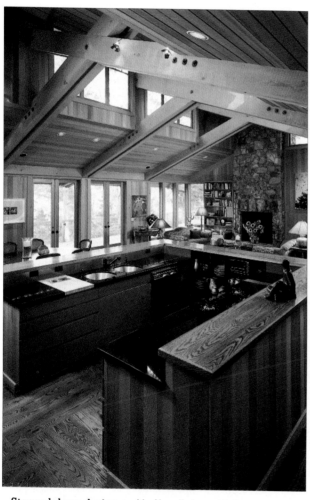

ARCHITECT: RAYMOND L. LLOYD

Stepped-down design and half-walls keep kitchen separate
from informal living area without blocking views.

Bathrooms

DESIGNERS: LYNN ANDERSON AND CARLENE ANDERSON KITCHEN DESIGN, INC.

Enjoy a leisurely soak, a good book, and a leafy view in this
charming old-world setting.

Hanging shelves and a pot rack take advantage of all available wall space in this highly organized kitchen.

ARCHITECT: JOHN MORRIS

Natural light pours into stunning marble and tile bath through twin rooftop windows that also open for ventilation.

Pull-out bins organize and secure small, hard-to-store kitchen items.